A Beautiful Death

A Beautiful Death

Michelle Meier

© **2018 LoveJOYoga Therapy**

Published by: www.LoveJOYogaTherapy.com

Typesetting: Judith Huber - www.JudithHuberDesign.com

Cover Design: Judith Huber - www.JudithHuberDesign.com

A CIP record for this book is available from the Library of Congress Cataloging-in-Publication Data

ISBN-13: 978-1-7320686-1-2

Printed in USA

LoveJOYoga
THERAPY

Contents

Acknowledgements

First and foremost, I'd like to thank God for His unconditional love and for being here for me when I most needed it. Even when I closed my heart, lost my hope and doubted You, dear Lord, You've always shown me there is love. I would not be where I am or who I am without You.

This book is dedicated to God and to my mom, forever my "Mami", I love you with all my heart and soul. But I know you already know that (wink, wink).

Thank you, Papi, for the incredible support you've given me over the years. My Father in Heaven blessed me with the best father on earth I could imagine.

Thank you, Marita, for your unending sweetness, love and support. There is no better sister I could ask for than you.

Thank you, Cedric, for believing in me before I was even ready to believe in myself. The completion of this book would not have been possible without you.

Thank you, Jackie, for being a light for me during my darkest times. I can't imagine my life without you and our heart-to-heart talks.

Thank you, Judith, for your tremendous help in making this possible. May Kitty's loving presence live on in your heart.

Last but not least, I give a special thank you to all my family, friends and earth angels who have been an integral part of my journey. You are forever in my grateful heart.

Love and Joy,
Michelle

Introduction

Grief can come from a variety of triggers. Moving from a beloved home, going through the breakup of a relationship, a miscarriage, losing a job, losing a loved one or a cherished pet, or enduring a traumatic event are just some of the examples. We have all experienced loss at some level. It's a part of life and there is no escaping it.

The greatest heartbreak for me was bearing the loss of my mom who was everything to me. It triggered the creation of this book. If you, too, have endured the loss of a loved one my prayer is that my story somehow helps ease your pain.

I'm not here to tell you how to grieve. There is no right way. While we might experience similar feelings—sadness, emptiness, hopelessness, anger, depression, a broken heart—for each of us the journey is unique. Our relationship with whom or what we've lost is unique. And the way we handle life circumstances is unique.

What I do know is that the only way through it, is *through* it. We can only run away or avoid our feelings for so long. At some point they will resurface or manifest physically within our bodies if we keep stuffing them deep down inside and avoid addressing them.

There has been a tendency in our culture to gloss over, cover or hide things we don't want to face. Because not many talk openly about grief, death and loss, there is this unspoken expectation for us to bounce back after loss. We generally have to report back to work, pay bills, continue caring for other members of our families, and basically deal with "life." After a loss, life doesn't stop. It keeps moving forward and, so, we are often and easily swept up with it, only to sweep our own feelings under the rug in order to manage everything else.

The most important thing you must deal with is the grief! It can show up in so many ways. You might be picking out an avocado at the local grocery store and burst into tears because you remember how much your loved one enjoyed guacamole. You might suddenly bust out into laughter remembering a funny joke you'd shared with your loved one and then cry when you realize you can't call them in person. You might crawl under your covers and hide in your dark bedroom for days on end for fear of seeing the light of day, because your loved one is no longer in it. All of it is ok. And it's important to let it happen as it happens.

Only you can decide when you're ready to step back into life. Only you can decide when you're ready to begin the next chapter.

I remember less than two weeks after our mom died, my sister had to return to work. A colleague, whom I'm sure meant well but was entirely clueless, stepped into her office and asked if she was "back to normal" yet. I was shocked and saddened to hear this but this is a perfect example of the common mentality around death. Get over it and move on.

Yes, you will be able to move on at some point but you can't truly move on with your life until you face your grief.

So if I'm not here to show you what steps to take through the grieving process, why did I write this book? I began journaling during my mom's final months to help me make sense of my feelings and fears. Writing has always been cathartic for me, where I could face my innermost self with bold honesty and without holding back. Shortly before my mom died, I'd sat at her bedside holding her hand and told her I'd write a book in her honor. I remember her smiling, green eyes sparkling, and in a heartbeat the title came to me.

"It's going to be called 'A Beautiful Death'," I shared with her, "because thanks to God, thanks to you, and thanks to yoga, I've experienced so much beauty and magic during this time."

Then after she died, I couldn't bear to read any of my journals for about two years. I guess there was a part of me that wasn't yet ready to face the truth. Just after the three-year anniversary of her passing, the first chapter came to me unexpectedly. I often felt God moving through me and the words just poured out. Some of what you'll read is my recounting of memories to the best of my ability and other parts are direct excerpts from my journals, shown with the date, and written in the present moment. I took the liberty to change some names to respect privacy and am thankful to those who have allowed me to call them by name.

By sharing my heart and soul while going through the saddest yet most miraculous time of my life, I hope to shed some light on the topic of death and grief—a topic about which most of us become squeamish or from which we want to shut down altogether.

The truth is death and loss are what we all have in common. Not one of us can escape it. It is a natural part of life. So why does the thought about it hurt so much? What are we so afraid of?

Let's Talk About Death, Baby

"The few certainties in our existences are pain, death and bereavement."

~Jane Wilson-Howarth

From the moment we're born, we are dying. At the time of writing this, I Googled "how many people die in a day" and was blown away to see 6,316 people die every hour. In a day, 151,600. Those numbers seem staggering but we live in a big world. It's to be expected. Every one of us will die. Some of just sooner than others. The scary part for most of us, when we think about it, is not knowing how soon. The liberating part is we can do what we wish with the precious time we are given. Sure, there are always going to be circumstances that are beyond our control and may be completely unplanned for. But we get to choose how we feel about it all.

How we feel about death is not something we jump up to explore. It is generally not openly discussed in our culture. Have you noticed how people (this includes myself) often use the term "passed away" as in "my mom passed away" instead of "my mom died"? Saying someone died sounds so final. "To die" literally means "to cease to exist." Passed away implies they have passed on to a better existence. This I believe to be true.

Also when someone we know dies, people reach out to express their condolences. Automatically we say, "I'm sorry for your loss." Even after losing my mom, I say this to others when someone they love passes away. While I never felt the need to hear it from anyone else about my mom, I feel that others may need to hear that. But how can I really know? Everyone's path through grief is their own. It's the customary response and so I've spoken it without really thinking about why...we don't really think about death much, do we?

If we do give it thought, we generally think in terms of sadness, darkness and heaviness. But what about the joy, the love, the celebration of life, the beautiful memories we were blessed to experience and the passage of our souls to a higher existence? Can we see those things in death?

Absolutely we can choose to see them that way. *And* we can allow ourselves to cry and mourn and sit in darkness when we need to.

The key is not to get lost in there. We must remember our way back, to emerge as a transformed soul into a new chapter—the chapter of life *after* the person we love died.

"Incipit Vita Nova." That was the official motto of my college. "A New Life Begins." Who knew that first reading that as a freshman was the planting of the seed that is helping me blossom now? Indeed, here begins new life.

CHAPTER 1

Fire And Ice

"Don't cry because it's over, smile because it happened."
~Dr. Seuss

Her hands were as cold as ice, her fingers stiffly interlaced in prayer. Her oval-shaped manicured fingernails looked exactly the same as they did a couple of weeks ago when she was spiritedly cracking jokes.

I'd never touched a dead body before. Never did I expect my first time to be that of my mom's. Other than her fingernails, I didn't recognize her without the presence of her soul. It could've been that the funeral home's makeup artist gave her a look she'd never had a before. Kind of an odd time to do a makeover.

Her face was pale and at peace with crisp black eyeliner painted across her lash line and her lips painted red. She'd never worn black eyeliner before; instead, she'd loved her olive green eye shadow to bring out the green in her eyes. I tried to look for my Mami but could clearly recognize that "the lights were off and no one was home". Still futilely trying to reach for her, to somehow find her, I placed my hand on her forehead, again taken aback by the icy hardness of her skin. It definitely was not my mom. I couldn't cry; I think I was in shock. I mean, I knew for months this was going to happen but I didn't know what to expect.

It's not like people welcome talking about the death of a loved one. I wasn't given any sort of manual. The last time I was at a funeral was for my grandma on my dad's side several years before. It was the only other time in my life I'd seen my dad cry.

On this day, we stood over my mom laying in her wedding dress with white footsie socks—goodness, how could we have forgotten to give the funeral home a pair of decent shoes for her? On this day, my dad cried again.

My mom wanted to be cremated and my dad had requested a viewing so my sister and I nervously obliged. We weren't sure whether we were emotionally prepared to see her but we wanted to be supportive of our dad. It was so strange to see her body so...lifeless.

Dad stood with our mom as my sister and I stayed back, taking it all in. In typical Meier family fashion, my sister finds humor in the situation.

She leans in to ask me in a faint whisper, "Why are all funeral homes so hideously decorated?"

Eyeing the rust colored tufted leather chairs, I stifled a smile, confused as to whether or not it was ok to be amusing one another in that moment. It seemed so inappropriate yet so apropos at the same time.

At that moment the lights in the room flickered off and on. Without a doubt, that was our Mami agreeing on the awful decor and laughing about it with us. My sister and I couldn't help but let a chuckle slip out as we instinctively reached for each other's hands. I was comforted by those moments when we recognized our mom's presence with us, especially when it was in moments of laughter and joy.

When we each felt we had the time we needed with the shell of our Mami, the funeral director wheeled her body to the crematorium with her palms frozen in prayer and the three of us in tow.

I'll never forget the steps I took from the viewing room out into the gray hallway through a back door outside to the crematorium, dutifully following our mom in a cardboard box. She insisted we use the least expensive option. She wanted us, instead, to throw her a Celebration of Life party.

The crematorium was a very basic, sterile room with a big metal cremation chamber. It all happened so fast. The metal door opened, mom in her cardboard box was slipped into the flames and the door was instantly closed to retain the eighteen hundred degrees Fahrenheit used to vaporize flesh and bone. The director offered my dad to push the button to start the official incineration process, which he did. And that was that.

The loud noise abruptly consumed the room. I thought about one of Mami's favorite quotes.

"Diamonds are formed through intense heat and pressure," she used to remind me when I felt challenged by life.

As I heard the crackling flames consume her body, I smiled at the diamond my mom had become.

CHAPTER 2

It All Began With A Grilled Cheese Sandwich

*"It takes someone really brave to be a mother, someone strong
to raise a child, and someone special to love someone more
than herself."*

~Unknown

I hated being apart from her. It started in my first days in kindergarten. We lived in Boca Raton, Florida. I was nervous about being with other kids I didn't know, leaving the comfort of my days together with Mami by my side.

Every morning she would drive me to preschool and I felt ants in my pants the closer we got. There was a big bridge we'd cross on the way and, whenever we drove over it, Mami would turn to me with that familiar sparkle of love in her eyes that I'd come to know and start singing:

*"You are my sunshine, my only sunshine.
You make me happy when skies are gray.
You'll never know, dear, how much I love you.
Please don't take my sunshine away."*

Her voice was by no means a singer's voice (we were certainly not awarded the singing gene in our family) but it sure brought me comfort every time she sang.

We'd arrive at the schoolhouse and, hand in hand, Mami would walk me inside.

"Don't let me go," I'd plead with her, my eyes hopeful and round.

But she had to, for my own good.

Eventually I assimilated with the other kids. I even discovered how much I delighted in our group nap times. I mean, who doesn't love a good nap? Nonetheless I couldn't wait until the hands of the clock reached 1 PM and I could see my Mami who, regularly arriving a few minutes early, would stand right outside the door waiting patiently for me. I'd run to her and hug her legs with all my might. She'd smile at me, running her fingers through my hair, and ask me how my day was.

Every Friday after school she would take me to Dunkin Donuts, where I got a grilled cheese sandwich and she'd get a French cruller with a black coffee and sugar. It was always the same order for us both, our favorite treat. We'd sit across from each other at a table by the window, my little legs dangling off the edge of the bench, as I licked the gooey hot melted cheese from my fingers. Mami would ask me questions about kindergarten and my classmates. I would ask Mami why the clouds were shaped like Goofy or Big Bird.

It was nothing fancy, just us girls hanging out and eating at the local coffee shop, but it meant the world to me that she committed herself to this time together, just the two of us, every week.

One Friday afternoon when holding hands as we walked into the Dunkin Donuts, Mami stopped suddenly and pointed down to the sidewalk.

"Look, a penny! It's good luck!" she exclaimed, as she enticed me to pick it up.

Every time throughout my childhood when I'd find a penny thereafter, I'd pick it up to collect as much good luck as I could. And Mami would be by my side cheering me on.

Those were some of the first memories I recall and cherish of our time together.

CHAPTER 3

The Power Of Prayer

"Things have a way of working out. Never underestimate the power of prayer, faith, love. . .and, above all, never underestimate the power of God to see you through."

~Unknown

When I was growing up, my dad's job in international finance moved our family to a new city every few years. Because of my shyness I had trouble making friends. Mami stepped in and helped introduce me to my peers when in orientation together at new schools.

In Geneva, Switzerland I was an awkward pimply ten year-old. There I met Jamie, a classmate, who also happened to live in our neighborhood. We quickly became best friends hanging out after school playing jump rope, building forts in the woods and gabbing about our first boy crushes. Joey McIntyre of New Kids On The Block was at the top of our list if you must know. That was about the only thing we'd ever fought about, Jamie and me—which one of us would one day get to date him.

One afternoon we rode the school bus home together as usual when Jamie suddenly turned on me, making fun of me in front of our classmates. Holding her index finger and thumb an inch apart from each other and squinting to look at the tiny space between her fingers, she repeatedly called me a "shrimp". I was significantly shorter than her. And I was shocked that she was taunting me. I had done nothing to prompt her insults. She continued on and on the entire bus ride home until the other kids on the bus were laughing at me too.

I held back the tears; our bus stop couldn't have come any sooner. As soon as the door opened, I ran down the street until I was far enough away that she couldn't hear me cry as she headed in the opposite direction towards her house.

Mami was surprised to see the tears streaming down my face when I walked through the front door at home. After I'd recounted to her what happened she told me we must pray for Jamie.

What?! Why would I want to do that? She's the one who was ridiculing me! Mami explained that when someone is being mean to me, it's only because they're hurting inside. People who are happy within themselves would never make others feel bad. So we must pray for them.

She beckoned me to sit at the kitchen table with her and said she'd guide us into prayer. It hadn't quite sunk in what Mami said about mean people hurting inside so I really didn't feel like praying for Jamie. I was mad and I was hurt.

Not giving up, Mami held out her hands and, reluctantly, I reached for them as I sat down across from her.

"Heavenly Father, in the name of Christ, we come to you for our friend Jamie who needs you," she began to lead us into prayer.

Sniffling, I closed my eyes and listened to her as she prayed for Jamie to find happiness and be at peace. She prayed for several minutes. I may or may not have rolled my eyes a couple of times but Mami never caught on. Her eyes were closed and she squeezed my hands gently as she prayed in earnest. When she finished by thanking God for blessing Jamie, she opened her eyes and told me to start my homework.

That was it? I looked at her quizzically, mildly annoyed that she was being so nice in Jamie's favor. She looked at me again. She never had to do that more than once so, straightaway, I pulled out my textbooks right there at the kitchen table to start working.

She got up to grab some food from the fridge to prepare a snack for us when ten minutes later the doorbell rang. Coring an apple, she asked me to answer it.

I did not expect to see Jamie standing on our doorstep, her eyes and cheeks red with tears. I stood there figuring out what to say but she started first with an apology. She explained that she and her mom had gotten into a big fight before school that morning and then she had a problem in school with a teacher and it was basically her worst day ever.

"I took it out on you; you didn't do anything and I'm sorry!" she cried.

With my mouth agape, I turned my head back towards the kitchen where I heard Mami humming the notes to "Amazing Grace." I swear I could hear her smiling.

So this prayer thing really worked! Jamie and I embraced and were playing together again later that afternoon, after our homework was done of course.

CHAPTER 4

Behind Closed Doors

"Sometimes the strongest among us are the ones who smile through silent pain, cry behind closed doors, and fight battles nobody knows about."

~Unknown

A cold gust of wind blew several dead leaves across the lawn. The trees had turned different shades of red, orange and yellow. It was fall and we were living in Stamford, Connecticut at the time.

Only one year earlier had I started high school. I'll never forget trying to navigate the new school grounds as a freshman on my first day. Completely lost, I'd ended up in the wing for the seniors and, when the bell rang, I realized I was going to be late for my first class. I scrambled with my backpack, full of books, running towards a flight of stairs going down. And that's just what I did. I went down. Literally, I fell down not one but two flights of stairs only to be saved by the strap of my backpack that had gotten caught on one of the hooks around the banister. The stairwell was packed with seniors who all started laughing at the clumsy new girl. Thankfully no broken bones; only a broken ego.

For weeks at school I was approached with, "Hahaha!! You're the girl who fell down the stairs!"

And I thought I was awkward when I was ten.

While I finally got past that mortifying incident that my classmates initially wouldn't let me live down, in my sophomore year I was still navigating my sensitive emotions, my rapidly changing hormones and all that "fun" stuff that comes with being a teenager.

It was almost dinnertime and Papi (my dad) was home early from work for a change. I remember how fast he'd walk through the house; it was as if he was always on a mission. His energy made me feel nervous. In a way I feared him, not because he was mean or a bad father. In fact, it was just the opposite. He worked very hard to provide for our family. I didn't see him too much while growing up. He was often away on business trips in other countries or working late at the office. It took me years to realize that this was his way of showing his love for us. But because he never told me "I love you" when I was a kid, I took it that he didn't. We have a way of creating stories in our minds that can rule us for better or for worse.

Papi speed walked into the kitchen where I stood in front of the open fridge, jamming a piece of whole wheat bread in my mouth (I had an obsession with snacking on bread back then; I could've downed a whole loaf in one episode if I'd wanted!).

"Why are you eating now?" he questioned me, "Mami's going to start cooking dinner any moment."

I glared at him chewing a mouthful of baked flour and yeast and dramatically rolled the open end of the plastic bag in which the bread was stored, crisscrossing the twist tie emphatically around it to seal it shut. I shoved it back in the fridge, closing the door loudly and firmly before I marched off.

"Michelle!!" he called after me, perturbed.

I stomped up the stairs ignoring him. That day at school I was made fun of by one of my boy crushes and I didn't want to be bothered anymore by "men."

When retreating to my room, I passed by Mami and Papi's room and thought I heard a noise behind the closed door. I stopped momentarily and held my breath as I put my ear to it. I heard several sniffles and then crying. My heart stopped. It was Mami crying alone in her room.

Several weeks earlier she'd been diagnosed with breast cancer and was immediately put on chemotherapy. She'd started losing some of her shoulder length champagne blonde hair, had become bloated and her fingertips were continuously inflamed from the needle pricks administered weekly by her doctor for blood work.

We were deeply saddened by the diagnosis but Mami had downplayed the news to my older (and only) sister, Marita, and me, convincing us it wasn't life threatening.

Marita had followed Papi's footsteps working for the same company he did but was living and working in a Southwest Florida branch at the time. She felt so far away and I missed her. She had always been a good sister to me—sweet, kind and loving—even when I'd annoy her as a hyperactive little kid.

Mami, in the meantime, put on a very convincing brave face and remained strong as her body and her hair began to radically change before our eyes.

Hearing her cry now on the other side of her door, all alone, I wanted to burst through the door to hug her. I stood there hesitating though. I got the sense that she needed to continue crying and I knew if I were to come in, she'd swallow it down and valiantly put on her coat of armor again.

To this day I still feel guilty that I never went in to hold her. I wasn't sure how to be there for my Mami then. I was struggling within my own matrix of teenage emotions; I couldn't even begin to fathom the depth of pain that she was feeling with cancer ravaging her body. Nothing made sense anymore.

I retreated to my room, closed my door, and cried alone for Mami.

CHAPTER 5

Mami's Best Friend

"Fall in love with a dog, and in many ways you enter a new orbit,
a universe that features not just new colors but new rituals, new rules,
a new way of experiencing attachment."

~Caroline Knapp

The sun arched high and luminous across the backdrop of a clear blue sky. Palm trees swayed in a warm gentle breeze. It was April more than ten years later and Miami, Florida was now home to us. I was living on my own not far from the home Mami and Papi had moved into post-retirement and proudly named "The Sanctuary". While the cancer had not taken Mami's life it had returned several times. She kept bouncing back. She was a true warrior.

She loved living in Miami and going out with Papi and their friends; they had an active social life and weren't going to take retirement "lying down". Papi continued traveling, only this time for pleasure. He was an avid diver with a thirst for adventure. Mami understood his need to explore the world; however, she didn't have the same energy after the repeated chemotherapy and radiation she'd gone through in the previous years. She wanted nothing more than for her family to be happy so she prompted Papi to continue his travels. It was during one of his trips away when Mami decided she wanted to have a dog again.

Marita and I both grew up with dogs in our lives; first a patient miniature schnauzer named Goliath then a spirited cocker spaniel named Rusty. They were a source of unconditional love and constant companionship. Mami wanted to have that again and Papi agreed it was time. She explained that since he was away at times, she wanted a "big, black dog" that would protect her and make her feel safe when alone at the house.

I still don't understand why she chose a standard poodle but Arco was the cutest puppy I'd ever seen—jet black silky soft and curly hair with big round timid eyes. He wanted to lick everything in sight and, whenever I'd come over, he'd lick me with a thousand kisses and his tail wagging as if he couldn't be happier to see anyone else in the world. Then he'd give the same amount of love and attention to Mami, then to Papi and also to Marita or anyone else who visited the house for that matter. Arco had this way of making you feel like you were his one and only love. We'd tease Mami about wishing for a protector dog; we were convinced if someone would've broken into the house Arco would've wagged his tail, retrieved his toys for a game of fetch and possibly lick the perpetrator to death.

It didn't matter, though; Arco was the apple of Mami's eye. She was so proud of her baby boy whom she claimed was one of the best-behaved dogs in his training school. He would "heel" obediently at her side upon command. He would sit and lie down when requested. He would give only one cautionary bark if someone knocked at the front door. He displayed none of these skills, however, when we were around. Just placing your hand on his back to pet him would send him into a joyful frenzy, walking in circles over and over again until you got dizzy and were forced to stop him. He could keep licking your hands for hours, too, if you didn't stop him. But, wait, he'd keep trying over and over again so one firm "No" was never enough. Mami rather fancied at times when he'd incessantly lick her hand. She swore her skin was smoother, like he was her personal exfoliator.

The funniest part about her getting a protector dog was when she bought him a matching collar and leash. They were mint green leather studded with rhinestones. She completed the look by painting his toenails gold. I was seriously debating sharing this memory because, as I write it, I realize how kooky she sounded. We'd never seen Mami like this with any of our other dogs. But both Mami and Arco were content, gold toenails and all, and The Sanctuary was that much more jovial because of his presence.

When Arco was only two years old, his hair turned gray. We couldn't figure out why; his life being doted on by Mami and the rest of us was in no way stressful. Well, he may not have been much of a guard dog and he was no longer black but he was still big and he had an even bigger heart full of endless love for us, his family.

CHAPTER 6

Where Is God?

"Trust in the Lord with all your heart; and lean not unto your own understanding."

~ *Proverbs 3:5*

For years I'd toiled away in the corporate world, making a living and getting by. I had all the benefits one could dream of—a 401K, health, vision and dental insurance along with plenty of bonuses. My boss was down-to-earth, had a great sense of humor and was generous and kind. Imagine marble floors, cherry wood desks and an unobstructed view of the Atlantic Ocean from downtown Miami. That was the office building where I worked. You could say I had it all.

Yet day after day, having more often than not put in extra hours, I came home late from work to an apartment all by myself, cooked myself dinner and watched one show on TV before tucking myself into bed. Then I'd get up and do it all over again the next day and the next and the next. I couldn't wait for the weekends; except then I'd have to catch up on laundry, go food shopping and clean my apartment. Before I knew it, Monday would arrive again and the monotony of the week played itself out over and over again, week after week, month after month, year after year.

I thought I was doing well. I thought I'd done the right thing in finding suitable job stability and making my dad proud. I remember him often saying that a sure path to success was finding a good job in an office and climbing the corporate ladder. This is how he'd achieved his dreams. But, inside, I felt unsettled. On the outside I began to notice bouts of upper back pain and breakouts on my skin. It was when I started losing hair that I became alarmed. I needed an outlet. I needed something other than work and household chores to fill my life.

That's when I began to research local dance classes. I wondered about giving ballroom dance a try or, living in Miami, perhaps signing up for salsa classes. Having grown up taking gymnastics and an array of jazz, tap, ballet and flamenco lessons, I felt this would be a fun and constructive way to express myself. Then the online ad popped up for *pole dance* classes. It was the latest fitness craze sweeping the nation and a new school had just opened in Miami. I was intrigued.

Finally I left work on time so I could make it to my first class. I wasn't sure what to expect when walking into the studio. All of the walls, except for one, were painted red; the fourth was mirrored. Dimmed ceiling lights illuminated ten dance poles. I was apprehensive. What had I stepped into? An hour and a half later I walked out feeling like a new woman. Pole dance had challenged me physically in ways I couldn't have imagined and I felt a sense of confidence that had me strutting into the office the next morning.

Every Tuesday night from thereon, instead of working late, I'd leave the office on time to make it to my pole dance classes. For that one hour and a half I felt free from any obligations and stress. I felt free to be me.

I stuck with every class until I'd graduated from all six levels the studio offered. Many other students had dropped out when we started learning how to climb and invert. But I was drawn to the challenge and creativity it brought out in me when figuring out how to transition from one move into another in one fluid motion, connecting to my heart and soul. Dance for me was poetry in motion. I lived for Tuesday nights and, so upon completion of all the levels, the studio owner asked me if I'd be interested in teaching. I felt a nervous rush when I thought about having to be in front of others, speaking and demonstrating with people watching me. Eeek! But, after the much needed boost of self-confidence and strength that pole dance had given me, I felt compelled to share this with other women. I wanted to empower them to feel confident and beautiful within themselves too. So I said yes.

Subsequently, aside from working full time at the office, I was creating choreography and a syllabus to teach my students every week. It was exciting and terrifying at the same time. I'd found my outlet.

Over time, though, it wasn't enough. My hair loss returned with even greater amounts of stress as I took on more responsibilities at the office. I began thinking about what my life were to look like one year from then doing the same thing I was doing at the time and I felt uneasy. Then I thought what my life would be like five years from then and I felt nauseous. Then I imagined what my life would be like fifteen years from then like this. That's when a wave of panic overcame me. What was I doing with my life?

Sure, teaching dance was amazing. Choreography came naturally to me. Connecting with my students felt so rewarding. Plus I was getting paid to work out and have fun. The office part of my life became less and less fulfilling and more about merely getting a paycheck. I'd always admired my sister who had excelled as a high-powered executive in the corporate world. I just wasn't her. And I wasn't my dad either. So who was I?

One weekday I awoke feeling queasy and like I was coming down with something so I called into work sick. I knew exactly why I was feeling sick. I couldn't take another day working in the office. It was like something triggered inside me and there was no turning back. What was I going to do? My income from teaching dance was certainly not going to pay rent. I picked up the phone to call my dad for advice. Any other time Mami would've been the first person I'd want to talk with but, that day, I knew it had to be Papi. I felt like I had pop rocks in my stomach anticipating how I was going to bring up the fact that I wanted to quit my job to my dad who had been so proud of me for getting it in the first place. I decided I'd rather go through the discomfort of bearing the news to him than sucking it up and going day after day, year after year, to a job that for me was unfulfilling.

I invited him over to my place. This was one of those conversations that needed to be had in person. He came by just before noon and offered to take me to lunch. I'd told him I'd called in sick to the office this morning. He must've known I was sick for reasons other than an actual cold or flu. He must've known something was up. I waited until after we ordered our food at the restaurant to open that conversation. My stomach was in knots and I gulped down some water before clearing my throat to confess to him how unhappy I was. I poured out my heart to him, expecting him to be upset and disappointed with me.

To my surprise, he reached for my hand across the table and assured me everything was going to be ok. To my greater surprise, he proposed that I move back in with him and Mami during this time of transition. My eyes filled with tears, I was so grateful for this unexpected offer and for his considerable generosity. I got up and walked around the table to hug him and we agreed that I would tender my resignation and move back home while figuring out what I want to do with my life.

At first I beat myself up that there I was, thirty years old and moving back in with my parents, but eventually I began to enjoy this unexpected time together as adults. I was thrilled to be home with Mami again too. Mother and daughter—best friends—now living together under the same roof.

I took on more dance classes and some temp jobs to cover my other expenses and was so happy to come home everyday to Mami for our heart-to-heart conversations. Sometimes we'd share a glass of wine on the patio and talk about life. Sometimes we'd sit in the living room and watch one of our favorite TV shows, "The Big Bang Theory", laughing hysterically over Sheldon's odd quirks and sarcastic remarks.

While I still wasn't quite sure what my new career path would look like, life was pretty darn good.

Then came New Year's Eve; a time for magic, love and new beginnings. My family was happy and healthy and we were all very close. And I was falling in love.

I'd first met Lucas while in my office job. We worked for the same company but he was married at the time and I was in a relationship so the extent of our connection was nothing more than the occasional coffee conversation in the office kitchen. It wasn't until after I'd left the company and he'd divorced that we fortuitously ran into each other, both single, at a community event. My mom had been with me at the time and elbowed me when she saw him approach with a big smile to tell me how great it was to run into each other there.

"He's *cute*!!" she said loudly enough for everyone, especially him, to hear.

"Ohhh, Mami, how I love you!" I thought to myself as I wished to be swallowed by the earth from embarrassment.

"Why haven't you two ever gone out on a date?" she persisted.

Lucas and I both laughed and he took that as his cue to ask me out for one.

We'd been on several dates regularly since and had really been enjoying each other's company. It just flowed between us. I was thrilled to spend New Year's Eve together with him at a local party where many of my friends would be.

I remember that night putting on a hot pink dress with rhinestones that made me feel like a princess and kissing my parents goodbye, giggling that I'd see them "next year."

Mami winked at me and said, "You kids have fun!"

And we sure did. We danced a lot throughout the night and, if we weren't dancing, we were kissing like two teenagers at a high school dance. We didn't want our time together to end so we went out for a bite at a nearby sandwich shop around 3 AM (it's amazing what's open in Miami at all hours of the night) and stayed up talking for hours. From that night forward we knew there was something special happening between us. He reluctantly dropped me off at my parent's house. The sun was already up and we giggled and kissed in the car before we were finally able to pull away from each other.

I slipped through the front door, took off my heels and tiptoed through the hallway to find Mami's door open and her reading a book in bed. She looked at me and we both grinned at each other so I waltzed into her room and curled up into her bed by her side. She gripped my hand close to her heart and, without a word (for I know she was beckoning me to spill the beans), I shared with her about our night and all the giddiness I felt with my new boyfriend. I felt so carefree and open, like anything was possible. She continued to squeeze my hand and smile as I recounted everything I was feeling. She was so happy for me, saying that she'd been praying for me to find the right man. Her prayers had been answered we both gleefully thought.

My relationship with Lucas continued to grow and flourish and Mami was right there by my side whenever I'd return home from our dates. I loved coming home to her and having our "girl time" together. It was like I was back in high school, except better since we were both adults now and could relate to each other on even more levels.

In February Papi, Marita and I embarked on our annual father-daughter trip. Every year we explore somewhere new together. It was one of our favorite family traditions over the past seven years and this year we were psyched to discover Belize and Guatemala. Mami was always supportive of the three of us going away to bond with each other. She relished having the house to herself for a bit; it was like a vacation for her too.

That was the last time period I remember feeling like everything was perfect, like everything in my life was coming together. That was the last time I remember feeling completely carefree and happy.

When we came back from our weeklong adventure, we found out that Mami didn't have much of a vacation with the house to herself. In fact, she told us—or, rather, casually mentioned—that while we were out of the country, there was one day where she couldn't physically get out of her bed. When pressing her with questions about it, she admitted that she was stuck from pain that had frozen her into an immobile heap. She'd been unable to go to the bathroom, to get food or water and, worse, to call for help.

I was shocked and horrified to imagine our Mami completely helpless and all alone. Meanwhile we'd been out having fun all week entirely unaware of what she was going through back home. Typical Mami, she downplayed it, claiming her lower back was most likely hurting because she'd danced her heart out on New Year's Eve. She attributed it to "old age" and her resistance to working out, not to mention the hours she spent hunched over her iPad playing games like "Pet Hotel". Because of her lack of exercise and since she's been known to dance the night away on special occasions, it was an entirely plausible theory in my mind. So, like her, I let it go at that.

She had no interest in going to a doctor. Since the first time she'd gotten cancer almost eighteen years ago, it had returned about every two years giving her a tally of eight bouts with cancer. Mami had undergone chemotherapy, radiation, a double mastectomy, countless follow-up surgeries, and was put on a regimen of all sorts of doctor-prescribed medications. After being poked and prodded by medical professionals for years, she was over it. I got that.

But her back pain kept resurfacing through April and right before my birthday, after several attempts, Papi finally convinced her to get a checkup. Reluctantly she went and she was even more reluctant to share with us the doctor's diagnosis. She brushed it off, letting us know everything was ok, just age kicking in.

She started a daily regimen of walking around the perimeter of the backyard several times for exercise, convincing us it was helping her decrease the aches in her back. She was getting up and moving from her formerly sedentary lifestyle. It was a positive change in my eyes.

I remember the sun shining on her face as she walked out there, circle after circle around the pool. She looked so grateful to be out in the fresh air.

With Mother's Day around the corner, Marita called to tell me she was coming to Miami to celebrate with Mami in person. She lived two and a half hours away in Naples. Over the previous years she'd been sending thoughtful cards and flowers and, this year, I recognized my sister's voice was marked with anxiety.

I couldn't understand why so when I asked her about it she replied, "This could be Mami's last Mother's Day."

I laughed at the absurdity of the notion and then became uneasy.

"What do you mean? What's different this year?" I questioned.

She couldn't explain why; she chalked it up to a gut feeling. I didn't like this feeling one bit. Neither did Marita so she insisted on being there.

Mami wanted to relax at home with us on her special day so we made her brunch and ate out on the patio. Marita brought her Vitamix blender to prepare some flavorful green smoothies for us. While we've generally been pretty healthy eaters in our family, this was our first foray into the world of liquefied greens. Marita was clever enough to add mango and banana and we found ourselves actually enjoying drinking kale and spinach. It was Marita's hope to help Mami regain her health through nutrition. Of course our family brunch would not be complete until we had one more thing.

The "POP!" of a cork suddenly burst from the champagne bottle Papi opened. It was a sound that made Mami grin every single time. We constantly found reasons to celebrate life as a family and this was one of the best we could think of: celebrating our beloved Mami. Arco, still gray but full of life at seven years old, was down for a party anytime too. Whenever we got together he yearned to be the life of the party, getting in the middle of everything and being cute with a mere wag of his pom pom tail. But we all knew Mami was really always the life of the party. Arco seemed to have resigned himself to this as he lounged in his patio bed while we ate until our bellies were full. While we hadn't given presents in our family for years (time with each other had always been our greatest gift), we presented Mami with a couple of small offerings. Marita had a coffee mug made for Mami. It was covered in several pictures of us girls with her and a colorful backdrop with the big block letters "L-O-V-E" spelled out on it.

It was serendipitous that the lavender and green gift bag she put the mug in perfectly matched the giant lavender and green felt flower I'd thought to get. Its plush lavender petals surrounded a smiley face and buried beneath the soft felt of its stalk was a malleable wire so that the flower could be molded into any shape or position.

Mami, after a couple of glasses of champagne (or, really, just because she was naturally silly), reshaped the stalk of the flower to wrap it around her head so it appeared to be growing out of her cranium. We couldn't help but laugh. Arco, in the meantime, had ransacked the tissue paper from the gift bag and was licking and savoring it like it was his own Sunday brunch. I shook my head. It was tough to be upset with him when he was so gosh darn adorable.

The sun was out, the birds were chirping. There was the soft gurgle of the fountain in the backyard. In the calm of the afternoon, Mami opened up to us to let us know the doctor had discovered the cancer returned. Oddly enough I felt rather indifferent at first hearing the diagnosis this time. Given that she'd fought cancer so many times before, I didn't take the news too hard. I hated that she had to go through it over and over, and I would've given anything for her not to be dealt that hand yet again, but at least she was consistently strong and resilient.

I'd actually thought to myself, "Well she's gone through this before and she's strong enough to do it again...we're here for her through this. No biggie."

Marita started to cry with the news and as a result of her gut feeling. She quickly removed her napkin from her lap and got up to embrace Mami on the other side of the table. I kept thinking I didn't believe her intuition that this could be Mami's last Mother's Day. The truth was I didn't want to believe it. But seeing Marita's reaction clinging to Mami with tears rolling down her cheeks hit me hard. This initiated a cry fest for us all. Mami almost immediately thereafter pulled back, emphatically waved her hands and her head, and said she didn't want to make this a sad thing. That, and the fact that the felt flower stayed put on her head when she was shaking it, prompted us to smile again.

She put my questioning mind at ease by confirming how she's gone through it before and will go through it again. She sounded so confident.

Marita sat down, blotting the tears from her face with her napkin, as we talked about the green smoothies and dietary changes we could make as a family to support Mami. She noted that she really enjoyed Marita's smoothie and would love to have a Vitamix blender too. Her wish was our command. Marita and Papi grabbed a laptop to start looking up nearby stores so we could immediately pick one up for her but every one of them was out of stock. The closest available one they could locate was at a store one and a half hours away. Marita and Papi made the long drive to get it for her that very day. We had to make changes. We were going to save Mami.

When It Became Real

"They will have no fear of bad news; their hearts are steadfast,
trusting in the Lord."
~*Psalm 112:7*

Everyday for the next two weeks we made green smoothies with several different recipes Marita had suggested for us. She had to return home to Naples after Mother's Day but we stayed in touch regularly and were grateful for her guidance on nutrition. She'd done a lot of research on her own and was quite knowledgeable in the field.

At some point Mami wanted to give juicing a try. Again her wish was our command. Several times a day our kitchen was abuzz with the sound of either the blender or the juicer. Peeling, coring, cutting and chopping veggies and fruit became a daily meditation.

Mami continued her daily walks in the backyard, increasing her time outside. I bounded out of bed with greater ease. Papi, who was always on the move anyway, gained enough fuel for all of us combined. We bonded during our time in the kitchen preparing juices, smoothies, salads and other healthy meals together. It was a far cry from the days I was inhaling loaves of bread and giving Papi the "dagger eyes". This was a revival, both physically and emotionally, for our family. Things were looking up.

Until the day they came crashing down. Over Memorial Day weekend, without warning, Mami was rendered immobile from pain in her entire body. She couldn't move an inch from her bed without gasping for air and had to be immediately hospitalized. Marita drove back to be with us right away and we were in there with her for about two days. That's when the truth came out.

Towards the end of her stay, a hospice care professional stepped into Mami's room to introduce herself. I noticed Marita's face grew somber. Uncomfortable with the palpable change in mood of the room and unfamiliar with hospice, I leaned in to ask her about it. She explained to me in a whisper that it's palliative care for people who are in their final months of life.

Mami finally confessed to Marita and me the entire diagnosis she'd received back in April. Her orthopedic doctor who initially checked her back said there was nothing he could for her. He requested she be sent to another doctor for an MRI. When the tests results came back, the new doctor had asked Mami if she had a will.

There were tumors growing all over her body. The cancer had metastasized into her bones, from her skull down to her feet. She was advised to do radiation but the doctor could only radiate certain points and it would only be to reduce pain. It could not save her. Her doctor also recommended chemo but Mami and Papi both adamantly agreed there was no way she'd go through it again. The cancer was too far out of control at that point anyway.

Mami and Papi chose not to communicate this to us because they still had an inkling of hope back then and they wanted to protect us girls as much as possible. I could also imagine Mami wouldn't have wanted to wish me a happy birthday by telling me she was going to die soon.

The doctor had told her she had about six months left to live.

Math had never been my forte but I figured it out fast. Way too fast. Mami was supposed to die in about four months. Everything stopped for me in that moment. I wanted to freeze that moment together with my mom and never have to go beyond that. At least right there in that moment, I could hug her. I could laugh with her. I could share with her my stories of love and triumph and hear her stories of wisdom and laughter. At least in that moment, I could keep her.

I think I must've sat in silence for several more moments as precious time continued ticking. I was too stunned to believe the words coming out of Mami's mouth. It was as if someone had sounded a bell to begin a race, one in which I never wanted either of us to cross the finish line.

It's All In The Name

*"I don't think that anything happens by coincidence...No one is
here by accident...Everyone who crosses our path has a message
for us. Otherwise they would have taken another path, or left
earlier or later. The fact that these people are here means that
they are here for some reason."*

~James Redfield

The day after Mami was discharged from the hospital was her first
official day of hospice care back home. The main nurse who would be
overseeing Mami's case arrived early in the morning. Hailing from Puerto
Rico, Rosie was a no-nonsense kind of woman with a kind heart and a
spirited sense of humor, quite like Mami. They instantly hit it off, as if
they'd been friends for years.

Rosie gave it to her straight explaining that, moving forward, Mami
would be hooked up to an IV with Dilaudid, a heavy-duty pain medication,
and have twenty-four-hour round-the-clock care. She vowed that she and her
team would do everything in their power to reduce the inevitable pain she'd
face and make her as comfortable as possible during these final months.
Mami looked her square in the eyes and, with her pointer finger extended,
raised her hand in the air and proclaimed that she would be the first person
to ever make it out of hospice alive.

Until this day I'm still uncertain if she said this to be positive and brave
or if she really believed this to be true. She was so confident in her statement
that I believed it. I thought there's surely a chance she can make it out alive
and I clung to that hope like it was my lifeline.

Her first few weeks in hospice were promising. She woke up every morning with considerable energy and would walk around the house with her rolling IV stand, albeit slowly but surely. Her two major destinations in the house were either the dining room to play solitaire or the living room to watch TV. She'd spend no more than a couple of hours in either spot, then return to her bed to read, play on her iPad or animatedly converse with either Papi, Marita (when she was visiting) or me and her nurses.

Each of the daily nurses we met over time had a name that resonated with Mami. Claudette reminded her of her close spiritual friend Claudia who used to live in Caracas, Venezuela where Mami and Papi had lived for many years early on in their marriage and where Marita was born. Then there was Nurse Karen. Karin (spelled differently but pronounced the same) had been her younger sister's name. She'd passed away decades earlier and Mami felt her presence like an angel watching over her in the nurse who shared her name. Nurse Evelyn ironically had the same name as Mami's older sister who was still living in Toronto, Canada where Mami and Papi had first met and fallen in love. Rosie, Mami told us, made her think of the rose tattoo she'd gotten just below the center of her collarbone to cover the scar from her cancer port years ago. Ever since she'd acquired the permanent red rose inked onto her skin, she'd proudly worn off-the-shoulder tops to show off her pretty tattoo. Mami had effectively turned a source of pain into beauty. That was just her way.

Then there was her main specialist, Dr. Iglesias, whose name took her back to her and Papi's favorite love songs by Julio Iglesias. When growing up, I remember them often slow dancing with each other in the living room to his passionate melodies. Mami remarked about God's sense of humor, love and irony. She felt they were all reminders to her of the many angels that were around protecting her.

Hearing this from her fueled my waning hope when one afternoon Mami started having almost paralyzing back spasms. She'd been sitting at the dining room table when she suddenly shook involuntarily, her face contorting in pain.

"Mami, what's wrong?" I asked, alarmed and reaching for her.

Never one to complain, she took a deep breath and swallowed. But she couldn't even answer.

Her nurse was already on her feet to help her back to bed but the short walk proved immeasurably long with the waves of pain that hit Mami like a tsunami, one after the other, with each agonizing step. She never cried.

But she was out of breath by the time she made it to her room, holding everything in before she collapsed onto her bed. Her nurse immediately increased her pain medication and she was knocked into a deep sleep the rest of the day. It scared me to have seen Mami so wickedly debilitated but what scared me even more was the lingering thought that what if she doesn't wake up?

Watching her nurse lovingly rest her hand on Mami's, her eyes closed and uttering a prayer over her, gave me comfort.

While Mami slept, the nurse determined with Papi that she would need a wheelchair because, if she were hit by another wave of such intense back spasms while standing, she'd surely fall and risk breaking her bones.

Another scary thought. But we trusted in Mami's well-intentioned nurses and, most of all, we trusted in the Lord.

The next couple of days were touch and go with Mami's extended periods of sleep and grogginess in response to the increased medication she'd required. But soon thereafter she re-emerged, with the same smile and the same spitfire sense of humor that we loved about her. Every morning when she awoke she'd raise her arms up in the air, rejoicing to the Lord.

"Thank you, God, for all the love in my life. Thank you for my family, for my nurses, for my home. Thank you for the joy You put in my heart. Thank You, Jesus," she'd utter over and over again, swaying as if in a glorious reverie.

But this was real life or, rather, real death we were talking about here. Mami had ultimately not only come to terms with her death sentence; she'd willingly embraced it. She was calm and collected when she shared this with us. I was impressed by her peaceful acceptance as opposed to dejected resignation of her final stretch of life on this earth. I wasn't sure I was yet ready to accept this fate.

When Rosie was back checking in on her, Mami graciously thanked her for the help she'd been receiving from her and her team. She expressed that she wished to die right there at home in the comfort of her own bed and the familiarity of her favorite surroundings. We all agreed that would be best and made the necessary arrangements with hospice to make it possible.

The following week a new nurse, Shirley, showed up. It was a name that drew a blank for both Mami and me; we couldn't figure out a connection with it to anyone in her life. A kind Trinidadian lady, Shirley had sincere eyes and radiated a calm, soothing energy. She especially enjoyed sharing stories with us as we watched over Mami.

When she'd first arrived, she'd unpacked her purse to settle in and put a book on the table next to Mami's bed where she sat. I was drawn to its vibrant yellow and orange cover. "The Power of Positive Thinking" by Norman Vincent Peale. I mentioned that it looked like a good read and Shirley confirmed so. She began opening up to us explaining how, years ago after going through a difficult divorce, she'd held so much frustration and anger towards her ex-husband. Her nerves and anxiety had overcome her until her sister stepped in and told her she must let her anger go. Her sister had sent her some books from televangelist Joel Osteen, which opened the doors to her healing. She'd been reading inspirational books ever since.

I noted how much I loved listening to Joel Osteen speak. Lucas had introduced me to his sermons and, every time I heard him preach, it's as if he were speaking directly to me.

Shirley nodded her head spiritedly and said, "It's amazing, isn't it? How he always has a message for you?"

We both smiled at each other before I excused myself to work. I was working as a sales associate for a relatively new all women's fitness club where I also taught pole dance. The owners were sympathetic to my situation with Mami and allowed me to work on sales from home. There were so many ways I felt God's blessings working through us when we most needed it and this was one of them.

Later when I was sitting at the kitchen table reviewing notes for work, Shirley walked in and asked if I could show her how to use the microwave so she could heat up her lunch. It was hard to focus on work; my heart and mind had been continuously with Mami. So I welcomed the break.

While her food was reheating and I was grabbing some utensils for her, Shirley noted how sweet Mami is and what a positive attitude she has. I agreed and told her that my mom has been my greatest inspiration, especially going through this.

Shirley shared with me that she'd lost her mother many years ago to ovarian cancer and had traveled back and forth to spend as much time as she could with her before she died. She recounted how she'd flown back one afternoon to visit her and, as she got to the baggage claim to pick up her luggage, her sister called. She wondered why she'd called so soon, knowing her plane had landed only minutes prior. Then she heard her other sister in the background saying, "Just tell her". Immediately anxiety swept over her as her sister stammered that their mom had passed away moments earlier. Shirley let out a mournful shriek that resonated throughout the airport and said how deeply she'd regretted not being there in time. It had haunted her for years afterwards. I felt my heart break into pieces with her as she spoke about her grief. I wondered if I'd get to be there with Mami when she took her last breath. I didn't want to imagine it any other way.

Placing my hand on Shirley's arm, I reassured her that while she couldn't have made it physically to her mom's bedside, she was there with her all along in spirit. Her mother, without a doubt I claimed, had felt her presence there through God.

"Thank you," she whispered as she took my hand in hers and smiled.

She continued to share with me that her father passed away only three years later of prostate cancer. This time she'd moved in with him to provide twenty-four-hour assistance as she does now for patients through hospice. She noted that it was hard for him to accept that death was imminent so she'd gone to Target to buy those relaxation CDs that include tranquil sounds of the ocean and forests with birds singing. They helped significantly to calm him during his troublesome transition. She was grateful to have been there every step of the way, including witnessing the very moment his spirit left his body.

I fought back the tears as I felt the ache of her heart as much as I felt my own. It was all so close now. Shirley looked at me with genuine interest and a warm understanding in her eyes and asked how I was doing. Nobody had really asked me that up until then; they'd generally asked how Mami was doing. I found myself confessing to her everything.

35

"I have faith that there's more to this life than what we see. I believe in life after death and that my mom's spirit will be eternally connected with mine. I know in my heart that God has a beautiful Kingdom that awaits her. I know she will be safe. Most of all, I know she'll be free—free of everything that ails her here physically," I declared.

I shared with her how Mami had named Marita the "Daughter of her Heart" and I was the "Daughter of her Soul". Shirley listened with a sort of gentle openness. I went on, divulging to her what weighed on me.

"It's been hard to see my mom in such agonizing pain and immobility. I hate that she's physically suffering so much. A couple of days ago, I'd cried and cried and cried and couldn't stop, I was like an open faucet. And then I cried and communed with God later that same night because I didn't want Him to feel that I doubted Him. But sometimes I feel scared and lost when I think of what life would be like without my best friend and soulmate, without the one person in my life who has not only loved me unconditionally but who has always truly and deeply seen me. This week I was sitting with my mom in her bed telling her how she's been the spiritual glue of our family and she confided in me that I'd be the one to continue being so for us. On one hand, I'm honored that she feels that I'm strong and giving enough to be so for all of us. On the other hand, I'm incredibly scared of falling apart and not being able to live up to her faith in me…She's always had this way of looking at me like she's looking at my highest self."

I was shaking as I let my thoughts and feelings pour out. Tears welled in my eyes. Shirley opened her arms to hug me and I felt myself almost collapse in them. As she held me close she whispered in my ear.

"God has a Divine plan and will help you get through anything in life. You can always call on the Father, the Son and the Holy Spirit as your guides and trust that you are protected and strengthened by them," she assured me.

We held each other for several minutes, long after the microwave had sounded off. I felt washed in comfort and peace.

"You are such a blessing to everyone in your life, both family and patients. Thank you for being not only my mom's angel but for being mine today too. May God bless you greatly," I wished her.

Only hours earlier I'd wondered how Shirley's name was a connection to Mami's life. It didn't matter; by that afternoon I knew that, no matter how long or short her time with us, she'd come into our lives for a reason.

CHAPTER 9

Mami's Last Wish

"One day, you will wake and there won't be any more time to do the things you've always wanted. Do it now."
~Paulo Coelho

Sometime shortly after the reality sank in that Mami's life was coming to an end in a matter of months we thought about her upcoming birthday on October 1st, right around the time her life sentence would be up.

It would be the big 7-0; I could see her all thrilled about that. Not! Mami had often said she didn't want to get old. "Old", of course, is relative and a frame of mind but I wondered if she had spoken that into existence for herself. Regardless, we felt that turning seventy was a cause for celebration despite her being mostly bedridden by that point. While she wasn't really into celebrating her own birthdays anymore, she'd always made ours special for us.

Papi, Marita and I started masterminding ideas of inviting our family who predominantly lived in Germany and Canada to come celebrate this milestone birthday. But Mami wasn't interested in celebrating her last one. My heart fell when she said that. I couldn't blame her, though, for her lack of interest.

She was, however, inspired to celebrate her 50th wedding anniversary with Papi, which happened to be nine days prior to her birthday on September 22nd. It was her last wish. My disappointment of a missed opportunity to celebrate Mami morphed back into excitement for the anticipated and unprecedented family party of a lifetime.

Planning their 50th wedding anniversary gave us all a sense of purpose and provided us the opportunity to do something meaningful for Mami.

We got wrapped up in our plan to invite everyone to the house where Mami might be able to hang out in the living room in her wheel chair. Papi came up with party rental ideas to provide tables and chairs for everyone. Marita pitched in ideas about food. I came up with wedding anniversary themed decorating concepts. We agreed we'd have food, cake, music and, of course, champagne. When eagerly sharing our party proposal with Mami at her bedside, her pursed lips revealed she was not buying what we were selling. As usual, the woman had her own ideas.

She shared with us that she'd love for the family to visit but she wanted us to all go to Natasha's, a restaurant and nightclub about an hour north of us, to enjoy a fun dinner, cabaret and a night of dancing. And she wanted us to do it in style, heading there and back in a stretch limo.

We sat around her with question marks bugging out of our eyes. I mean, she could barely move an inch some days with the debilitating pain of the cancer gnawing away at her bones.

But when your dying mom has a wish, you'd do anything to fulfill it for her. Even if that dying mom is a stubborn German woman intent on partying.

So we started working on it immediately. We got the family across the continents on board with travel dates, flights and hotel. We made reservations at Natasha's. We searched for limos that could not only accommodate a family of fourteen but a wheelchair too. Papi built a ramp for the front entrance of the house so we could wheel her down the front step and back up into the limo.

All the while, though, in the back of our minds, we wondered how the heck would Mami actually be able to make it out? We racked our minds and it never quite made sense. So from there we secretly devised Plan B; we didn't want to let her in on it so she wouldn't lose hope for her last wish. Given she was "touch and go" some days, we just knew it would be smart to have another plan in place—a safety net—should she not be feeling well enough on the anniversary.

And it went like this: we'd rent tables and chairs for the house and dress them up with white linen chair covers and white linen table cloths to be adorned with bouquets of white roses and faux diamonds. We'd offer food and snacks along with a vegan white and gold fondant 50th wedding anniversary cake, complementing the theme with gold silverware and gold napkins. It would be a wedding anniversary party made of dreams, all in the comfort of our home right at Mami's fingertips.

We planned to rent everything for the weekend so that if we actually did make it to the nightclub on Friday evening, we'd have the family over on Saturday for a "Part 2" of the celebration. If partying on Friday turned out to be a no-go, we'd have everything in place for the family to come over then. We simply told Mami that we were setting up for a two-day celebration. She was amenable. It was a win-win.

She had one last request. For years she'd longed to have a name necklace but not with her own name on it. She wanted to have Jesus' name around her neck. It was her wish to let everyone know that Jesus had healed her. Many may have not understood how Jesus could heal her when she was so obviously and painfully dying but that was missing the point. Through the trials she was enduring, He had healed her spirit. This is not to say God's healing is always unpleasant. Sometimes it's gentle and instantaneous. This was simply the path Mami's soul had signed up to take and, I imagine, that only when one is facing death, can one know this. Mami innately understood this and she wanted everyone else to know it too. God's healing may not come in the way we expect but He will always readily heal our spirits in the way we need.

CHAPTER 10

God And My Yoga Mat

*"Yoga is the joining of our mind, body and spirit. It is like
nature, everything is always recycled and brought full circle.
I find that I can heal myself if I do what nature does. It's taken
away stress and has helped me through crisis."*

~Tao Porchon-Lynch

One afternoon while lying in bed, Mami was leafing through a magazine
when she came across an article about Tao Porchon-Lynch. She is celebrated
for being the world's oldest living yoga teacher; however, she is anything
but old. The article featured a picture of her—ninety-three years young at the
time—in peacock pose, an advanced arm balance that requires some serious
core strength, arm stability and equipoise. In the accompanying interview
Tao spoke of the benefits of yoga throughout her life. With a mind-boggling
eighty-six years of practice, yoga had not only kept her young, strong and
limber, it had helped her find peace and eradicate fear even in times of crisis.

Drawn to this vivacious yogini's outlook on life, Mami called me into
her room to share the article with me. She proposed that I train to become
a yoga teacher. Pointing to Tao's picture she half jokingly suggested there
looks to be more longevity in teaching yoga than in pole dance. I laughed
because I did rather fancy myself still swinging adeptly around a pole well
into my eighties but she had a point.

I'd practiced yoga off and on over the years. Papi had taken me to my
first class when I was home on summer break after my freshman year of
college. Instantly I could see the strength and flexibility it would afford
me and I was most interested in learning to wrap my leg behind my head

because I thought that would be cool. Little did I know that yoga would someday become my lifeline during the biggest heartbreak of my life.

Mami knew me best so I took her advice seriously and began, at once, researching yoga teacher training programs. But there was really no need for me to investigate any further. 305 Yoga happened to be a studio right above the fitness club where I was teaching dance. I don't believe in coincidences. I called the studio's owner, Terri Cooper, who was offering a one-year long training program with rotating modules, one of which had just started. After asking her several questions about her Karma Yoga program, which is based on a path of service, I knew this would be the right fit for me. By the following week I was officially a teacher-in-training.

Just as when I was a kid in school, it took me awhile before I opened up to our group. During the first module I quietly observed and studied as much as I could. Sometimes I sat there wondering if anyone would understand the pain I held inside me of watching my mom slip away day by day back home. I often thought, "Nobody could fathom what I'm going through…I'm in this alone", which was a fallacy of course, but it was how I felt.

It wasn't until the second module that the shift occurred. Our homework assignments included journaling about our life experiences and relating them to renowned yoga teacher Judith Lasater's enlightening book "Living Your Yoga". It was the first time in several years I'd started writing again, a love I'd first discovered when I was eight and, after laying dormant for what felt like ages, had finally been rekindled. Writing helped me make sense of my emotions as I mentally prepared to let go of Mami. In our classes Terri prompted us to take turns sharing what we'd written. When I began hearing my classmates' own battles with heartbreak and grief in its many forms I learned that I was not alone. Every one of us was dealing with something in our lives. And then I began to open up.

When we allowed ourselves to be vulnerable with each other, an unshakeable bond between us inevitably formed. While we each came from different backgrounds and walks of life, we soon became each other's cheerleaders and shoulders to cry on.

Then came the physical component of our training—the asanas (yoga poses) and sequencing we learned. Getting on my yoga mat was an unspoken inquiry into myself. It gave me something my journaling could not. Sometimes I feel that putting into words our experiences, in a way, dilutes the meaning behind them. Sometimes we simply need to feel into our bodies without creating a narrative around it.

Terri would remind us that the way we are on our mats reflects the way we are in life. Say, for instance, I'm in a challenging balance pose and I keep falling over. Do I get frustrated with myself and give up? Do I laugh and, if I do, is it because I'm nervous about the way I might be perceived by others in class or because I'm enjoying the process of learning? Can I accept where I am in this moment? My mat became my mirror.

Somewhere between the rhythmic cadence of breath merged with mindful movement, I began to uncover my strength, my vulnerability, my love and my fears. I began peeling away the layers of myself to reveal the truth of my being that lies within me. For the first time in my life I had a glimpse of the fact that "I am" and just that is enough.

This is when I learned yoga is so much more than being able to wrap my leg around my head or looking badass in a headstand in a pair of Lululemon leggings. It really doesn't matter whether I can do those things or not. The beauty of the practice of yoga is that some days I feel stronger and more flexible and can go for more challenging poses and other days I feel tired and tight and can give myself permission to be gentler in my stretching, rest in a Child's Pose or simply sit and breathe. It ebbs and flows with me, just like life does.

Yoga is an ancient practice, a tool to explore the depths of oneself. The word "yoga" derives from the Sanskrit word "yuj", meaning "to yoke" or "to unite" and it was a system devised thousands of years ago to help human beings unite with Divine consciousness. It has been erroneously believed to be religious since it was born in India's Hindu culture. Rather, it can be a deeply spiritual path of self-discovery and self-actualization for anyone—regardless of religion, race, gender or creed.

Yoga classes became wildly popular in the Western world having originally been touted as a powerful full-body workout. (And it can be!) While many studios and teachers offer a deeper practice now to a growing and thirsty audience, the focus on the physical movements and poses represent only one limb of the eight-limbed path of yoga devised by the sage Patanjali to live a meaningful and purposeful life.

The first limb, *yama*, focuses on one's ethical standards to live by. The most noted yamas are "ahimsa" (non-violence), "satya" (truthfulness), "asteya" (non-stealing), "brahmacharya" (continence or moderation) and "aparigraha" (non-covetousness).

The second limb, *niyama,* concentrates on one's self-discipline and spiritual observances. The main niyamas are "saucha" (cleanliness), "samtosa" (contentment), "tapas" (meaning heat or spiritual austerities), "svadhyaya" (study of sacred texts and of oneself) and "isvara pranidhana" (surrender to God or the Universe, if you will).

The third and most famous limb is *asana* which are the physical postures practiced in yoga. The body is the temple of spirit and so we must discipline it in order to grow spiritually.

The fourth limb, *pranayama,* illuminates the importance of breath control. Prana is the Sanskrit word for "life force." The breath is life and when we learn to master the various techniques of breathing we recognize the connection between our breath, our mind and our emotions.

As we ascend from the first four limbs, focusing on understanding and connecting with our bodies and our emotions, we can move forward to the next four limbs, concentrating on our senses, our minds and, ultimately, achieving an enlightened state of consciousness.

The fifth limb is known as *pratyahara* or withdrawal of the senses. Here we begin to draw away from the external stimuli of the world to observe our habits and cravings, some of which may thwart our spiritual growth.

Once we've eliminated the distractions of the outside world, we come to the sixth limb, *dharana* (concentration), where we can now face the distractions within our own minds. We learn to concentrate on one specific focal point, such as a candle flame, a sacred image, or the silent repetition of a simple sound.

This brings us to *dhyana,* the seventh limb, which is meditation. The difference between concentration and meditation is that concentration is focusing on one single point while meditation is the state of being profoundly aware without a particular focus.

The eighth limb *samadhi* is known as the state of transcendence or ecstasy. This is when we transcend the self and experience oneness with our Creator and with the Universe as well as the interconnectedness to all other beings. Here we recognize our union with the Divine, that we are all one and the same.[1]

Make no mistake; following these limbs is no easy task, which is why yoga is called a *practice* and not an end result. The deeper I've delved into studying and practicing yoga over the years, the more I realize how much I have yet to learn.

While first studying these eight major steps to transcendence, I wondered if Mami had any idea just how meaningful yoga would become in my life and not just a way I could earn a living by teaching. This entire system helped me navigate through the murky and unknown ocean of grief.

There were many days I had zero desire or energy to practice but getting on my mat proved to be a great antidote. In fact, the more I practiced, the more I realized how much I needed it.

I sobbed often during the sweaty Vinyasa flow classes from our training sessions, tuning into Terri's words of wisdom and into my own inner wisdom that lay deep within my body beneath the layers of hurt and heartbreak. Every backbend, every forward bend, every twist helped me release the pain I harbored inside. And without fail, after every class, I came home feeling more and more ready to face Mami's imminent death.

As our training in Karma Yoga continued, we were given an opportunity to serve as volunteers for an upcoming fundraiser, The Yoga Aid Challenge, to benefit kids in underserved communities. Terri also announced that she'd be leading her annual retreat to Rishikesh, India beginning the first week of the New Year where, she noted, we'd have a chance to dive deeper into our yoga practice and be of service to the locals. The idea of practicing yoga in its birthplace of India captivated me. At the same time my heart sank knowing that Mami would no longer be around next year, let alone for the fundraiser two months away. I knew how much I'd need India, or at least somewhere else other than here so I could remove myself from the hell that our family had been facing this year. I'd need time to process everything. At times it felt like too much to bear. I wanted to get away. And India was far, far away.

---

1 Paraphrased from "Get To Know The Eight Limbs of Yoga" by Mara Carrico, www.yogajournal.com.

With that in mind, Terri led us through another dynamic practice that unlocked the floodgate to my anticipatory grief and knocked down the protective walls I kept putting up around my heart. It felt cathartic and liberating to face my fears head on about losing Mami. After toweling off my sweat and tears and rolling up my yoga mat, I felt present to the harmony and synchronicity of the circle of life and death. I felt deep gratitude that I was blessed to have the relationship with my mom that I did. I felt connected and present. Because of the way yoga makes me feel, I now often share with people how the top two things I turn to in life are God and my yoga mat.

CHAPTER 11

Mambo Jambo

"When he to whom a person speaks does not understand, and he who speaks does not understand himself, that is metaphysics."

~Voltaire

Back on the home front, Mami was giving into her vices. There were several days here and there where she'd devour guava pastels, drink coffee and make requests for various food cravings like potato salad and German potato pancakes with applesauce. Even though she never really exercised in her more recent years, she had constantly watched what she was eating to maintain her figure. We got a kick out of seeing her enjoy herself like this.

Thankfully Marita, with her noteworthy cooking skills, had Mami's cravings covered whenever she was in town, which was gaining more frequency the less time we had left with her.

With the cocktail of medications she was on, Mami's days and nights had turned wonky. She'd sleep at random hours throughout the day, sometimes nodding off then suddenly pulling her head back up to utter something cute and nonsensical. Sometimes she was completely cognizant and either recalling a memory or wisecracking with us. We never knew what we'd get so we simply went with it.

One afternoon I'd asked her if I could borrow her magnifying mirror so I could tweeze my eyebrows. Without hesitation, she facetiously exclaimed that I should be ashamed of myself for walking around with unkempt brows. This prompted me to show her my toes and point out how I needed to fix my pedi too. She acted horrified.

We had a good laugh and then she grabbed my hand and spontaneously said in German, "Come, lets go to the underworld".

I responded in my rather choppy German, "I don't want to go to the underworld. I'd rather go to Heaven and you're going there anyway!"

Mami agreed that, "Ok, we'll go all the way around", demonstrating by circling her pointer finger in the air. Going with her train of thought, I told her that, yes, we'd take the scenic route.

Later Papi came in to give her a kiss and ask her about lunch to which Mami responded, "No, Michelle's on the same page!"

Also going with it, Papi asked which page that would be.

"We took care of the triangle window and we had it replaced," she responded matter-of-factly.

She grinned at Papi before he headed back, baffled, to the kitchen to figure out what kind of food to prepare for her.

Once he'd left, Mami murmured to me that my husband and I would have "a Biblical home" to come to one day. She said that once she's gone that she's leaving her part of the home to Marita and me. She said she could imagine creating another entrance in the house to split it up and have Papi live in one part and Lucas and me in the other. I gently explained to her that it would be up to Papi what he'd like to do with The Sanctuary. She nodded her head in agreement and noted that she didn't want Marita or me to have the burden of work anymore. She didn't want us to have to slave away for a job in order to live. I reassured her not to worry of such things, that God would always take care of us.

When Karen, her nurse on duty at the time, was administering her next dose of morphine, Mami smiled and explained to us, "It's like when you take your car in to retune it, like for an oil change."

As often as she'd left us in confusion, sometimes her seemingly random thoughts made sense. She then nodded off only to wake up and ask me very earnestly to come sit by her side on her bed. I did so, being as careful as I could to not hurt her legs. She took my hand and told me that there would be a lot of things left around the house after she's gone. I gulped at the thought. She explained that she and Papi have a camping set that included a new stovetop grill, plates and champagne. She said that she'd kept it around, thinking I might like it one day and that it'd be nice for Lucas and me to use if we want. But she didn't want us to feel bad that it was kind of a cheap set. She made sure to indicate though that it was brand new.

Mami and Papi did indeed have a camping set over forty years ago but that was long gone.

With our continued conversations, I'd become aware that there was a fine line between loopiness from heavy-duty medication and what Mami was really thinking, feeling and experiencing in her mind and body. I was careful not to negate or shut down what she wished to share, even if it didn't make a lick of sense. At the same time I wanted to maintain my honesty in response.

Squeezing her hand, I said, "I appreciate your sweet thoughtfulness, Mami. I was never much of a camping-in-the-outdoors kind of girl but, hey, it might be kind of fun if I were to give it a try!"

Her eyelids became heavy and the smile on her face already faded as she drifted off to sleep before I finished the sentence.

CHAPTER 12

The End Of Days Roller Coaster Ride

"Life is like a roller coaster. You can either scream every time there is a bump or you can throw your hands up and enjoy the ride."

~Ben Busko

As the end of days drew nearer, Mami's condition rapidly shifted back and forth from one day to the next. She'd had yet another dreadful day overwrought by waves of excruciating back spasms that forced her into submission. She squirmed and shook under her covers. Her body was worn out. She was under attack from the inside out. It pained me to see her grimace and tightly ball up her fists, holding her breath, when a spasm would bolt through. I hated seeing them fight their way through her fragile body. I couldn't begin to imagine the level of pain she felt. All I could do was pray and gently remind her to breathe deeply to allow them to pass. It broke my heart every time it happened and I'd have given anything to take away the anguish she must've carried. She never let it show.

I've always believed that everything happens for a reason yet I wondered what the reason was behind these spasms. What was it that was eating her from the inside? Aside from the physical damage of the cancer that insatiably ravaged her body, I questioned whether there was spiritual growth that she'd been undertaking while still there in this body, in this School of Life. Only God knew that. I gathered that, deep down perhaps on a subconscious level, Mami knew why too. All we could do was take it one day at a time with her.

After a day of spasms that had shaken her to her core, she requested an increase in pain medication. She continued to undermine her pain to us, nonetheless. She refused to talk about how serious it was. We fully supported her wish for pain management. Every time there was an increase in meds, however, we prepared ourselves that there would also be an increase in drowsiness and sleep.

This time she was out of it almost the entire day, from morning through night. She had a small rectangular pillow covered in a soft yellow cloth with smiley faces printed on it. Her head tilted back against the pillow and her mouth hung wide open, the corners of her lips pulled down from the distress she bore, slowly breathing life in and out. Within those hours upon hours of sleep, she had one or two moments of wakefulness when I noticed her having hushed conversations with Papi. I left the both of them to speak privately and headed into the kitchen to clean.

Later when anxiously scrubbing the countertops, I heard Papi come in. I noticed him wiping away tears that had begun to form in the rims of his eyes. It broke my heart to see him so crushed. I couldn't imagine what it would be like to lose the one and only partner of your life, the one with whom you shared everything.

I dropped the sponge and wrapped my arms around him. He held on for all of a moment and then pulled back to tell me he was sorry for crying. I let him know to never apologize for that and reminded him we're always here for each other, to pick each other up.

He explained that he and Mami had talked about her will and that he needed to see their lawyer as soon as possible that week. He was unsure of how much longer she could hold on, let alone if she'd even make it through next week.

I felt a lump in my throat. It was at least one month sooner than we'd anticipated. But Mami's body was deteriorating rapidly.

All the while, preparations had to be made for a tropical storm possibly upgrading to a Category 1 hurricane heading our way. Rosie let us know that we may have to transport Mami to a hospital. Even though we had a generator at home that would help us in a power outage, Mami needed twenty-four-hour nurse care. Should a hurricane come, Rosie had explained, the nurses would be stuck and unable to provide the assistance needed. Not to mention that, God forbid, Mami's medication was to run out. We would've had no way of getting it for her.

I'd asked God for His protection. I knew He had complete understanding of our situation and how difficult and painful it would be for Mami to have to move. God was our shield. The storm didn't prove to be a menace; rather, it brought heavy rainfall and exceptionally gusty winds followed by long, quiet periods of dark clouds looming overhead. It wasn't enough to put us in danger and, so, I thanked God for the turn of events in our favor.

Despite the steady downpour that continued to dump on us the rest of the day, Mami was back in high spirits and telling stories to Karen and me. After four half vials of morphine, the slight smile on Mami's face revealed she was relaxed. She had quieted down momentarily and Karen stepped out of the room for a quick break.

Mami's tired green eyes still sparkled as she turned to me. She urged me to sit with her and, happily, I came closer to kneel on the floor beside her bed. I reached for her hand over the covers. I thought that maybe she was feeling a little loopy but the exchange that followed was articulate and deeply thoughtful.

I don't quite remember how we got into the conversation. Heck, I couldn't even remember which day it was…one day of sadness had blurred into one day of joy and back and forth like that until all the days of the previous months had merged into one colossal emotional rollercoaster.

What I do recall is that she asked me if it was ok for her to go. I took a deep breath and before I could answer, she brought up her own mom, Omi Lies'chen, as we'd affectionately called her. Omi lay in a hospital bed for two years before she passed away. Mami frequently flew from New York to Berlin to be with her. She relayed to me that while on one of her visits she'd asked her mom if she was ready to go. Omi had told her then not quite yet, that she still was processing some life lessons in her heart.

I looked into Mami's eyes and asked her if she felt she was ready or if she felt she still needed to learn any other life lessons. She said she was ready but was afraid that she didn't do enough in this life. She thought she should've gone to cancer centers and other support groups to share her story and help other people go through this. I told her not to worry of such things and that she did exactly what she was meant to do at every given moment in her life. I also reminded her that, no matter what, Mami would be leaving her legacy with us. Papi, Marita and I would be sure to carry it on in our own lives.

Mami and I continued to hold hands as she confessed to me that she was hanging on mostly for Papi. Tearing up, she said that she could never imagine having to go through losing him and feared how devastating it would be for him to lose her. At the same time, she was concerned about the financial and emotional costs of her holding on. I asked her if she truly felt it was better—for *her*—to hang on if she stayed in her condition for another year or several more years. I let her know not to worry about Papi, Marita or me as God would be our guide, no matter where life would take us. I reminded her that the most important concern was that of her own spirit and what her spirit's needs are.

"If you feel that your spirit still needs to learn something and be here in this physical body," I continued to tell her, "then this is where you should be. And if you feel that your spirit has completed its work in this lifetime and you're ready to move forward, then that is where you need to go."

She quietly listened, searching my face as if for answers.

"We support whatever you need. And, most importantly, God will be with you every step of the way, just as He will be with all of us," I reassured her.

She laid her head back on her little yellow pillow and squeezed my hand.

"Thank you, I needed that," she said and closed her eyes. I sat there in the silence of the room and watched her sleep, tracing the silhouette of her face in my mind's eye, committing to memory every curve and line.

The next day turned out to be another tough one for Mami. She'd start talking and then lose her train of thought in mid-sentence from recurrent memory lapses. A large bruise had formed on her arm where the IV was inserted. Despite a history of bruising easily, she claimed the nurse wasn't doing her job right. She unexpectedly got irritable with Papi when he came in to kiss her as he'd been doing everyday, several times a day. By day's end when we were by her bedside desperately trying to keep her happy, Mami leaned forward to move one of the ice packs from under her back.

"No, I don't need a hand!" she shouted at me. I hadn't done anything. Her own hand fidgeting with her lower back had confused her.

"Leave me alone," she said staunchly. I stood there, momentarily frozen. She looked at me, distraught. "I don't want you here."

Mami's words stung. I retreated to my bedroom and cried. I knew she didn't mean it, that she was just confused, but it hurt nonetheless. I didn't kiss her goodnight because I was afraid to upset her more. I prayed that night that she'd still be alive the next day. I couldn't bear it if that were the way we'd left things.

The following morning I awoke groggy and stiff but was thankful to find Mami alert and cheerful.

Meanwhile, unbeknownst to us, Marita was patiently waiting in her car in our driveway. She'd left Naples in the wee morning hours to visit us again and, upon arrival, had tried calling the house phone, Papi's cell phone and mine, too, because she didn't want to ring the doorbell and disturb Mami. Ironically Mami was on the house phone talking with one of her best friends for the first time in several weeks, Papi was at the gym, and I'd left my cell phone on silent.

Fortunately it wasn't too long before I noticed her parked outside. I ran outside and we embraced before laughing over her sitting patiently alone out there while we were "up and at it" inside.

"C'mon," I grinned and whisked her inside with her overnight bags to join Mami's bedside. Mami was lucid and talkative all day.

I don't know how she found the time between her frequent visits to Miami, her work and her married life, but Marita managed to make some DVDs compiling family photos alongside soundtracks of songs that were meaningful to us.

She'd asked Mami if she'd be up for watching the new one she'd brought and she was game. Papi had come home by then so we gathered around Mami's bed to watch the history of our family, told in pictures and highlighted by the songs, "Amazing" by Seal, "Wind Beneath My Wings" by Bette Midler, and "Por Ti Volare" by Andrea Bocelli.

When "Wind Beneath My Wings" began, Mami remembered how that had been her special song she'd dedicated to Papi and, before we knew it, it had triggered a waterfall of tears for her. As pictures of our happy family flashed across the TV screen, Mami sobbed heavily.

"I'm not ready to go!" she cried out, "I can't possibly leave you guys now." Tears were streaming down her cheeks.

Magnetically drawn to her and overwhelmed by our yearning to somehow save her from this mess, we instantly leaned in closely over Mami, grabbing each other's hands. Together we formed a tight circle with Mami around her bed. Witnessing her fear of missing out on life, revealed in her frightened eyes, elicited an onset of tears from the rest of us.

The four of us watched our lives pass before our eyes, as images of old family pictures with our younger and smiling faces morphed into more recent pictures of us still together and joyful. We gripped each other's hands with a love beyond what we could express in the physical realm. It all felt so unreal, yet at the same time, so deep that it cut right into my core, as if slicing me in half and there fell my heart upon the floor by my feet.

I closed my eyes trying to hold back the tears but all I could do was grip even more tightly Mami's and Papi's hands, connected with Marita's across from mine. In that moment huddled over Mami, I wanted to signal how deeply my love extended to each of them. I felt that surge of love returning to me in the circle of love we held together. We each looked at one another without uttering a word, basking in God's presence there with us in the depths of devotion we undeniably felt for each other as a family.

CHAPTER 13

It Takes A Village

"We cannot accomplish all that we need to do without working together."

~Bill Richardson

Marita took time off from her demanding career to drive back and forth between Miami and Naples every two weeks to be there for Mami. When she wasn't able to be there in person, she called and checked in with us daily. She cooked while staying with us and also brought us homemade soups we could freeze and eat later.

One evening after savoring one of her soups, Papi snuck back into the kitchen for a late-night snack. I walked in to discover him with a piece of crispbread slathering the last of the artichoke spinach "hoomus" (as he pronounces it, his slight German accent prominent) *on top of* the last of the crunchy peanut butter that we'd agreed was not from our favorite brand. I stood there and stared at him, attempting to hold in my laughter. He looked at me with a goofy grin, explaining that he was simply trying to finish up the items in the fridge that we no longer wanted. Unable to keep my mouth shut, I asked him if he was for real. Peanut butter and hummus?! Stubborn as Papi is—and we wonder from where I get it—he looked at me with a forced smile and said it would taste great together because each of them are great on their own. Umm, yeah, ok…I stood there and watched him like a hawk until he sat down at the kitchen table and finally, not to mention somewhat reluctantly, took the first bite of his creative concoction.

Returning my stare, he grinned and said, "See, it's good!" as he ever so slightly winced and swallowed the smattering of disparate ingredients.

I couldn't help laughing at this point. It was the little things that brought us satisfaction. For Papi, it was peanut butter and hummus. For me, it was chuckling over his adorable antics.

He may have a unique set of taste buds, but he was still the man of the house. Papi handled the financial arrangements, phone calls and necessary paperwork preparing for Mami's death.

I cleaned the house, did the laundry and took care of Arco.

We spent time sitting and talking with Mami or watching over her, generally along with one of the nurses. In our own ways, the three of us gave her a lot of love.

Marita often reminded us, "it takes a village". She was right. We each brought something to the table, creating a collective network of care.

The time we individually dedicated to being there for Mami was demanding but we never saw it that way. We'd survived many challenges throughout our lives but nothing like this. This was by far the most life-changing event we all had to go through. Mami's need for our love and our being there for her brought us together in a way like never before. We'd always been a close and loving family. The time we spent caring for her in her final months, though, deepened our connection and our compassion far beyond what we'd already experienced. I felt a tenderness; a softening happening in my heart. Every morning Papi hugged me and told me he loves me.

When either of us felt down, we stepped in more readily and lovingly than ever before to lift each other up.

Outside of our family I felt the tremendous support of my dear friends including those in the yoga community. How and why this all came together the way it did and with the timing that it did, I'll never know. But I had this persistent feeling that there was something greater coming from all of this.

In the darkest hours of the night I learned that it is not the way through life itself; it is the company you keep along the way that can make or break it.

CHAPTER 14

A Legacy Of Love And Joy

"She (my mother) became a warrior far superior to any epic hero. She became a giant on her knees. With a sword in one hand she battled the enemies of death and disease, and with her other hand stretched toward heaven she kept beseeching God's help and His mercy."

~Bishop T.D. Jakes

In Mami's darkest hours, she held fast to the Lord. She continued to praise and thank Him each and every day *in the face of death.* For most of us it's hard to be grateful when things aren't going our way. But to have seen Mami give thanks to God in spite of the physical trauma her body endured as it shut down piece by piece blew me away. She was my hero.

Even after a day when she couldn't move her leg an inch because of excruciating agony, she noted how she had absolutely no reason to complain about life and remained focused on the supportive and good people she had on her side.

On that day I sat with her in her bed, far enough away that I wouldn't mistakenly sit on any part of her but close enough that I could lay my hands on her leg. I did so in far-fetched hopes of magically healing her bones or at least offering a sense of relief for her. I told her how much I admired her for her strength.

"It's not about being strong. It's about accepting my situation and either giving up altogether or just saying, 'Ok, I can do this!' and making the best of it I can," she wisely spoke.

She'd obviously chosen the latter option and it made perfect sense to me. Of course we must make the best out of everything in life. Nonetheless I was amazed that she could do so under such dire and presumably depressing circumstances. Here was death hovering, staring right at her, accompanied by relentless pain spiked by fluxes of unbearable spasms. This was not to mention the rapid deterioration of her bones that I was afraid could've pulverized at any given moment. And Mami was *still* praising God and choosing to see all the good in her life.

She proudly wore the Jesus necklace Papi had gifted her, per her last wishes. One afternoon when I came in to see her she told me that she wanted me to have the necklace after she was gone. I didn't quite know how to respond and Mami could sense my apprehension.

"I know it's rather bold to wear His name around your neck like this. I don't expect you to wear it. But I want you to have it."

With that, she kissed me and I thanked her for her gift.

Everyday she showed her gratitude to us and to her nurses for taking care of her. Whenever someone did something for her, whether making her something to eat, changing her sheets or giving her medication, she'd smile and thank them as if it were the grandest gesture anyone could've made for her.

One afternoon when passing by Mami's room in between one of my laundry runs, I overheard her talking with her nurse who had brought up some difficult family issues she was facing.

"When we feel deeply hurt or upset with someone we love, instead of getting angry with our loved ones, we must give our feelings to God. We cannot always carry the burden of our own pain. It's often overwhelming. And that's when we can ask God to help us carry it because we don't have to do it alone in life," Mami spoke as she put her hand on the nurse's.

Her nurse wiped a tear from her eye and thanked her. I smiled as I walked back to the laundry room.

Mami didn't want her friends to break down if they were to see her so, for the first time, our technologically challenged mom requested an email account on her iPad, which she'd previously used for games like solitaire when she couldn't make it out to the dining room table. She didn't even know how to turn on a computer at the time; she'd never had a need for one. She might've been the last of her kind for all I know.

Marita set her up with a new email account, explaining the ins and outs of her new inbox. When she pointed out to Mami that she could have her own automatic signature stamp with each email, she beamed and asked her if she could type it in herself. Marita gave her the iPad and when Mami handed it back it read:

"Love and Joy,
Christa"

It was perfect. Mami embodied Love and Joy. She remained loving despite the feeling that her body hated her. She remained joyful despite the sadness that her life was to end sooner than any of us had hoped for.

When Mami was able to make it out to the dining room in her wheelchair one afternoon, I sat with her and her nurse at the table and we delved into a discussion about death. Mami was open about everything. I loved that about her.

We began asking each other questions. What is it that we fear about death so much? Do we fear that it is the "be all, end all" of everything? Are we afraid that we will no longer be heard or no longer feel loved? When cutting through our egos and fears and stories and dramas, what is it that remains? Don't we intrinsically feel that there is something more there? Something greater out there, yet *within* us, too? What is the soul? The spirit? What is the truth at our core? And isn't that something that co-exists at all times—past, present, and future—in fact, transcending time. . .something that is eternal and infinite?

Knowing that there is something greater within us, a God spark, and, even grander, God himself...doesn't that bring us comfort?

"Praise God," her nurse chimed in. Mami and I nodded our heads and continued.

Even though what happens after death is mostly unknown, aside from stories of people who've, through accidents, experienced momentary pulls to "the other side" and into the Light, we have yet to overcome our fear of this unknown. Just because we do not know it doesn't mean it's bad.

Dying is an inevitable fact of life in our physical bodies on this earth. Not one single human being has escaped it in the history of mankind. So why can we not be more accepting of this and more loving to ourselves in our transition from this physical body into the spiritual realm? Why can we not praise God in this magical journey and trust that we are leaving this life a more evolved soul than when we came in? We are graduating from the School of Life and moving into a new and advanced level, whether that means reincarnation to learn our next lessons or vibrating at a spiritually higher level.

"Death," Mami noted, "is merely a transition into something even more beautiful than we experience here in our bodies. Our bodies are simply our transport system in this lifetime and will get us as far as our spirits need to go during this life lesson."

She paused then looked at her nurse and me and said, "I want to share with people that dying can be the most beautiful experience we ever go through."

Mami was the ultimate example that, through our mindset and, really, our "heartset", we can choose to see the beauty and happiness in our lives and beyond. Mami was proving to us that death is not a sad end; rather, it is a gateway and an opportunity for the growth of our spirits. It is a new beginning.

CHAPTER 15

Closer To The Finish Line

"Goodbyes are only for those who love with their eyes. Because for those who love with heart and soul there is no such thing as separation."

~*Rumi*

I awoke to the persistent pounding of a pressure washer pointed at the windows of my room. With the upcoming anniversary celebration, Papi wanted the house in mint condition so he'd hired someone to help us take care of various jobs we couldn't get to. The constant drone of the pressure washer lasted for hours, reverberating within the confines of my head, as the handyman worked his way around our home and across the patio deck.

Between the house projects, having a nurse there everyday and the recurring visits from Rosie and Mami's doctor, it hadn't really felt peaceful at The Sanctuary for a while. We were grateful for the help but, having always kept our home quiet and private, it felt strange constantly having other people around.

I felt unsettled and found myself restlessly doing loads of laundry, clearing out parts of the house where work needed to be done, and discussing with Marita Plan A and Plan B for the anniversary party. Marita's frequent presence at the house was a blessing not just for Mami but for me too.

Some days it was hard to be with Mami all of the time. Marita, unable to be with us every single day, took to Mami's side whenever she was in town. It was a relief to have her company but, at the same time, the guilt burned inside of me for not being there one hundred percent for Mami. Sometimes I felt the need to disconnect from it all and watch a mindless movie or read a book. Sometimes I needed an escape from the weight of everything.

Often, though, I couldn't even will myself to go out and socialize let alone take a walk on my own in nature. I was afraid that to my friends, both in and out of the yoga community as well as the people with whom I worked at the fitness club, I sounded like a broken record. When they asked how things were going with Mami, what could I say? She was dying and we were doing the best we can. She was strong, courageous and joyful. As hard as it was, she made things easier on us through her optimistic attitude towards death. No matter how much I talked about her, though, they were incredibly supportive. I often felt overwhelmed by the outpouring of love and compassion our family was experiencing from friends, co-workers and strangers alike. It rekindled my hope that there are good people out there. Everyday I was grateful for the enormous net of support that held us up and kept us going.

But the guilt of disconnecting from Mami gnawed away at me. Because of my struggle with being with her on a constant basis and my lack of desire to go out, I felt like I was in limbo.

Within this odd state of uncertainty, I wrestled with a plethora of emotions. Love, fear, joy, sadness, connection, disconnection, anticipation, exhaustion, guilt, anguish, solace, peace…feeling such a wide range of human emotion in such a short span of time left me wondering if it's possible for a human being to short circuit.

To top it all off, Lucas and I had reached an impasse in our relationship. He feared commitment and I'd dreamed of marriage and having a family one day. It was hard for me to come to terms with it, especially with the amplified emotions battling within me everyday. He was still there for me but I knew it wouldn't go anywhere long-term. On one hand, I needed the comfort of affection but, on the other hand, I was afraid to invest my heart any further. I wasn't yet ready to let go of him. Not when I knew I'd have to let go of Mami so soon. We still saw each other but I held back every time, knowing that we, too, would soon come to an end.

One evening as the blanket of night crept over our house and time ticked forward, I felt a pang of loneliness. I suddenly feared crawling into bed alone. I wanted to call Lucas but my need to make things right with Mami won over. I was uneasy with not always spending the whole day with her, especially not knowing exactly how much longer we would have together in this life.

She was tucked under her covers with her hair gathered in a little side ponytail and rolled up in a soft pink curler. I melted looking at her, like a mother would look at her baby. Amidst the daily chaos in the house and because Mami had somewhat stabilized, we'd cut out the night shift nurses. So I double-checked her bedtime medications and she was thankful I remembered her Valium and nighttime laxative she'd nicknamed "Sweet Daddy" for its sugary flavor.

I turned off the overhead lights in her room and the dim light of a lamp from Papi's night table softly illuminated the background. Sitting down at her bedside I looked at her beautiful face and sighed.

"Mami, I'm sorry that I haven't been spending much time with you throughout the day. I want to be with you, I want to soak up every moment we can together—I feel like it's never enough—but at times it feels like too much. I feel like I need a break. It's not from you...it's just from... *everything*," I explained.

She dismissively waved her hand in the air.

"I don't want you to be here with me all the time because it would be too much for me too. With the nurse also here, we tend to talk more often and sometimes I'd prefer to have quiet. Sometimes I just want to close my eyes and be left on my own," she told me.

It was then that I realized that neither of us had been feeling a sense of peace at home. What a relief we both understood each other's need for silence and time alone.

"I know you already know this but I'm always here for you, even when we're not together in the same room," I said, taking her hand and placing it on my heart.

"Thank you, I know," she whispered and squeezed my hand.

That night I fell asleep fast. I felt like a burden had been lifted.

The following afternoon, when sitting in front of the TV with Mami and her nurse, the nurse handed me a booklet from hospice. Imprinted on the cover in italics, it read "A Sacred Journey". Curious, I skimmed the first couple of pages, noticing titles such as "Understanding the Dying Process", "Appetite", "Bodily Functions" and "Confusion/Disorientation". I felt that familiar pit of fear in my stomach again. How would we actually deal with Mami's last moments when the time came? How would we deal with the aftermath? I tried to focus on my faith in God to usher Mami home and lead us through the transition of moving forward in our lives without her physical presence. I was balancing precariously on a tightrope between faith and fear. I closed the book and set it aside for another time.

That evening when the house was quiet and Mami was alone I walked to her door and stuck my head in. She looked at me and smiled.

"Are you up for some company now?" I asked.

"Yes, of course, sweetie," she replied.

Gripping her hand as I sat down, I said, "You know when you're, umm, gone from your body, we'll always be connected via spirit and can reconnect at any time."

Her eyelids fluttered a bit as she smiled and asked, "What would you like my ringtone to be when I call you from the other side?"

I grinned and, as I pondered some clever ideas, Mami lightheartedly suggested, "Ding-a-ling-a-ling!"

"Ok, simple enough!" I agreed, chuckling.

"Hmm," she thought aloud. "Or maybe we can go with…CAW! CAW! CAW!" she cackled like a crow.

Laughing, I said, "No, no! Let's stick with the first!"

She confirmed then that it would be "Ding-a-ling-a-ling" and determined that my answering tone should be "Ding-a-ling".

We giggled together at our spontaneous, silly creativity. Hearing her laughter reverberate through my heart—and filed away for future memories—reminded me that our eternal spiritual connection can never be broken.

A Milestone

"And we know in all things God works for the good of those who love Him."

~Romans 8:28

The big day had arrived. No, not that big day, thank God not yet. It was the 50th anniversary celebration for Mami and Papi. Our family had flown in from Germany and Canada and had booked themselves all together in a nearby hotel. Not wanting to disturb us before the anniversary, they went sightseeing around town. Mami had barely moved from her bed in the days leading up to this much anticipated milestone and we were nervous that we'd have to go straight to Plan B, hosting the party at home only. Mami hadn't left the house since going to the hospital on Memorial Day weekend, about four months earlier. We knew she wanted more than anything to go out for one last hurrah.

That morning we apprehensively checked in with her to see if she'd be able to (with help, of course) get out of bed, get dressed up, get into her wheelchair and bear the hour long drive up north to sit for hours in a nightclub with music and entertainment before another hour long drive back home. The thought of the drive alone made me wince thinking about every possible bump on the road that could trigger the pain of her bones being eaten alive.

Her eyes widened and, with a grin akin to Alice in Wonderland's Cheshire cat, she said, "YES!"

When there's a will, there's a way. Especially if there's a stubborn German woman behind the will. So that was that. It was going to happen.

Mami had planned to wear an expensive, elegant and somewhat subdued dress that night but opted instead for a fun and funky twenty-dollar dress Marita and I had bought for her weeks earlier at a local Brazilian shop. We both beamed as we helped her into the vibrant teal and gold ensemble that afternoon. It was much more fitting for her than the plain olive green dress she'd initially thought of wearing.

We'd hired a hair and makeup artist to help her get ready in her bed and had asked Rosie to join us for the night. She had become a part of our family and we knew we'd be in good hands, God forbid, anything happened to Mami while out. Rosie had the foresight to switch Mami to Fentanyl patches weeks earlier to get rid of the IV attached to her side.

Meanwhile in the dining room we'd made the finishing touches to the tables and chairs that had been delivered the day prior for Plan B, which would at that point be saved for Day 2 of the celebration. Decked in white linens with gold place settings and gold cutlery the table held a centerpiece of white roses and faux diamonds, which we'd put together ourselves. It was just as we'd envisioned. We oohed and ahhed at our own creation before disappearing to primp ourselves for the festivities.

Once Mami was all dolled up in her wheelchair and ready to go we couldn't believe our eyes. She didn't even look sick. The power of the mind and of the will is far greater than we think. So powerful, I believe, that we can choose the timing of our death.

The stretch limo arrived with the rest of the family already in it. We were elated to be reunited. Given that they lived so far away, we rarely saw each other but, when we did, it was with immense delight. Everyone cheered when we hoisted Mami into the limo. It was a feat that not only were we all reunited but also that Mami had made it.

The "POP!" of a champagne bottle opening from the mini bar table resounded inside the limo. You must've known that was coming, didn't you? Mami clapped and grinned as we raised our glasses to her and to each other.

An hour and a couple of champagne bottles later we pulled up in good spirits to the restaurant and nightclub. Its humble exterior nestled within a strip mall bespoke nothing of its theatrical décor inside. Crystal chandeliers dripped from cathedral ceilings alongside long curtains of crystal beads. Ornate Persian rugs covered the floors surrounding a giant dance floor and stage. We had a large rectangular table reserved to accommodate our group; Mami sat at its center facing the stage.

Large portions of food and endlessly flowing vodka and champagne were served before the live entertainment began, which ranged from singers, dancers and Cirque-du-Soleil type performers. The spectacular performance roused us into applause at the show's end right before the hosts opened the dance floor to the patrons. Music and dancing: this was our domain and we took to it like thieves in the night.

As we danced to the beat of the music, I could feel time stealing away. Often I'd gaze over at Mami and stop by the table to check in with her, but to see her fully enjoying herself and raising her hands up in the air along with the music and lights elated me. Before I knew it, I lost myself in the music and movement, the vodka and laughter, and the family and fun. For the first time in months, it felt like everything was right again. If even for just a moment.

We caroused late into the evening when I noticed Mami and Papi solemnly speaking to each other at the table. Papi corralled Marita and me into a corner away from the rest of the family to let us know Mami had reached her pain threshold and he'd be taking her home in a taxi. He expressed that they both wanted the rest of the family to continue the party and take the limo home at the end of the night. Mami didn't want to say goodbye to anyone on such a high note; they may have wondered if it would be their last time saying goodbye. Maybe she was uncertain if she'd feel up for Day 2 of the anniversary celebration so Papi wheeled her out quickly and quietly before even Marita or I had a chance to kiss her goodnight.

I didn't like not having that opportunity but I fully understood and respected her wishes to leave discreetly. Marita and I obediently rejoined everyone in their revelry and, only when asked, did we explain that it had been time for Mami to go home and rest.

We didn't leave until well after midnight so sleeping in the next day was in order for everyone. My feet were swollen from dancing most of the night in strappy heels but I was over the moon that we'd fulfilled Mami's last wish and everyone, including Mami, had a fantastic time.

She'd slept soundly through the entire following morning and when she came to, she was still pumped up to have everyone come over that afternoon for the second part of the celebration. We were floored. She was obviously tired and in pain but all she was focused on was enjoying every moment with our family.

Prior to their arrival, Marita, Papi and I had set up snack plates, restocked the bar, put on peppy dance music and spruced up the flower arrangements both at the table and around the house. Once everyone was settled in with a cocktail in hand, Mami's nurse wheeled her out in her wheelchair with Arco loyally walking by her side before he noticed all the people in our house and excitedly ran up to everyone, wagging his tail and seeing whose hands he could lick. No takers on the licking but, damn, he was thrilled at the copious amounts of love he registered he'd be getting and giving that day.

A happy dog means a happy mom. She laughed at Arco's exuberance and was just as enthusiastically greeted by everyone's hugs, kisses and smiles. Throughout the afternoon I noticed Mami having one-on-one conversations with just about everyone before we sat down at the table for a German tradition of afternoon coffee with cake. The fondant cake we had specially designed was exquisite and several people had stood up to toast to Mami and Papi's fifty years together. Both of my aunts had prepared such heartfelt speeches detailing the history of Mami and Papi's relationship from the beginning onward. I felt like I'd relived their special moments with them, like their first kiss outside of a hardware store under the light of a full moon and their wild days living in Caracas, Venezuela as VIPs of the top nightclub at the time and camping trips at their favorite beach in Morrocoy.

Marita had also prepared a speech but forgotten it at the hotel so she chose to speak from her heart, almost immediately breaking down into tears before we all laughed together because we expected that to happen. Marita is a big softy; it's one of the things I love about her most. I realized amidst everything we'd been handling as party planners aside from being there everyday for Mami, I had nothing prepared so I, too, spoke from my heart.

We each hugged and kissed Mami and Papi with tears of joy and a touch of sadness that it would soon be over—the party, the togetherness of the family, Mami's life and, in turn, Mami and Papi's remarkable marriage.

Mami, not wanting it to turn into a mournful event, announced to everyone that her mouth was getting dry and she, therefore, required a refill of her champagne glass. She always knew how to turn things around. Everyone laughed and resumed side conversations with each other around the table.

Just as she did the night before, when Mami had reached her threshold, she quietly excused herself with the nurse to retreat to her room without officially saying goodbye to anyone. It was exactly what she'd wanted and we couldn't have asked for a better time celebrating such a momentous occasion for not one but two days in a row.

CHAPTER 17

The Beginning Of The End

"Sometimes you will never know the value of a moment until it becomes a memory."

~Dr. Seuss

We were still abuzz from the family festivities over the weekend. Sunday was the clean up day as we began to dismantle the decorations, the rental tables and chairs. As we pulled the linens from the main table where Mami had sat and laughed the day before toasting to fifty years of marriage I thought of how quickly everything passes. We'd planned for months for this special occasion; it was the last hurrah before Mami was to leave this earth and now it was over.

It's that feeling you get after the high of an amazing life event and then you go back to everyday life. Only our everyday life lately had been nurses, medications, emotions and staying as close to Mami as possible.

Mami was exhausted from all the partying so she was in bed sleeping most of the day but it was one of those accomplished rests…that kind of feeling when you go to bed knowing that you achieved everything you'd set your heart on. Mami had had her celebration with Papi and had gotten to see our family in its entirety. And there were never any goodbyes. Rather, there were animated conversations about the fun times they shared. There was dancing. There was laughing. Yes, there were some tears too. But, overall, it was the most fun we'd had all together within the larger part of our family in any of our lifetimes.

As I reassembled the centerpiece of roses and faux diamonds, I felt overwhelmed with joy at how beautifully everything had come together. We each had a hand in making this happen and I was filled with gratitude for our amazing family. At the same time, I felt how quickly it was all slipping away. I'd never have these moments again. Even if we got together again as a family with a fun celebration, Mami would be missing. It wouldn't be the same.

But so is life. Moments are just moments. They are fleeting and to try to catch one and stay with it is an impossibility. That's why it's so important to enjoy every single moment we are given. It is a precious gift that you'll never know for sure how long it'll last. You've heard that saying, "Make every moment count." How do you do that? You just be with it and let it pass. Don't get attached. Appreciate it. Enjoy it. Then let it go. That is probably the hardest lesson I've had to learn in life.

I walked back through the hallway towards my room, suddenly aware of every step I was taking. And each step was another moment that got me closer to Mami's room; each step another moment closer to Mami's death. My breath was slow and drawn out as I peered through her door. There she lay napping with the covers tucked beneath her underarms and a peaceful smile on her face. I smiled and watched her for awhile. Her pale skin looked somewhat worn but was still aglow. Eventually I retreated into my room for a nap.

The following evening we'd fully returned back to normal, or what normal had become for us in those days. The party rental company had retrieved the rentals, the dining room was pieced back together, and Mami was still in her bed dozing on and off. Our extended family was still in town but understood Mami needed to rest and that we wanted to be there with her. She didn't want anyone else to visit; she'd ended on such a high note with everyone and wanted to keep it that way. Marita had left the day before to go back to work. It was hard to see her go and I knew it was even harder on her to have to leave again. I imagined she was afraid that she'd miss Mami's last breath. I think we all shared that fear.

Papi had cooked dinner on that fateful night and he and I sat with Mami, balancing our plates on our laps while Mami held her plate in bed on her yellow pillow balanced across her chest. She wasn't particularly hungry but she nodded in delight when we offered her some leftover cake. We all partook in the vegan delight and then left Mami so we could clean up dishes in the kitchen. I found comfort in the monotonous flow of Papi washing plates and cutlery, placing them one by one on top of a towel on the countertop while I dried each one as they came. We had a rhythm going. We didn't talk much. The sound of the water splashing onto the dishes and washing them clean brought a sense of calm to us both.

Sometime in the late evening when we were getting ready for bed, Mami needed help to get to her commode, which was placed right beside her bed. She'd barely been able to move since the wedding anniversary. We no longer had the nighttime nurses since Mami had been doing relatively fine up until the weekend. So both Papi and I came to assist. Usually Papi and the nurse would help her onto it and then give her some privacy until she called out for help back into bed. This time was different.

She'd sat up in bed while Papi placed his arm under hers to gently pull her closer to the edge of the bed. He signaled for me to place my arm under her other so we could hoist her together onto the commode. It took a couple of attempts, as we tried to be as gentle as possible with her. She seemed to be doing ok so we decided on the count of three we'd get her to standing, which she did. We guided her hands to the handles on either side of the commode and she gripped on tightly, standing as tall as she could. I noticed Papi and I holding our breath, still holding her up and nervous to let go. She said she was fine and asked us to leave, giving her some privacy. I sucked in another breath and held it as Papi and I looked at each other. But Mami was firm, she wanted her privacy and, that, we completely understood and empathized with.

Slowly Papi and I both removed our arms from under hers, looking to Mami for any signs of protest in her face. She waited patiently and, as we slipped the last of our fingers through, we heard a loud crack as Mami collapsed and screamed. My stomach dropped to the floor with her and we somehow managed to get her up to the edge of her bed again. It wasn't until I looked down at her leg that I realized what the source of the loud cracking noise had been. It was her femur bone. The bone had split in half and was now pushing into the side of her thigh causing a large protrusion.

Until this day I still don't know how I kept it together. I attribute it first to God and also mainly to Mami. After her first scream she remained calm and was just focused with Papi on how to get her back into bed so we could assess the situation and get help. Papi didn't want any more hands on deck and I could imagine the pain he felt alongside her as he tried to maneuver her back into place in her bed, every movement giving way to another moan from Mami. I think I'd have been screaming bloody murder by then had I been in her place. Papi managed to get her lying down back in bed and I sprung into action. I briefly scanned her med schedule while grabbing her morphine and promptly fed her twice her regular dose. She opened her mouth and looked up at me as I dropped the "bird feeder", as we called it, under her tongue. Neither of us said a word but as we locked eyes, I felt so much love exchanged between us in that one moment that no words were needed. All the years that Mami had selflessly taken care of me when I was sick or hurt came flooding back culminating into that one moment where I could, for once, take care of her when she needed it most. The look of love in her eyes overrode, for that brief moment, all the pain that had erupted moments earlier. That look of love was what kept me going instead of breaking down, sitting in a corner and rocking myself from the trauma of witnessing my mom break before my eyes.

As soon as I'd administered the morphine, I bolted into the kitchen to grab some ice packs and thin towels. Upon returning in a flash, I placed them as gingerly as I could over the side of her thigh, which had rapidly grown into the size of half a soccer ball. I'd never seen anything like it.

As I retracted my hand from her thigh, I reached for the phone and called the emergency line for hospice to explain the situation. This all must've happened in less than five minutes. Papi sat down momentarily behind her, recovering from having hoisted her onto the bed and also processing the reality of what just happened. I confirmed that a nurse was on the way to determine what we could do and then looked at the clock. It was after midnight but I knew I had to make the call. I knew I had to wake up Marita and ask her to come back from Naples.

Papi had gone into the kitchen to get more ice and possibly for a moment alone to take it all in. I was running on pure adrenaline by that point. I knelt down on the floor by Mami's bedside trying to mask the horror I felt when looking at her mangled leg and then looked up to meet her eyes, feeling the love between us well up inside again. I wanted to touch her, to hold her, but I was afraid she would break even more.

78

As if she knew I was holding back, she reached for my hand and with the most heartfelt smile said, "You're my angel tonight, thank you."

Then, almost in a whisper, she said, "I know you felt bad about moving back in with us but this was never about you. God knew I'd need you during this time so He planned it this way."

That was all it took for me to finally burst into tears. I kissed her hand over and over, now salty with my tears, and thanked her for letting me be her angel, if even for one night, when she'd been my angel my entire life.

It was almost 3 in the morning and Papi and I were bleary-eyed keeping watch over Mami who was by then thankfully long asleep. Marita pulled her car into the driveway and we hugged at the door, shuddering in each other's arms. We tiptoed into Mami's room so as not to wake her. It wasn't so much the tiredness but the sadness I could see in Marita's eyes as she slowly looked over Mami's body, putting together what had happened only hours earlier. We sat on the chaise lounge by Mami's bed, scooting close to each other less because of the small sitting space and more because of the comfort we needed. I started to doze and Marita nudged me to go get some sleep. She'd stay by Mami's bedside through the rest of the night. I kissed her goodnight and sent a beam of loving thoughts in my mind to Mami as I walked out to my room.

The sun was streaming through the windows when I awoke the next morning and I sat up immediately, tuning into the hushed voices I heard from Mami's bedroom. The hospice nurse was there and they were discussing how to alleviate more of Mami's pain. I could imagine it was through the roof though she never let on. We waited for her main doctor to arrive and ascertain how we could best help her. He arrived within the hour and it was quickly decided that the only way to seriously dial up her pain meds would be to get her to the hospital. It was not the route any of us wanted to take. Mami had envisioned her final days slipping away into a peaceful sleep at home. But with her continuously disintegrating bones, it was no longer an option.

Papi made the arrangements to get an ambulance while we packed up what we needed. Mami didn't have the desire to bring much. What was the point? But I couldn't resist packing the cute felt flower with the smiley face that we'd given her for Mother's Day and the teddy bear she'd given me when I was nine. Marita remembered her little yellow pillow and Papi had the good sense to pack some toiletries to keep her more comfortable.

It was the fourth time someone had pulled into the driveway for Mami in a matter of hours. First Marita, then Mami's nurse, then her main doctor and this time it was the ambulance. I heard the doors open and close with a foreboding shut. I knew that once Mami was out the door, she'd never be back home again. I looked around at the living room, already feeling the emptiness. But that feeling was nothing compared to what was yet to come.

The paramedics came in with the stretcher pulling it down the hallway towards Mami's room. At the end of the hallway, they stopped. The narrow space between the corners of the hallway and the bedroom door couldn't accommodate the stretcher. They tried several times to angle it in different directions but it was impossible to get into her bedroom with it. They would have to carry her out by her bed sheets.

I wanted to be there to help but knew I'd be in the way and, so I stood back, at the same time scared of seeing Mami go through any sort of movement again with her broken leg. The paramedics had put the stretcher back outside of the front door and returned to Mami's bed, beginning to pull the ends of the sheets up and around her, relaying to each other how they would hoist her on a count of three.

"One," they counted and each wrapped the corners of the sheets around their forearms and wrists gripping extra tightly with their hands so as not to drop her.

"Two," they counted and signaled to one another who would walk out backwards first.

I braced myself and cowered back into my bedroom unable to face what Mami was about to face.

"Three," I heard from behind the wall.

Her screams echoed in the hallway as I glimpsed them carrying her, her broken body swaying helplessly back and forth, in the sheets. I could sense her gulping in deep breaths trying to hold back before screaming again in agony, that last one echoing in my heart and deep into my belly. I felt as broken as she was. Shattered. I stood there at the doorway, momentarily paralyzed and sobbing for my Mami.

Papi and Marita were right by her side as the paramedics hoisted her onto the stretcher then into the ambulance and it was as if I were sleep walking a few steps behind everything. My heart was still in the hallway and the rest seemed a blur. Papi climbed into the ambulance with Mami who had already passed out from shock and, with a brief glance and head nod, Marita and I agreed we'd meet them at the hospital.

As the paramedics began to close the door on Mami in the stretcher with Papi by her side, I caught Papi's eye and then looked to Marita. It was such a brief moment but it was replete with all the fears and sadness we'd felt building up over the past few months. In that moment, we all knew this was the beginning of the end.

The ambulance pulled out of the driveway and Marita went back inside to finish packing and getting things ready for us. She was always so great at staying levelheaded and getting things done no matter what her feelings were. I admired her for her strength. I slowly stepped back into the house staring at the living room. It already seemed darker inside. A light had gone out here at home. And in my mind I could still hear Mami's screams echoing in the hallway.

CHAPTER 18

Rise And Fall

"The fear of death follows from the fear of life.
A man who lives fully is prepared to die at any time."
~Mark Twain

Monday, September 24, 2012

Except for the subtle rise and fall of her chest, she could already be dead. Papi, Marita and I stood there looking at Mami as if our own hearts had stopped beating. The kind of pain she'd been through to get here was the kind of pain I wish nobody in this world would have to feel.

The hospital was cold and there was a strong smell of sterility in the air. Mami was unconscious. The big question that was thrashing its way to escape our mouths but remained silent out of fear was, "How much longer?" The fear was two-fold. Fear that I was actually losing her. Fear that she had to still live through this level of pain for God only knew how long.

That's the thing. Some deaths are unexpected. My heart shudders, for I can't begin to imagine losing a loved one suddenly like in a car accident or from a heart attack or, God forbid, a murder. The doctors had given my mom a six-month sentence, which she'd fully divulged to us almost two months in. So we had about four months to "prepare" for the arrival of the end. The truth is, no amount of time and nothing really prepares you. You have this idea in your mind that, ok, my loved one is going to die in a few months but then you're a few months in and you won't ever know the exact day, hour or second of that last breath.

It's the waiting that got to me.

The doctors at the hospital were insistent on getting her into surgery to reattach the broken halves of her femur bone and insert a metal rod into her leg. That thought alone made me want to throw up and cry. How could they want to push her into surgery? This woman is dying!! But that's what doctors at hospitals are trained to do: keep patients alive. Meanwhile, Mami seemed ready to step out of this physically intolerable state. She couldn't speak for herself so we had to fight for her. We couldn't let them put her under the knife at such a critical time. It would be too much. She couldn't have handled it. When we knocked out the option to perform surgery, the doctor advised putting her in traction. NOOOO!!! Don't move her! The vision of her broken body swaying in the sheets as the paramedics carried her out of our house was more than I could handle. More than she could handle. She needed to stay right where she was, in the hospital bed. Just let her be. Papi did all the talking and it took everything inside of me to subdue the rage I felt to shout at the doctor to just let our Mami die in peace.

Finally the doctor noted that while he respects our wishes for opting out of surgery and traction, the hospital did require Mami to be moved into a different bed in another wing. For crying out loud, the woman had holes in her bones. Any movement could've literally further shattered her into pieces. Why did we have to move her to another bed? Why couldn't we just keep her lying there and move the bed—which had wheels—into the other wing? All this hospital policy and no heart or respect for the wishes of a dying woman and her family.

Papi didn't give up fighting for her. We were eventually able to have her wheeled in the same bed to her new room in the other wing of the hospital. This was it. She could be there as long as she needed to be without being disturbed again. I felt that we could then also settle in. How long we'd be there, none of us had any idea.

It had been a long day. Night was falling upon us fast and the three of us stood around Mami's bedside watching her lay quiet and still. Was this it? Will I ever get to say goodbye to her or did I miss my chance the night before when we were holding hands and looking into each other's eyes after her leg broke? It felt like when you watch a movie and you're all into it and then—BOOM!—the screen goes black and the credits start rolling. You're grabbing your hair at the roots, wondering, "What??!! That was it??" But those are movies. This was real life. This was my mom.

I couldn't decide if I was more tired or nauseous or sad but none of that mattered. What mattered is that we were there with her. And then there was that. Standing in this tiny hospital room, with one chair next to the bed, how would we all stay there together with her? That's when we realized how real this had become. We knew without a doubt that we didn't want to leave her alone at any time. Yet we really didn't know how long this would take. So we decided as a family—as a team—to take turns being here for her. Between the three of us we could each take an eight-hour shift with her and, of course, we could double up and stay longer if we wished. But for our own comfort, sanity and, most importantly, our ability to be there for her, this was the only way it made sense.

At the same time, I had a sense of guilt and fear leaving her to go back home. Guilt that I wasn't really being there for her. Fear that what if she died while I wasn't there? But somehow the rational won over the emotional. We were only human and we needed to sleep in a bed and not in a chair or standing up until we became delirious. We still needed our faculties to not only be there for Mami but to be there for each other.

Marita and I hugged Papi and kissed Mami on her forehead as we reluctantly left the hospital for the night. The drive home was relatively short but it felt like a long ride. Marita intuitively turned on the radio tuning into some soft music to diffuse the somber energy. The melodic flute of Sting's "Fields of Gold" bled into the car. "You'll remember me when the west wind moves…" came his haunting voice and that's all it took before the tears silently filled my eyes in the dark of the moving car.

I fell into a deep slumber that night. In my dreams, I was walking through the hallway of our house, the one where the paramedics had carried Mami, swinging with her broken leg in her bed sheets. The image was borne into my brain. Other than the faint remnants of her cries of anguish, there was nothing there. It was empty. I paced back and forth down the hallway. All of it felt empty. And then, just before I awoke, I heard her voice. I never figured out what exactly she was saying but I knew she'd spoken to me to let me know her presence would always be with me, even long after she's gone.

Tuesday, September 25, 2012

I awoke with tears in my eyes and a sense of urgency to get back to the hospital. Marita was already in high gear and on the same page. Papi called and delivered good news. Mami was awake, alert and smiling.

We couldn't get there fast enough. Speed walking into her hospital room and seeing her smile filled me up so much, I couldn't contain it. I ran to her bedside and kissed her all over as Marita did the same. Poor Mami being smothered by us but, really, we were all just overjoyed to see each other.

After catching up, I stepped outside the room to call Lucas. Today, of all days, was his birthday. I felt horrible that it had ended up like this. He was more than understanding that we would not be celebrating his special day and asked if I wanted him to be there. I did but I didn't want to overload Mami so we agreed to touch base later. He just knew when to step forward and when to step back. For that I was grateful. After having gone through losing his own dad to cancer, I felt he could identify with what I needed.

I then called my friend Nicole. Nicole and I had met in my yoga teacher training program. We hit it off and were talking after class in the parking lot one day, getting to know each other better, when she shared with me that she's a music therapist working with hospice.

When I asked her which one I was surprised to discover it was the same one that had been helping Mami in her transition.

She'd asked who my mom was and looked equally surprised when I told her.

"I know your mom!" she said exuberantly and continued, "I've come to your house to sing for her."

I was floored. Nicole turned out to be a blessing sent to us from God. So she was the first friend I called from the hospital to let her know my mom had been admitted there. Nicole was at work, about an hour drive up north, but she dropped everything to come down and be with us.

I'm always touched by people's compassion when in extreme situations. Sometimes tough times bring out the worst in us and sometimes they bring out the best.

While Nicole was on her way down, the hospital Chaplain, Steve, came in to greet us. Mami was elated for his arrival and asked for some time alone with him to make peace with whatever else she still held in her heart.

I never knew what that conversation entailed but, seeing Mami afterwards, I'd noticed a shift in her energy. She was truly ready to go.

Nicole knocked on the door and peeked in with her sparkling brown eyes and a guitar case, almost as big as her, in her slender arms. We each got up to embrace her before she came around Mami's bedside, gently placing her hand onto Mami's. Nicole offered to sing for us and Mami's smile grew bigger as we all chimed in, "Yes!"

She circled around to the foot of the bed where she'd momentarily put down her guitar case and emerged with the guitar in her hands, her dainty fingers perched upon the strings, ready and waiting. Papi, Marita, and I along with Steve the Chaplain, who was still with us, stood around Mami's bed in a circle, and reached for each other's hands. Marita was holding Mami's right hand and I was on the other side of the bed holding her left hand. Papi stood by my side, holding my other hand. We were all connected.

Nicole began strumming her guitar, the first notes immediately I recognized to be "Amazing Grace". Mami's favorite song. And it's one of those songs that unwittingly brings me to tears every time I hear it. Nicole's angelic voice filled the room and I noticed we'd all begun to sway side to side ever so slightly, enough to feel the rhythm of the live music flow through us.

I noticed Mami had closed her eyes and, with a soft smile, I could see her melt into the music as if her spirit could fade right into the sound. Nicole's enchanting voice, the strumming of the guitar, the Chaplain with his eyes closed, too, and whispering prayers…"This", I thought, "would be the perfect last moment."

Closing my eyes, I began speaking to Mami in my mind, visualizing her spirit hearing my words.

"It's ok, Mami, I love you and I release you. Follow the light. Go be with God and know that we're cheering you on through this journey as you go. It's ok to go." I squeezed her hand. "It's ok to go…it's ok to go." I still swayed with the music.

I later found out Marita was doing the same thing streaming her thoughts to Mami in her mind at that time too. We had given her permission to go. We wanted her to be free.

The song came to an end and Nicole ever so lightly swept her fingers up and down the chords, as if in a low background music. I felt Mami's hand soften in mine. I peeked through the smallest slit between my upper and lower eyelids, blinking to look at Mami's face through my tears. Her smile had faded and her face had softened too. She looked so peaceful. I held my breath and prepared for the final release.

"It's ok to go, Mami, I love you, it's ok," I kept thinking as I closed my eyes again.

I tried not to grip her hand too hard. I didn't want to send the wrong message. After several more seconds passed, which really felt like hours, I looked to Mami again to check for the disappearance of any signs of life. Mami suddenly blinked her eyes wide open, looked at her watch, and then looked at all of us.

"How much longer is this gonna take?!" she exclaimed.

It was all we could do but break into laughter. Still looking at us, she animatedly went on.

"Seriously, I feel like I'm sitting on the runway in my private jet but the pilot's gone missing…Yeah, I mean, I know some of you have to get back to work so don't let my absentee pilot keep you waiting!"

Yup, that was our Mami. In the darkest, toughest moments, without fail, she was right there with her spunk and spitfire comedy.

Wednesday, September 26, 2012 – Sunday, September 30, 2012

The rest of our extended family was still in town but Mami was firm that she didn't want any visitors, whether family or friends, other than Papi, Marita and me in the hospital with her. The 50th anniversary party had given her the opportunity to say goodbye to the rest of the family without actually saying goodbye. We were dressed up, celebrating, dancing and toasting during those two days and that felt like the perfect end for her. She didn't want everyone hovering over her bed, crying and watching her wither away as her body, bit by bit, began to fail her in the end. While it had been months since she'd seen some of her friends, she was content that the last time she saw most of them was during a local Friday night happy hour that she went to with Papi. That was how she wanted to be remembered.

I wondered if she'd felt the same towards us girls, Marita and me, that she wouldn't want her daughters to see her go like this but, whether she did or not, she didn't say. If anything, she knew how much more important it was for the four of us to be together through the end.

While it was heartbreaking to see our Mami's broken body, her leg contorted at an inhumanly frightening angle, her bright spirit and silly jokes fueled our energy in the days that followed.

She continued on heavy-duty pain medication with a nonstop stream of Dilaudid dripping into her veins. Mami always wanted to be the strong one. She never gave away the full extent of her pain. Whenever the doctor would come by on his rounds to check on her, he'd ask her to rate on a scale of 1 to 10 what her pain level was.

She'd quietly say, "Hmm…a 3." We'd narrow our eyes, looking at her, and sometimes she'd budge and say, "Maybe a 4."

It wasn't until days later that the truth came out. She'd expressed that she was ready to go and asked if there was any way to speed up the process. When we called the doctor, he explained that while the hospital can't assist death for patients, he could continue upping her pain medication, depending on her pain levels, and eventually her systems would begin to shut down because of the high doses. So when he asked her again on a scale of 1 to 10 what her pain was, she got really quiet for a moment before tears came to her eyes and her bottom lip quivered.

"It's 100!!" she burst out.

We knew she wasn't just saying that so that the doctor would increase the meds to speed up her process of dying. It was real. She'd been holding it in for so long, trying to be strong for us, and it finally came gushing out.

It felt like somebody was strangling my heart when I thought of the overwhelming pain she'd endured over the past year. The first major signs of it had already taken a hold of her body in February. With her most recent x-rays we could physically see the large holes in her bones from the cancer eating away at her. The head of her femur bone had dislodged from her hip socket. I was horrified and, at the same time, amazed how she could still genuinely laugh and smile the way she had been with us.

The doctor immediately increased her medication. Just as when she was in hospice care back home, whenever her medication was increased, she would pass out and sleep for hours on end. And, every single time, I'd wonder if she'd wake up again.

Now at the hospital, every time she did wake up, I was buoyed to see her precious smile. But over time she became slowly incoherent and faded in and out of sleeping and waking states. Sometimes she was confused and would look at the pulse reader connected to her finger, which intermittently flashed a red light. She'd then repeatedly push her finger to her lips, tipping her head back. Marita figured out she was trying to sip her finger, meaning she was thirsty and needed water. So one of us would grab her plastic cup and position the straw to her mouth so she could sip. She would look up and smile to whomever had given her what she needed. It was the cutest thing, her confusion.

Then she would look either one of us squarely in the face and say over and over again, "thank you…thank you…thank you," in a breathy voice. She had to muster up all her energy to do this. In those moments especially I could feel how deep her love ran for all of us. And her love was profoundly reciprocated.

Other times she was lucid and would talk to us or the friendly nurses who would come to our room; some to check on her, others to simply meet the amazing dying woman they'd heard about on their floor who was brightening everyone's days.

Back home I took silly pictures of Arco and me to share with to her so she could still see her baby boy. She'd told us that, when she died, she wanted Papi to take care of Arco for the first three months and, after that, I would permanently inherit him. Everyday Arco waited patiently by her bedside for Mami to come home. He was so hopeful and loyal. We gave him lots of extra love when we were home. It must've been so hard on him too. Waiting and waiting and waiting for his Mami. But deep down I think he knew what was going on.

One of the afternoons this week we met with a hospice grief counselor who came to the hospital to let us know how she could be there for us in the pending aftermath. Mami was sleeping and we met with her briefly in a room across the hall so that she wouldn't have to hear our conversation about how to handle her death. Even though our meeting was relatively short, I felt uneasy leaving Mami alone simply because I feared she could potentially die while none of us were by her side. I was itching to get up and go.

After we'd gotten the counselor's contact info the three of us congregated outside of Mami's hospital room and that's when I noticed tears glistening on Papi's cheeks. Marita and I wrapped our arms around him and, almost immediately, he took a deep breath and sucked it all back in, claiming that he was ok. It pained me to see that Papi didn't feel comfortable crying with us or letting us be there for him. At the same time, I'm aware he grew up in the aftermath of World War II in Berlin where stoicism was needed to survive. And I'm sure he felt that, as the patriarch of our family, he had to hold it together and "be the man". I wanted him to be able to let go with us but I understood why he held back in that moment.

We walked back into the hospital room where Mami was still asleep, not yet dead, and realized how exhausted we all were. The level of emotions around death can feel overwhelming and entirely draining. It was the sheer force of God moving through us at this point, animating us to do what we needed to do to be there for Mami and for each other.

Reverting back to our original plan of eight-hour shifts, we decided that either Marita or Papi will spend the nights with Mami and I will take one of the daytime shifts. We all laughed and agreed that I was not fun to be around if I didn't get my eight hours. Marita and Papi were better equipped for that. They were naturally early risers.

Once rested, I couldn't wait to come back to be with Mami. I cherished our waning moments together. When she awoke one afternoon from another nap, she blinked open her eyes and instantly smiled when she saw me. I could never forget the way she looked at me, the same way she always had my whole life—like she saw the best version of me already manifested before her very eyes. She looked at me with such love.

And with all that love in her heart pouring through her eyes, the windows of her soul, she told me that she was hungry. I giggled. It's funny how quickly her belly started talking to her in that tender moment between us. I offered to go downstairs to the cafeteria to get her something but she pointed to the side table by her bed where we'd been collecting snacks in case anyone needed a pick-me-up. There was a banana, a bar of dark chocolate and a single serving cup of creamy peanut butter. The perfect combo of sweet and salty.

She watched me quietly as I peeled and cut the banana into bitable pieces with a plastic knife we'd retrieved from the cafeteria and then scraped each piece with peanut butter, topping it with a piece of chocolate to create a mouthwatering trifecta. Feeding her one piece at a time, she slowly chewed and smiled back at me. We didn't exchange any words. Instead, we simply looked at each other as I continued to hand feed her. I thought of all the times she must've fed me as a baby. I couldn't have been more grateful to return the love to her, even in this smallest of ways, after all the sacrifices she had made as a mom to nurture and raise me.

She made it through only half the banana when she put her hand up, waving off the rest. She was full.

She looked into my eyes and whispered, "Thank you." I smiled at her, stroking my hand across her arm. It was barely anything, the bites she'd taken, and I knew this meant we were getting closer to "D-Day."

During another one of my afternoon shifts with Mami, she was awake but, at first, rather loopy it appeared. At one point she kept pointing to the foot of her bed and asked me if I saw him.

"Who?" I asked, "Who's there?"

She told me that there was a man standing there. She went on to describe that he was wearing all black. I asked her if he was a good man. She responded that, yes, he was. He was there to help her pass through. I looked good and hard to the foot of her bed and saw nothing but I knew she was telling the truth. I knew she saw this man. I thanked him out loud for being there to help her.

Before I knew it the week had passed and by Friday I felt like a mess. I wasn't sure how we could continue pulling through these long shifts at the hospital in constant vigilance over Mami and prayer for her release. My body ached for release too. I'd felt that, when this time is over, I'd need at least three consecutive days of uninterrupted sleep. A couple of days ago I'd promised to go out with my cousin and Lucas tonight though and, as much as I'd wanted to be with them, I was extraordinarily tired. Somehow I pushed through the whole day at the hospital and made it through the evening with them. I even managed to have a pleasant time with our lighthearted conversation and martinis. Little had I known that it would end up helping me feel better.

Every night that Mami and I kissed each other goodbye grew harder and harder. I knew with each day that passed we were getting closer and closer but the not knowing when was the hardest. I'd kiss and hug her and look her in her eyes, reminding her how much I love her. I began to feel like a broken record and every night I wanted to linger longer, trying to feel satisfied and complete with the way we were leaving things.

Tomorrow would be her birthday and I kept having thoughts that maybe she'll die on her birthday and it would be completely sealing the circle of her life, from birth to death. I looked at her face, trying to imprint every inch of her last look at me into my memory. Her delicate bone structure, her pale skin and green eyes smiling back at me. I wanted our final goodbye to be perfect. And then I had to go.

The three of us hadn't been able to spend much time with the rest of the family still in town so Papi, who would be staying with Mami overnight, had generously given Marita and me his credit card to take them out to dinner on South Beach. It was strange stepping out into the real world again. Part of me felt guilty that here we were enjoying a night out on the town while Mami was in the hospital dying. The other part of me felt thankful and relieved for the opportunity to blow off some steam. Life had been so serious and heavy lately.

With our bellies full and a slight buzz from the generous amounts of wine we imbibed, we strolled over to Española Way afterwards, a charming pedestrian friendly area where Spanish colonial architecture, art galleries, restaurants and bars abound. You can almost imagine yourself walking through the lively streets of Madrid here; the place transports you.

We settled in at Tapas y Tintos, a tapas bar as the name suggests, with vintage furniture and authentic Spanish décor. The dim lights added to the romantic ambience but it was the flamenco show that was about to begin that really made the night. Sharing pitchers of sangrias, we gazed in awe at the live performance.

The guitarist, donning a black dress shirt, black slacks and black leather shoes, strummed his notes while singing with soulful passion not unlike the Gipsy Kings. The percussionist, in a gray chest-hugging t-shirt paired with a black vest and a pair of fitted jeans and black leather shoes, bobbed his head with the beat as he rhythmically tapped his fingers and clapped his hands on a cajon, a wooden box that perfectly complements the sounds of the guitar. The rhythm of the night was all tied together by the flamenco dancer who pounded her shoes ever so rapidly into the wooden floor of the tiny stage upon which the three of them performed. She wore a fitted black top with the signature flouncy sleeves over a black flamenco skirt with large blue polka dots that fell over her well-worn flamenco shoes. Her short black hair was tied back tightly and little strands of it began to fall into her cheeks as she tapped her heels harder and harder into the rickety stage. You could see the glisten of sweat across her brows, furrowed with fire and ardor, as she curled her fingers with each fervent move.

As small as that stage was and as close as the performers were to one another, the flamenco dancer utilized every square inch of space, extending her body with beautiful curvature and throwing her hands out into the air just millimeters away from the percussionist's face. I winced in some of those moments yet the percussionist continued to play, as if in a musical trance, and not the slightest bit fazed by the dancer's powerful movements. We were entranced.

It was a welcome reprieve for Marita and me to get out and do something entertaining with the rest of our family, something non-hospital related. After all this I realized the imperative need for caretakers to take care of themselves too. And to not feel guilty when doing so. I believe we can do a better job of caring for others when we first take care of ourselves. That means good sleep, food, exercise and a healthy dose of fun. Of course we live in an imperfect world where things happen unexpectedly and sometimes we won't be able to focus on all of these components for ourselves. Reminding ourselves that we are doing the best we can is what matters most.

Monday, October 1, 2012

Marita and I woke up at home around 8 AM, physically tired yet emotionally renewed from the delightful time we had with the family last night.

Today was Mami's birthday, or rebirthday as I liked to call it this year. It would be the day, I imagined, she shall be born again into God's Kingdom, cradled in our Lord's arms. I, too, felt rebirthed. Since I was a kid Mami had

94

always joked that we were still attached by the umbilical cord. She couldn't have been more right.

The past week has yielded a rise and fall of emotions. I recall going home from the hospital last Wednesday night after our heartwarming day with Nicole and Steven when I felt this sense of magic, almost like it was Christmas Eve. I couldn't understand or shake the feeling, nor did I want to because I warmly welcomed being able to feel the light, the magic and the growing excitement of something so special.

Last night when we'd gotten home, I'd purposely left the lights on outside the house, as if a signal to Mami that she can stop by our sanctuary as she makes her way to Heaven. I felt like this was it. Today was her day.

So it felt almost like a letdown when Papi reported to us over the phone from the hospital that Mami was still alive.

But something had changed. She was no longer conscious. It dawned on me in that moment that last night, in a way, really had been our final goodbye with each other.

I thought back to the irony of how Mami had told us months ago when we first learned of her death sentence that she wasn't interested in celebrating her 70th birthday. All that had mattered to her was celebrating fifty years of marriage with Papi. So she had gotten her wishes. For that I was thankful. It floored me that, even though she hasn't yet passed on, she is no longer responsive today—the day she explicitly stated she didn't want to commemorate. It's like she had either decided for herself or her soul already knew that today, on the day of her birth, would be goodbye for her.

Papi, Marita and I, on the other hand, had yet to say goodbye for good. I wondered again when that would be. That answer, I knew, would continue to remain elusive until it actually happened.

Papi encouraged us to get some more rest and visit Mami today at noon for a change. With relief, I crawled back into bed for a much needed nap before getting up again to finish preparing for another day at the hospital.

During that short but deep sleep, Mami visited me. I'd dreamed that I was right where I was in my bedroom taking that nap and I'd heard Papi come home with Mami in the wheelchair. I overheard Marita welcome them both home and the joy in Mami's voice as she elatedly recounted her memories of our home. I heard her note how she used to sit in the dining room looking out at the view of the backyard and also how she used to sit out on the patio enjoying the view inside the house. She went on pointing out her favorite spots in the house. In my dream, I'd awakened to her voice sharing her fondest memories here and, so, I stepped out of my room to embrace Mami and welcome her back too. When I turned the corner in the hallway, Papi was standing there pushing her wheelchair but it was empty. I asked where Mami was and Papi said she wasn't here, that he was just bringing the wheelchair back home. When I awoke from this dream, I smiled knowing that Mami's spirit was there with us to let us know how much she'd cherished our treasured home and all the special places in which she used to sit admiring the beauty of life around her.

Back at the hospital Mami's tenacious spirit willed her to stay alive, lying contorted beneath the thin crisp blankets on the hospital bed. Every night that either of us left the hospital, we hoped and prayed for God to summon our beloved Mami, not only to take her out of her pain but because we knew those were her wishes too.

Mami was completely shut down today, no more food, not even a sip of water. Her breathing had become shallower and her head, adorned on either side by adorable pigtails, had flopped to her right shoulder. We noticed her skin had also become more pallid. She was propped upright with pillows and, despite the blanket covering her, her body felt cool to the touch. All signs that she was making her transition.

Marita brought up a good point that Mami had mentioned, while still lucid, to Steven the Chaplain during her confession. She'd admitted that she was always a "closet Christian" and had been ashamed to share her beliefs with others. This was something I'd struggled with, too, for so many years. I loved and honored my mom and, out of respect for her beliefs, I'd prayed almost every night of my life to a Lord I couldn't see or fully comprehend. I'd prayed from childhood on and, even though I had witnessed its power, it was like I'd prayed out of obedience. It was what a good girl should do. My questioning had started in senior year of high school with my favorite philosophy class. It was there that I discovered Nietzsche and fell in love with his idea of the "uebermensch", the one who questions authority and society's beliefs and decides for himself what is right and what is wrong.

The wave of questioning continued in my years away at college, where I found myself falling into periods of melancholy and self-abuse.

While I did start to pray more avidly again years later, it still felt forced at times. I felt I didn't really know how to talk with God nor did I understand who He was and what He stood for in my life. It turns out that it was up to me to stand for Him, and not the other way around. God never forces us to come to Him; instead, He patiently awaits us to come around when we're ready.

It wasn't really until these recent months since Mami's condition began deteriorating and death was looming that I began to know who God is. I felt ashamed that it took me the prospect and ensuing reality of losing my mom to make me truly believe in Him. At the same time I was grateful that I felt no fear for her and no anger towards God for "taking her away from me". Somehow, feeling God in our presence these days, I could accept the truth of life and the truth of death.

And death, as we'd talked about, isn't really an end. It's the beginning of something far greater and far more beautiful than the human mind, I imagine, can comprehend. But our spirits know. Deep down, we know the truth.

Even as Mami lies here now, no longer awakened by a single noise, I know that her soul knows. I know that her soul understands God and understands how we feel. Words are no longer needed. Not even a brief look into each other's eyes is needed. It has stretched far beyond that now.

I find myself continuously checking her heart rate and oxygen level on the monitors behind her head. Somehow I feel more relief when I see both levels drop, indicating that her body is finally shutting down. Then I feel frustration at times when I see how high both levels spike again. When this happens, I have to remind myself to relinquish myself to God's will. As Mami used to tell me, "I trust in the will of God and lean not unto my own understanding."

Mami had still wanted to share with others that God had healed her. And God surely did. He mended and healed her spirit so perfectly and, now, even with the little communication she had left in the past couple of days, she was able to touch so many nurses' lives. One of the night nurses, Joyce (as in rejoicing), had asked Marita if Mami was a Christian. When Marita affirmed so, Joyce noted how she could see Jesus in Mami's face. Each of the nurses cried with joy when being in Mami's presence. This, I believe, is

97

why Mami was still alive this week, longer than we'd thought or hoped. She was still working out her spirit's wishes and finishing up whatever work she knew she needed to do before returning Home.

She also knows the legacy of love and joy that she's leaving with Papi, Marita and me—to feel loving and joyful through everything in life, even in the face of death. It is something we will continue to share with each other and with others for the rest of our lives. It has brought our family closer than ever and I believe it will make our deaths, or transitions, as I see them, much easier when our own times come.

As beautifully as everything has been working out, this week has really worn on us. We were all exhausted, with aching necks and backs, and not quite thinking coherently all the time. We've been incredibly understanding and sensitive to each other's needs.

We had to decide the details for Mami's cremation. Wait, we had to make arrangements with a funeral home first! With everything going on, it only just occurred to us we had yet to do so. It was down to the wire now. Papi and Marita left together in a hurry to sort it out while I stayed back with Mami. When returning to the hospital several hours later with a booking and a plan, they discussed with me the specifics. We all agreed we wished for Mami's body to be properly cleaned before being placed in the fire. We also thought it appropriate for her to be dressed up, as she'd always loved to do. Initially Marita suggested the idea of putting her to rest in the bright and beautiful sorbet colored dress Mami had fancied and worn during Part 2 of the 50th anniversary celebration. Then Papi suggested her wedding dress. We knew that was the perfect dress for her. I'd recalled her mentioning once, many years ago, that she'd want to be buried, or cremated rather, in her wedding dress. At that time she was concerned she would never fit into it again. But now that she was almost skin and bones—and yet somehow still so radiantly beautiful—we knew she'd more than easily fit in it. Papi affirmed these had been her wishes so it was set.

I'd let Papi know on the ride home from the hospital that I could help him find Mami's wedding dress, which was most likely stored in the hallway closet. Though from the moment we got home, the phone was ringing with calls from anxious family members and friends, to whom Papi tiredly attended. I pre-heated the oven for a pizza for us when Marita called to report that Mami's oxygen levels had dropped to the mid-80s and her heart rate had dropped to 72 bpm. This was good news, of course, and what we all wanted for Mami, as per her wishes, but I could see Papi tense up over the kitchen counter. His eyes began to water as he struggled to remain calm. Marita was concerned that the oxygen monitor would begin beeping when it dropped below a certain point and asked what she should do in that case. Since the breathing tube wasn't a life-sustaining apparatus, it didn't matter that we left it in. It was there simply to make Mami a little more comfortable. We suggested she speak with the night nurse and we encouraged each other with the reminder that it was Mami's wish to die. Marita later texted me that the nurse had said she could simply turn off the machine when it started beeping but that it was nothing they needed to do just yet. I let Marita know to call us if anything changes and promised to keep my phone on all night.

After pizza, I settled in on the couch to search for a movie I could get lost in and Papi began to dig in the hallway closet. I'd completely forgotten about our conversation only hours earlier. With a loud crackle of plastic, Papi removed the cover from over Mami's wedding dress and swung it out as I stood up like a magnet drawn to it. I cleared a stack of freshly folded laundry from the couch to make room for him to place the dress there and, again, I noticed Papi fighting back the tears. It broke my heart to see him so heartbroken. I couldn't even begin to fathom what it'd be like to lose the love of your life, the one person with and for whom you've lived life for fifty years. I hugged him a lot that night, probably too much to a point that may have annoyed him but I figured you can never give someone too much love.

Later once Papi had retired to bed, I took care of Arco's monthly flea medication and started shutting down the rest of the lights around the house. With only the bar lights left on, I was drawn to the couch where Papi had carefully draped Mami's dress. The light of the bar softly illuminated her ivory lace and taffeta wedding gown and I couldn't help but fall to my knees before it and reach out for Mami, hoping to commune with her. I apologized to her for not always having been a good daughter and for all the mistakes I'd made over the years. I told her I wanted to be a good child of God, as was she, and I thanked her for having always seen me for who I really am.

When the loss of having the only person in my life who completely saw and understood the real me settled in, the tears came pouring out. I thought to myself, "If not Mami, then who will really take the time to understand me and to love me unconditionally as she'd so selflessly done my whole life?"

I became aware in that moment that it was up to me to know my true self. It was up to me to love myself unconditionally as I am. Only I could dependably give that to myself before anyone else could. And I knew that Mami would always be here with me, that she'd still continue to see me, to know me, to love me.

It would be years before I grasped that it is God, above all, who sees my true self and who loves me unconditionally. And because of His absolute love, I can love myself unconditionally too.

Wednesday, October 3, 2012

It has been nine days since Mami was first taken to the hospital. She still lies here with us, completely unresponsive. Mucus has been forming in her throat and nose. Because suctioning would've been too disturbing and painful, we each cleaned her out during our shifts, delicately collecting mouthfuls and nosefuls of it into wads of tissues. She was entirely helpless. Her head was, as always since she'd stopped responding, tilted to her right side. It was so far now that she appears to almost be kissing her shoulder. Her skin has paled even more and bruises have appeared on her fragile twisted legs. Her toenails still look so pretty with the gold nail polish from the pedicure she had done before the anniversary celebration.

Sometimes I've wondered how I've been able to handle this all fairly well, given that I am losing my mother, my best friend, my soul mate…I've managed to stay strong and emotionally steady overall, understanding that Mami will be in a much better place and that this is best for her spirit.

But it's wearing on me to see her lying there like this. Each day that passes by stretches on and all the days continue blurring together in one long painful—yet still magical—mess. I'm thankful that she doesn't seem to be suffering physically anymore. If she's so deeply asleep, she must not feel the pain. Or at least I hope so.

The days have been long and we're all downright depleted. I feel like we're in this state of limbo now that Mami is unresponsive yet we are all still taking care of her. It feels like when you pull off a Band-Aid too slowly, ripping your skin inch by inch by inch. Rather than a quick tug, letting the wound be exposed to air so that it can finally heal. It feels like this is drawing out the healing process, both for Mami and for us. And I'm becoming more and more aware of the giant void gaping before me, the empty space I know we'll have to one day come home to, knowing that it is no longer filled at the hospital either.

It has been an intense odyssey of emotions over the past six months— from the joy, the laughs and the memories we shared, holding each other's hands, tenderly and openly looking into each other's eyes to the tears, the fears and the pain, both physical and emotional. Kissing each other goodnight every night, wondering if it would be our last…it was so beautiful, our time together, yet so fleeting.

I prayed everyday for Mami to go quickly into God's arms so she could be free. At the same time, I wanted to be able to keep looking into her eyes, which beheld a lifetime of warmth and love and cherished memories together. It was when she stopped responding a couple of days ago that it became even harder. Now that she was actually and finally slipping away, I wanted desperately to hold on, to keep her here. There was the urge inside of me of wanting to kiss her now, to stroke her hand, to lay my hand gently on her forehead waiting for her warm smile to inevitably follow. I felt I had to stifle that urge though; I was afraid that any touch magnetized by that feeling of me wanting to hold on instead of letting her go would somehow bring her back to this life. This was something we knew she did not want. So I quietly watched over her in that moment, holding back the tears, and prayed.

The hospital grounds were nicely manicured and, nestled within one of the courtyards, was a Prayer Garden. I'd walked downstairs to it the other day, circling around the koi pond over and over again. I wondered how many people had prayed here before me and how many more were yet to come with prayers and pleas for help. I apologized to God for asking for Mami's release. I knew I shouldn't have any expectations. I knew God had a plan. Who was I to question that? There in the garden I gave up my need to figure out the time Mami should go. I asked God to release me from my frustration and confusion of what it was that was taking so long. I asked Him to give me the strength (I knew Mami had it) and I let Him know I trusted Him to walk us through the process, no matter how long it took. I don't know, maybe it was Papi who needed her here a little longer. We know how much it's breaking his heart too. The fact that Mami is still lying here in the hospital has still given us reason to live, to be here for each other. Maybe it is Mami's spirit that is working some things out. Maybe it's me who needs her here longer. I just don't know. But it is not for me to know or understand. This is where faith comes in. And that's what I asked God for that afternoon in the garden.

Thankfully our weariness this past week, instead of making us more abrupt and short with each other, has softened us and made us more loving with one another. We have become more bonded than ever as a family. Well, we always did say that Mami was our spiritual glue. Here she is—still the glue—simply by lying passively in the hospital bed. I was nervous about taking over this role of hers as she'd entrusted to me months ago. Mami didn't even bat an eyelash then. She said she knew I'd rise to the occasion and that, through it all, God would walk with me and the rest of our family. She had so much faith. In God. In herself. In me.

It was her faith in me that had always given me strength, confidence and the inner peace that, above all, I have a good heart and good intentions. This is something that I want to always remember, especially during times of greatest need: to have faith in myself.

Thursday, October 4, 2012

This morning I awoke back home to Arco, a.k.a. "Bark-o", doing what he does second best. Barking. (Licking would be the first, of course). Our biweekly housekeeper had come earlier than usual, thinking it'd be a good idea to give us some extra help. While her heart and sentiments were in the right place, I wasn't exactly thrilled to be forced awake earlier than planned, given the amounts of sleep I so desperately needed to catch up on. She was dismayed and saddened to hear about Mami having gone to the hospital and told us she's been praying for her to get better. I thanked her and let her know that Mami is peaceful and joyful; she had expressed her wishes to be with God again. Even if she were to miraculously wake up, I couldn't bear to see her living the rest of her life with dysfunctional and disfigured legs, forcing her to be bedridden or in a wheelchair. Unless God could create the biggest miracle ever in restoring her to the perfect health she had before cancer had ever invaded her body over eighteen years ago, I wouldn't really feel right keeping her here with us.

Marita and I talked about it at the kitchen table over breakfast, which she'd prepared for us. We think Mami is hanging on for Papi. We know that she has been spiritually absolved and that she is at complete peace now with dying. I recall Mami telling me several weeks ago that she couldn't fathom leaving Papi behind. She'd felt that she couldn't bear to be without Papi if he had died before her and it tore her up that she'd be doing that to him. We, of course, understood this to be a natural process of life and that it'd be rare to go together. We also knew that we had to accept these circumstances and, once again, trust in God to guide us through. It did not make things any easier nor did it help us understand why it would happen this way. It just allowed us to be accepting of this fate.

Later at the hospital sitting with Mami, a brief but distinct memory from childhood vividly flashed through my mind. I must've been five or six years old. I'd grabbed Mami's hand and told her that, since we are soulmates, we'd always be together through everything and that we would one day go to Heaven together too…that when she dies, so would I.

Now I'm at her bedside watching her rest ever so peacefully as she slowly dies. I was so hopeful as a kid. I was also more spiritually aware, I think. I really did believe we would go to Heaven together at the same time, still holding hands. From the hospital chair I instinctively reached for her the way I did as a little girl. I guess the truth is that a part of me is dying with her. And the Heaven that I shall see is the strength and love that God is giving our family to endure this life-changing experience.

So here I sit, slowly dying with Mami. With her I also inhale and exhale, feeling our life energy in tandem, and watching the rise and fall, then pause, then rise and fall of her steadily shortening breath. I want so much to speak with her, to tell her how much I love her, to let her know we're all going to be ok when she's gone and that we're taking extra special care of Papi.

I struggled with where to place my hand on her body in an offer of comfort, love and support. Her free hand was on her right side and harder to get to with that side of the bed close to the wall in the corner of the room. Her left shoulder was bare, aside from the fentanyl patch applied to her skin, but I was afraid I could possibly wake her if I touched her there. I settled for gently placing my hand on top of her layered blankets under where her arm was and kept slowly and lovingly stroking my hand over the blanket, whispering how much I love her.

Still now I continue racking my brain as to why she's still here with us and I recognize it is not meant for me to know. I'm aware that I selfishly want her here because she has been a big reason for me for living. For so many months my life and my service have been dedicated completely to Mami, as it has been for Papi and Marita too. My fear is what will I do next? To whom can I dedicate my love and my service when I come home to the inevitable big hollow space in my life?

Marita gave me the answer today. My service shall go to Papi, as he will need it most when we move into the chapter after Mami's passing. I lament everyday to see how this affects Papi. I know he has given so much of himself to Mami especially this past year and, while he always had a lot of other stuff going on in life between work, traveling, diving and photography, he so deeply cherished his one true love. As we've seen, he would do anything for her. And knowing that he's been doing everything for her, I'm afraid in the immediate aftermath he may feel he has nothing left. So I must make it my mission to make sure he feels all the love and care in the world. I must give to him, for he's given so much to me my whole life. Mami and Papi sacrificed greatly for us kids. It is an honor to be able to care for Mami now that she's helpless, just as when Marita and I were helpless little babies in her arms.

Friday, October 5, 2012

The days have become a daze and the nights a fog, the three of us shuffling through our shifts as best as we could bearing the buildup of heavy emotions weighing more and more upon us each day. We've been twelve days in the hospital now with Mami. Somehow we still managed to find humor with each other, joking about Mami being a stubborn German woman since she's been taking her sweet time to cross over to the other side.

When I awoke at home earlier this morning, something came over me and I had a keen urge that I wanted to spend the night shift with Mami at the hospital tonight. I asked Marita and Papi if they'd be ok with switching and of course they were. We were all accommodating each other with everything that we could. They first asked me, though, if I was sure about it because the night shifts would guarantee little and uncomfortable sleep in the cramped guest chair by Mami's bedside. Yes, I was sure. It's not like I was sleeping much better overall at home away from her. I wanted the chance to have a sleepover with Mami.

Later, after an early dinner, I packed up my overnight stuff along with my laptop where I kept my playlists of music, which I'd planned to play for her. It's said that hearing is the last sense to go before dying.

Once at the hospital, I hugged and kissed Papi goodnight, relieving him of his shift. He reported no new developments before he hugged me once more and left. There I stood alone looking at Mami lying in her bed, her left leg crookedly bent and foot rolling to the side at a freakish angle...her contorted neck that had allowed her head to roll so far to the side, it was almost lying flat on her right shoulder now. Every time we'd tried to gently readjust her neck and head, it'd flop back down to the side. She looked incredibly uncomfortable but we didn't want to move her any further for fear of causing her any more pain. I softly placed my hand on her arm and whispered that I was here with her, then kissed her on her forehead.

I pushed the chair next to her bedside and silently prayed to God to let me know if her last breath is drawing near so that I could call Papi and Marita to get here. I wanted the three of us to be together with her in her last moment.

Opening my laptop, I pulled up some of the music that had always uplifted her. Christian music artist Chris Tomlin was among her latest favorites and I chose certain songs to play for her with a purpose.

- "Our God" (To remind Mami that she is in the best hands possible).
- "I'm Forgiven" (To let Mami know she's been absolved and that God forgives her and loves her unconditionally. I reminded her that she is perfect and whole exactly as she is).
- "I Lift My Hands" (To ask God to come into our lives, to connect with and place a bridge for Mami to cross into His arms).
- "I Will Rise" (For Mami's journey to God's Kingdom, that she'll leave behind her sorrow and pain and can rise into the Lord's arms...I kept lifting my arms up to the sky to that song, sometimes reaching with one arm for Mami's hand and with the other arm still

outstretched to Heaven, asking God to take her hand and walk her up to her beautiful new Sanctuary in the Sky).

- Singing along, I mixed in songs from Neil Diamond's Jonathan Livingston Seagull: "Skybird" series. I remember so many times in the past watching her move and sway to his magnificent compositions. Even though she hadn't moved an inch in days, tonight I could feel it moving her soul.
- I ended the night with one last song from Chris Tomlin, bringing it full circle with "Amazing Grace".

In my mind that night, I'd nicknamed myself DJ Angel in our own private nightclub called Gateway to Heaven. Never underestimate the power of humor, especially in the most trying times.

After the last song, even though I was singing in a somewhat hushed voice, I couldn't help but laugh out loud. I apologized to her that she was literally stuck listening to my horrible singing voice (really, I could crack glass). But I did not come to this earth to be the world's best singer. I came here to sing with joy. And I knew that Mami knew it had all come from my heart.

I sat there smiling at her, watching her slowly breathing in and out.

After I'd closed my laptop and put it aside, I reached for Mami's hand and prayed for her.

Mami's nurse stuck her head into the room to check on her and I confirmed that nothing had changed since she was last here. She nodded and empathetically smiled. The entire staff in this wing had been so kind and caring. I could tell they felt bad for everything we were going through as a family. At the same time, they'd told us how much we'd inspired them for the way we've pulled through together and been there for Mami and for each other. They witnessed so much love between us, each of them testified.

At some point sitting by Mami's side I nodded off in the chair, teetering somewhere between the line of reality and sleep. I was vaguely aware of the sound of Mami's heart monitor, which I'd repeatedly listened to for any signs of change.

Later around 1:30 AM, from deep within a dreamless sleep, I heard Mami suddenly gasp for air. It was the first sound I'd heard from her since she went unconscious five days earlier. I jumped to my feet with a million thoughts clamoring for my attention all at once. How can I help Mami? Do I call Marita and Papi now? Hold Mami's hand. Check her vitals. Call for help. Pray now.

She moaned and choked on the fluids rattling in the back of her throat. Within seconds I'd scanned all the machines she was hooked up to. My stomach turned when I saw the numbers plummet, her diastolic blood pressure having dropped all the way to 61 mmHG while her heart rate, which had been very slow and steady for days on end, now sharply hiked up to 123 bpm. I'd read about the combination of low blood pressure and cardiac arrest being telltale signs of a person right before death.

With my heart pumping just as fast, it felt, as Mami's, I decided in that moment to wait on calling Papi and Marita until after the nurse comes, which I rang for. As soon as I'd called for help, I stood there and called out to God. He was the one I knew would be our best line of help. As I reached for Mami's hand, hearing her gagging and choking, I implored God to please, please, please send forth all of His Angels to come protect and comfort Mami and to ease any pain she may be feeling from gasping for air. And, wouldn't you know, God sent them!

The lights over Mami's hospital bed started flickering repeatedly off and on, off and on, as if they'd gone haywire. I physically felt what I could only describe as a gust of wind blow sheer across my arms. It was so powerful my hairs stood on end. Almost instantly Mami's breathing stabilized and I felt relief. I smiled up towards the sky, thanking God and His Angels for their help. They are always there when you need to call upon them. Witnessing what I just did made me realize we're never really ever alone.

Moments later the nurse stepped into the room and I explained what happened to Mami. After checking Mami's vitals, she confirmed Mami was ok. The Dilaudid was supposed to be changed at that time so I asked the nurse for an increase to ease any pain she might've felt during that initially frightening episode.

I stayed up watching Mami and the continuing rise and fall of her chest for a long time, hours maybe, fighting the sleep that was trying to take me. Eventually sleep overcame me while slumped in my chair next to Mami's bed and the two of us, Mami and me, slept there together soundly.

CHAPTER 19

Four Pennies

"I found a penny today
Just laying on the ground,
But it's not just a penny
This little coin I've found.
"Found" pennies come from Heaven,
That's what my Grandpa told me…
He said when an angel misses you
They toss a penny down
Sometimes just to cheer you up,
Make a smile out of your frown.
So don't pass by that penny
When you're feeling blue;
It may be a penny from heaven
That an angel tossed to you.

~C. Mashburn

At 8 AM I awoke to the morning nurse's knock on the door; she'd come to check on Mami's vitals. When taking her temperature, she declared that Mami had a fever. She was burning up fast. I knew then it was time to call Papi and Marita and I urged them to come without delay.

They made it there before 9 AM and the three of us stood there watching Mami. She was lying quiet and still; the only motion we could detect was the movement of her breath, barely perceptible now in her chest. It had slowed down somewhat since the day before. The clock ticked. It felt as if I could hear time moving.

A couple of hours had passed like this as we stood in silence so as not to disturb her transition. What now? In Mami's own words last week, how much longer was this going to take? My stomach growled. Papi looked towards me and suggested that we girls go get lunch. We were tired of eating hospital food everyday so Marita had the bright idea to go to the farmer's market right by our house. Papi encouraged us to eat there, outside in the fresh air, and we let him know we'd bring him back something nice. He thanked us as he pulled out his laptop from his duffel bag on the floor next to the lone chair in the corner of the room. He said he'd be working on "The Celebration of Life" DVD. This was a compilation of Mami's life in pictures that he'd been scrupulously putting together for the commemoration party Mami requested we throw in her honor once she was gone.

When walking into the farmer's market, I noticed the warmth of the sun on my skin and smiled. It surprised me how much I appreciated the fresh air in that moment. I'd forgotten what it had felt like.

There were delicious organic vegetables, fresh-squeezed juices and various vegan delights laid out on picnic tables under a big tent. Marita and I grabbed three boxes, one for each of us, to load up on lunch.

We found a spot to sit at a nearby picnic table and ravenously dug into the fresh wholesome goodness. After thirteen days of hospital food, Dunkin Donuts runs and any other takeout food we could get our hands on, this was heaven sent. Marita and I talked about how strange everything felt. Marita's presence has always been a blessing in my life and, in that moment, I felt it more than ever. I couldn't have imagined commiserating with anyone else.

About three quarters of the way through the meal, Marita's phone rang. I'll never forget the two of us looking at it and seeing Papi's name come up on the screen. Before she even answered, she looked at me and we both knew. It was 1:06 PM Saturday, October 6, 2012. Mami had gone home to the Lord.

Marita and I burst into tears, holding and consoling each other, rocking together on the picnic bench. We may have even wailed because the next thing we knew, we noticed people around us who'd stopped to look at the spectacle. We looked at each other with tears streaming down our faces and snot coming out of our noses and started to laugh. Of course this would happen when we're in public and couldn't help making a scene because of the tsunami of emotions that swept over us from all the months leading up to this one moment.

On one hand, I felt such deep, cutting sadness that our Mami was really gone for good. On the other hand, I felt relief that she no longer had to suffer in her physical body.

Marita and I stood up from the table facing each other, eddying emotions magnetic between our hearts. We wiped each other's faces with our napkins, packed up the food and made our way to the car so we could go be with Papi.

On our way walking back to the car, Marita had called her husband to tell him the news and I called Lucas. While on the phone, I noticed a penny lying on the ground and, without thinking, picked it up.

Marita grabbed my arm, turned away from her phone, and exclaimed to me, "Do you see? It's a sign from Mami!"

It hadn't occurred to me in that moment. Of course it was; Mami had always told us they were good luck. We both grinned at one another as I picked it up and we returned to our phone conversations.

A couple of hundred feet later I noticed Marita stooping down to the ground. She'd discovered two more pennies lying close to each other and looked over to me, smiling wide again. By the time we got back to the house, we'd found four pennies altogether. It was so evident to us that it represented the four of us—Mami, Papi, Marita and me—and that we'll always be together. Mami couldn't have shown us more clearly.

Rebirthday

"Death—the last sleep? No, it is the final awakening."
~*Walter Scott*

I didn't really know what to expect when we got back to the hospital. I wasn't sure how exactly it worked once someone is pronounced dead. Mami's body was still lying in the room when we walked in and I looked to her and then to Papi, feeling torn. I needed to see Mami for myself but I knew that Papi needed us more. He was the one who was there when she took her last breath and who had been there with her body ever since.

He immediately explained to us how he'd been working on Mami's "Celebration of Life" DVD and, when he'd put the final picture in place and clicked "save", he looked up to see her take her final breath. It was as if she'd been waiting for him to finish it. I couldn't imagine how his heart must've ached when he noticed the final beat of his wife's for the last time. Marita and I both swung our arms around him, the three of us embracing each other next to Mami's body.

Once we started to pull away and regroup about what to do, I turned to look at Mami. She was still lying in the same position. I looked closely at her chest. It was so strange, after intently watching it rise and fall these past couple of weeks, to see it not moving at all anymore. Her body was not only motionless. It was soulless. There was a stark difference between life and death. It was the first time I'd ever witnessed it. I wished it didn't have to be with my Mami.

The next thing I knew the doctor and nurses came in to give their condolences and started rolling Mami's bed out of the room. They would have to take her body downstairs for an attendant from the funeral home to pick it up. It was like a bizarre dream watching my mom's body being wheeled out of the room that day. I thought to myself this is the last time I'll ever see her…I watched her head, then her chest, then her legs and finally her feet disappear as they rolled her out the door.

We stood there in a moment of silence in the empty hospital room, the place that had become our temporary home over the past couple of weeks. Everything that we had lived for these past few months had now vanished. It was time to go home.

We said our goodbyes and thanked the rest of the hospital staff before making our way downstairs. Once on the ground floor, Marita went ahead to get the car while Papi and I waited in front of the hospital entrance.

He turned to me and said, "I guess we'll have to start learning how to live our lives new now."

It was heavy to hear but it was the truth. I hugged him and reminded him that Marita and I are always here for him, just like we know he's here for us.

Back at the house, it felt empty and Arco was home alone, still waiting. I felt so bad that he couldn't be there by Mami's side like he'd always been. Everyday he'd been waiting for Mami to come back home and she hadn't. I hugged our baby boy and explained to him that his mommy had gone to Heaven. I told him he'll never be alone anymore, that we'd always be there for him. We are in this together. He seemed to understand. Dogs have a way of knowing that I think humans have yet to tap into. All I wanted to do was hold him.

Later that afternoon when I awoke from a brief nap, there was a hushed stillness in the house. I couldn't cry. It was like I was numb. What I did feel, however, was gratitude. I thought of how grateful I was for Lucas who had been by my side through everything and for Marita's husband for being so supportive and wonderful with her during this time. I thought of how surreal life had become when death draws near. Our lives had not, by any measure, been as we normally lead them but, goodness, were we blessed to have been able to take so much time to be there for our Mami and for each other. It will be strange to try to find our way back to our normal lives yet in a way in which we could move forward with the giant hole we have where Mami once was. Of course she's always still with us but I knew there would be that daunting physical void. It was this part that I was numb to. I knew that numbness would wear off at some point. The question was when. I didn't try to figure it out. It would come when it comes.

That night Papi suggested we go to Jaguar Café for dinner. It was within walking distance and we all felt we could use the walk. The October night sky was clear and there was a hint of coolness in the air. From time to time as we walked we held hands. At other times, where the sidewalk narrowed next to the main road, we walked single file. There were a couple of dark spots along the path where street lanterns were not working. As we walked past one of them it suddenly turned on. It happened again with another street lantern several hundred feet later. Perplexed, Papi said they must be new sensor lights (they'd never been that way before) but Marita and I were convinced it was Mami lighting up our path for us. The thought of that brought us much comfort.

As we approached the heart of the commercial neighborhood, we noticed four bright white spotlights circling the sky and felt even more connected with Mami. It reminded us of the four pennies we'd found earlier. The source of the lights was in the heart of the Grove near Johnny Rockets, a popular local diner. They'd rarely put spotlights like that anywhere in the Grove. We were touched to have that connection with Mami in the sky on her first night ascended. All through dinner, at a table outside on the sidewalk, we could see her lights circling above. It was like having her at dinner with us.

When we returned home, Papi announced he wanted to smoke a cigar. So we all got more comfortable and, while Papi dug into his humidor, Marita spooned out into three bowls the decadent banana tiramisu frozen yogurt with toffee candy we'd picked up on the way home.

I turned on one of Mami's favorite lights, the Bliss light, a laser projector that creates a galaxy of moving stars on the ceiling. Gazing at the green pinpoints of light expanding and contracting over a backdrop of blue nebula, we noted how much more beautiful the universe must look from Mami's viewpoint. During her hospital stay I'd gotten a Guardian Angel candle that we'd been burning for her each day. I lit it again in her honor; she, herself, had now become an angel.

We sat out on the patio with Arco enjoying dessert and drinks while reminiscing over all the fun, amazing, adventurous memories we shared with Mami. We laughed and smiled, just the way Mami would've wanted us to. And it came from our hearts.

While we were recounting stories, I'd begun to notice the light over our table flickering off and on. It wasn't until I mentioned it that Marita and Papi realized it too. After last night's encounter with Mami's angels in the hospital, I knew it was Mami right there, laughing and rejoicing, with us. It turned out to be a most beautiful and magical night, the three of us sitting around the same patio table where we'd sat together as a family for decades. And even though the fourth seat was empty now, our hearts were full of her love and her light.

Before turning in to bed, I beheld her in my mind's eye calling on her to say, "Thank you, Mami, for giving this special night to us. Thank you for giving and sacrificing all of yourself for us. You are our Angel. You are our Greatest Love, along with Jesus. *Hallelujah, sweet Mami; you are free!!!*"

CHAPTER 21

And Then There Were Three

"Believing that we are never alone and that we always have divine guidance will carry us when we are too tired to carry ourselves."

~Randi G. Fine

The three of us walked quietly out of the funeral home through the parking lot to the car. The sun was shining and there was a cool fall Floridian breeze against my skin. I pulled my pashmina over my bare arms, wrapping it around the light blue dress I'd worn. As lovely as that afternoon was, it felt weird, like I was sleepwalking through some bad dream.

I looked to the pavement with each leaden step. So that was it. It all seemed to happen in the blink of an eye. What had happened these past few months to make it fly by so fast? Every moment I'd shared with Mami now seemed so far away. It was not her in that cardboard box. Yet it was. How do you separate spirit from body? We come to know each other here on this earth as the trifecta of mind, body and spirit intricately woven together by God's hands. When He reclaims the spirit and we are left here with the body, how do we make sense of it?

As we walked across the black asphalt I couldn't stop thinking about how her body was being consumed by flames. That was all we were left with other than her personal items. I looked back at the building to where the crematorium was. I don't know what I expected. Smoke rising from my mom's ashes? A cloud in the shape of an angel telling me she's ok? The funeral director running out and telling us, "Our mistake, that was not your mom!" But nothing. Just the sun shining brightly in a deep blue sky. Just my sister's arms slipping over my shoulders. I realized at that moment that

I'd been holding my breath. I let out a sigh and wrapped my arm around my sister until we all packed up into the car and drove off.

We'd tried to live as "normally" as we could. On the way home, we stopped at our usual Cuban café for cortaditos and these cheesy guava pastries we love. What was normally a treat though now seemed like just plain food. As I bit into the flaky pastry, I flashed back to feeding Mami her last meal at the hospital before she became completely unresponsive. She was so cute propped up with pillows in her hospital bed and the napkin I'd placed over her chest like a bib. I smiled at that memory and looked back to Papi and Marita sitting across from me at the café.

Papi wolfed down his pastry and Marita sipped on her coffee. Yup, just like normal. We talked about our plans for Mami's Celebration of Life party, what music to play, what kind of food to offer, how many bottles of champagne to buy. We were going through the motions. And we were beyond tired. But there were moments where we could see humor and found ourselves at least smiling with each other. Sitting at the table with them, I was so grateful to not be alone. I was so grateful to have the dad and sister I do. To go through my worst nightmare, I can't imagine anyone better to be in it with me.

The cremation would last several hours, we were informed, and then they'd have to further break down and pulverize Mami's remains. We'd be able to pick up her ashes the following day.

She'd wished for her ashes to be spread in nature. But that's about as specific as she got on that front. She didn't indicate where. She trusted us to choose the right place.

We thought long and hard about it. We'd entertained several ideas, including flying to her home country, Germany, and bringing her ashes to the forests there. She'd always loved long walks in the woods and had a thing for pine trees. She'd even collected pinecones she'd picked up on our family travels and kept them in a papier-mâché bowl she'd crafted herself. But the more we thought about it, the more it didn't make sense to go through such lengths to get her there because then it would be that much harder to visit her thereafter.

So right here in South Florida is where we agreed to search. We took the day for a road trip to scope out possible locations. The first two stops we made were nice but we still felt uncertain if either was the right spot for Mami. We stopped a third time when we noticed all these pine trees around. In Florida! Venturing from the car into the trees, Papi led the way through some tall grass when suddenly we heard a disturbing rattling sound. We froze in our tracks, our eyes darting back and forth across the ground. Just ahead we spotted it—a rattlesnake in the path. With eyes fixated on the snake and in the slowest motion possible we quietly stepped back and back and back until we were far enough to run in the opposite direction. Whoa!! That was not the right place for Mami and she made that very clear. And it led us, right across the road from where we started, to walk directly towards a lake.

The Dade County pines, native to this area, leaped up from the ground, tall and glorious. The rays of the sun peaked through a passing cloud and we stood there in awe and excitement. There were pinecones dotting the ground and Marita and I crouched down to whisk up a couple to examine them as we walked further into this small forest. I looked ahead at the lake and noticed a lot of dragonflies darting back and forth. There was a sort of magic in the air. I could tell we all felt it.

We turned to each other, huddled together and smiling in silence. I looked down for a moment and noticed that a group of dragonflies had formed a perfect circle, hovering, around the three of us. Their wings were steady and taut and it appeared as if they were floating in place. I quietly tugged at Marita's arm, beckoning her to observe the unusual phenomenon, but both she and Papi had also already taken notice. We were all floored and it instantly confirmed what we already knew. This was the spot. This was where we'd spread Mami's ashes.

CHAPTER 22

The Visitor

*"Legend has it that dragonflies were given an extra set of wings
so that angels could ride on their back, smaller than small, yet
whenever you see a winged masterpiece, you can be certain that
an angel has come down from heaven to visit you."*

~Heather Fitzpatrick

Curious about the meaning of dragonflies, Marita Googled it for us once we'd left the area and regained cell phone reception. We learned that dragonflies spend much of their lives in a larvae stage in the muck underwater. In the final part of their life the graceful adult emerges with its wings, leaving the muck and water behind to fly into the world of air and sun. Its metamorphosis is said to represent death. Its rise above the water and emergence anew symbolizes life after death. It signifies transformation and renewal.[2]

We got goose bumps, recognizing that Mami was showing us that she lives on. We were connected through God's guidance and Mami's presence.

When returning home, Arco was loyally lying at the foot of Mami's bed. It was obvious he was grieving too. I knelt down beside him, rubbing behind his ears. He looked up at me with despondent eyes.

"I know," I sighed, looking back into his eyes and running my hands across his back.

It occurred to me that in the past couple of weeks between the anniversary and then the hospital stay none of us had picked up after Arco when we'd let him out in the backyard. It must've been a mess of dog droppings out there.

---

2 Paraphrased from https://animalsake.com/what-does-dragonfly-symbolize

"C'mon," I beckoned him. He halfheartedly got up and followed me out to the patio.

I grabbed several plastic bags before stepping outside and, refreshed by the sun, Arco bounded onto the lawn stopping to sniff various stalks of grass that drew his interest.

Indeed, Arco had left us many "gifts", most of which had hardened and dried by then. I walked around, searching and stooping down several times to collect his feces. The bag was filling up fast.

I thought about Mami, remembering how often she'd claim to us how proud she was of her baby boy but, when it came time to pick up after him, he was suddenly not her dog. Of course she'd take care of him but if there was the slight chance that one of us would do the dirty work she'd gladly relinquish her duties.

Laughing at the thought and with my hand clasping a big bag full of you-know-what, I pumped my arm up to the sky and sarcastically said, "Look at what you left me, Mami, *thanks!*"

In that instant, I noticed the shadow of something fluttering behind my shoulder. I knew exactly what it was. I turned to get a glimpse of it. There were two trees, several feet apart, to my left where Papi had tied off a rope to hang his scuba gear for when he went diving.

The dragonfly landed on this empty rope. I placed the bag to the ground and slowly walked over to her, avoiding any sudden movements so as not to frighten her away.

Before I knew it, I was having a conversation with this dragonfly, albeit a little one-sided. But she was a great listener. I thanked her for the signs she'd been giving us and for the love she and God had been showing us. I told her how weird it felt to be at home without her, that everything in life just felt weird, like I'd lost my footing. I didn't know how to get it back and was aware it would take time.

She must've sat with me for at least twenty minutes as I poured my heart out to her. I was amazed because dragonflies are known to flitter about, not stay in one place as this one was patiently doing.

I'm sure I must've looked like I'd lost my marbles having a conversation with a dragonfly but I didn't care. It gave me solace.

Admiring her spirit in this form, I said that I'd love to have a picture of her to remember this time together.

"Ok," I said putting my hands up in a stop position, "wait right here," I told her. "I'm going to run inside and get my camera," I explained matter-of-factly.

As I was saying this to the dragonfly quietly perched on the rope, I thought to myself, "This is crazy. She's probably going to fly away the moment I leave."

But I took my chances and sprinted into the house to dig up my camera from my room, which took a couple of minutes. Bolting back outside with it, I scanned the rope with bated breath.

There she was, still parked in the same spot as before. I breathed a sigh of relief. When I turned my camera on and zoomed the lens on her, she turned slightly and lowered her wings. I snapped a photo. Then she turned again, this time raising her wings. I snapped another photo. Every picture I took it was like she was posing for it. I laughed because she had been a model in her earlier years.

"Some things don't change, huh?" I prompted her.

By the end of our photoshoot, Arco came up, curious as to why I'd been spending so much time in that part of the backyard. I thanked Mami for the pictures and told her Arco wanted to say hello. He wagged his tail and looked up at me, his tongue hanging out the side of his mouth.

It was time to head in so I blew her a kiss goodbye. That would be the first of her daily visits, sitting with me either on the rope or on a nearby bromeliad, over the course of the next two months.

CHAPTER 23

Mother, Mother Earth

"By the sweat of your brow you will eat your food until you
return to the ground, since from it you were taken; for dust you
are and to dust you will return."

~*Genesis 3:19*

The following day it was time to pick up her ashes. As before with the cardboard box, Mami insisted we use the least expensive option for everything so instead of an ornate urn, we got her ashes in a plastic Ziploc bag. Literally. For a moment it seemed cruel and undignified but I completely understood and agreed with Mami's reasoning. Why spend the money on something or someone whose physical body no longer exists? It's the ones who are left behind that organize all this fanfare of fancy funeral ceremonies and burials in costly caskets or cremations in expensive urns with an abundance of flowers that only have the same fate as those who've died. But it makes us feel better. And it is tradition.

Most importantly, we were honoring Mami by following through on her wishes. So there we were with a big clear plastic bag of Mami's cremains.

When we returned to the spot she'd led us to choose, we made our own little ceremony of it. We'd brought our beach chairs, a picnic with a smorgasbord of snacks, some mementos of Mami including her little yellow pillow, my teddy bear with whom she cuddled in her final months, Marita's Bible and my iPod with a speaker to play a musical tribute to her. Marita had the good sense to also bring a Kleenex box. We set up shop under the pine trees and each took turns reading letters that we'd written to her.

I shared a letter I'd written to Mami for her birthday but never had the chance to read to her. I read it aloud to Mami's spirit that day with Marita and Papi my encouraging audience. I knew she'd heard what I wanted to tell her.

My sweet Mami, Mother of my Soul,

You have reached so many magnificent milestones in your life:

70 absolutely amazing years filled with love, gratitude, joy, adventure, immense spiritual growth, abundant blessings, and God by your side and in your heart every step of your path—even when unbeknownst to you.

50 beautiful years together with your wonderful, loving husband who would do anything for you and who utterly adores you more than words can express.

44 delightful years with your incredibly sweet and selfless first-born, Marita, Daughter of your Heart. She has blossomed into one of the most kindhearted, caring and giving women I know.

And 32 resplendent years with your second-born, Michelle, Daughter of your Soul. I am, thanks to you, growing into the compassionate and spiritually awakened being that my beautiful mother has become.

Everyday I am entirely grateful for the unconditionally loving and supportive family and friends with whom we've been blessed.

These are all remarkable milestones that you have manifested as a Child of God.

This is your life, Mami. And this is all the beauty you have created.

God has always been and always will be with you along your magical journey, paving the way.

You have been and forever will be so many things to me: my mother, my teacher, my best friend, my soulmate...

We've experienced many life lessons together on our journey, learning sometimes how to "muddle through" and, yet, somehow learning to be better souls when we leave our bodies in this life than when we entered it.

I fondly remember our deep, philosophical conversations out on the patio in The Sanctuary, waxing poetic over life and our greater purpose here and beyond. You have continuously inspired me to be more thoughtful about life and the way we choose to live, whether it was when standing in a circle of friends and stepping back to let someone else join in and be a part of the group or it was discovering the greatest within me that I can contribute in this life.

Mami, you have given me purpose in my life. Especially when often times I've felt lost and unsure of what I'm meant to be doing. When jumping from job to job, where I'd fall apart and lose my soulful joy for life...when I felt I haven't been enough...you've lifted me up and reminded me of my achievements and my devotion to my loved ones. You never stopped believing in me and you have invariably seen right through to my core, to who I really am. And just like they said in our favorite movie, "Avatar", I see you, too, Mami.

What I see is that you are the most beautiful, inspiring, loving and courageous human being I know. Your Light illuminates everything and everyone with whom you've come into contact.

From the moment you brought me to life and let me know that Jesus loves me, as do you, I've felt a connection with you that reaches beyond that of mother and child. That is why I've always called you my soulmate. I know that this physical life, here and now, is just a sliver of the eternal spiritual journey we share together. And you recently confirmed that with me by sharing the book, "Many Lives, Many Masters".

I guess it explains our timeless connection when we've shared many life lessons at the same time together or even way back when I was kid and you used to have a glass of wine and I'd somehow get giddy and silly around you. "We're still connected at the umbilical cord," you used to tease.

With that connection and your love that I imagine only a mother can have for her children, you have constantly supported me and trusted that I have a good head on my shoulders and that I have a good heart too. Well, I do because of you.

You have been my biggest inspiration in life: strong and determined as a warrior, compassionate and loving as an angel, and positive and thoughtful as a spiritual guide.

> *You have taught me to live honorably.*
> *You have taught me to learn open-heartedly.*
> *You have taught me to laugh uncontrollably.*
> *You have taught me to love unconditionally.*

Love is the highest vibration that exists and words cannot express just how dearly I love you, Mami. Not only am I wishing you a joyful 70th birthday, I wish you a most glorious rebirth-day. Remember that Jesus loves you. And I love you, too.

Forever the Daughter of your Soul,
Michi

As we shared our letters to her, we repeatedly reached for the Kleenex box. We also laughed and smiled over some of our favorite memories with Mami before we retrieved the portable speaker to play "Amazing Grace" in her honor.

The sun was hot and beads of sweat began to form on our foreheads. At last we got up and stood together in a circle in prayer. Papi picked up the plastic bag with Mami's ashes and, with bated breath, we gathered together watching him as he ever so gingerly opened it. We stood there, frozen, for another moment. We were all new to this. It is not everyday we dig into a Ziploc bag and pull out the pulverized remains of someone we love.

It was cool and dry to the touch, much finer and smoother than sand. The coolness felt like a relief from the sun's relentless heat out there. Mami's ashes quickly slipped through my fingers so I closed my hand to keep from losing more. I looked for a moment into my cupped hands filled with her ashes and then closed my eyes feeling her energy with me, as if absorbing her essence into my being. I could feel her there and this time, as the sun shone brightly, I felt filled with love and light. And with that overwhelming love in my heart, I threw my hands into the air, offering her ashes back to nature.

Fist after fist, we each took turns digging into the bag of Mami's ashes, holding her close, and scattering them around the trees and all over a circular clearing next to the lake. Every time I loosened my fingers around a fistful of her ashes, I watched them release from my grip and float down to the earth. I noticed how Papi thoughtfully let go of the ashes first in one spot, then in another. Marita spun around in circles, sprinkling the ashes over the grass and bushes. It became like a dance between the three of us—reaching, grasping, turning, releasing.

That day the trees, bushes and pinecones were blanketed in white. That day it looked like it was snowing in South Florida. That day, we gave our mother back to Mother Earth.

CHAPTER 24

The Aftermath

"All great changes are preceded by chaos."

~Deepak Chopra

Our home felt empty yet it was so full of Mami's things. Soon after we'd thrown Mami's Celebration of Life party there, Papi explained to me that he'd be putting the house on the market; it didn't make sense for the two of us to live together under the same roof. He was right. It just felt so sudden. I didn't know that I was ready to move from the place that held so many of our memories with Mami. But it was not for me to decide. Moreover, I understood that it might've felt like too much for Papi to come home everyday to the reminder that his beloved wife was gone.

He reassured me that it could take up to six months to sell the house so, not to worry, we would have time.

Marita continued to visit us regularly to help us go through Mami's belongings in the meantime. We spent hours upon hours combing through her closet, her toiletries, and her jewelry. I'm not sure that either of us was emotionally ready to do so but it had to be done, especially to prepare the house for the market. At the same time, we were still in a state of shock and numbness. We'd known this would happen for months but it still hadn't hit us, the reality that our Mami was dead.

Despite the graveness of the situation, we worked together as a great team. Divvying up Mami's clothes, deciding who would get what and what we'd give away, was rather easy with Marita. We never fought over any of the items. Aside from the fact that we had somewhat different wardrobe needs, we both were more concerned for each other's happiness with what we'd each get to keep from Mami. For the items we both wished to hang on to, we agreed to trade off with each other over time so each of us would have a chance to enjoy them.

Sitting on Mami and Papi's bedroom floor with Marita amidst piles of clothing and trinkets I thought again to myself how blessed I am to have such a wonderful sister who made the hardest things in life so much easier.

I also thought that while our house wasn't huge, Mami had accrued so much stuff over her lifetime. It felt overwhelming and tedious at times; so much so that we had to often take breaks to remove ourselves from it.

Then it was time to go through her bookshelves. This might not sound like anything exciting but Mami was an avid reader, having collected several hundred books that lined the shelves of the whole bedroom wall, from floor to ceiling. We went through each book, one by one, saving only a few for ourselves and giving the rest away to the local library.

We were on a first name basis with the staff at Goodwill. Every week we dropped off more things. Even so, Marita and I kept a sizeable amount of Mami's belongings for ourselves. We weren't yet ready to let go. We shed tears and smiled as we shared memories that popped up with particular articles of clothing we'd found, like Mami's favorite pair of jeans or the zebra print dress she'd loved to wear. I pulled out a slinky leopard print top that I'd bought for her a couple of years earlier, remembering that at the time I'd wished I could have the top for myself. Now I did have it but this was not the way I'd wanted to get it. Marita and I clung to each other whenever it became too emotional for either of us.

Arco sat with us through it all, looking on. I wondered what his doggy-mind was thinking watching everything unfold, as we completely cleared Mami's walk-in closet, bedroom dressers and her drawers in the bathroom. All that was left, in the end, were the sheets on her bed and the memories in our hearts.

On one of her trips to Miami, Marita had brought various beaded bracelets she'd strung herself with the words "LOVE" and "JOY" spelled out in singular letters per bead in the center. She'd made several in almost every color of the rainbow, inspired by our cousin who'd first come up with the idea and distributed them to our family during the Celebration of Life party. We each wore them as a reminder of Mami and the legacy she'd left with us. It was a most thoughtful gift and I loved being able to share the story about Mami when people would ask about them. In my mind it kept her alive with us.

It felt like I'd blinked my eyes when the Yoga Aid World Challenge fundraiser event had arrived. Our group of teachers in training came to support the event, many of us getting up before sunrise to help set up in advance. While I haven't always been an early riser, I love the quiet of early mornings. They make me feel spacious. Calm. In tune with myself and with God. I felt a surge of excitement on my way to 1111 Lincoln Road, the site of a newly designed and architecturally renowned parking garage. We'd be practicing one hundred and eight sun salutations together with hundreds of others on the top floor of this open-air garage overlooking the Miami skyline. The day was already abuzz with the kind of energy that compels even those with two left feet to get up and dance.

One hundred and eight consecutive sun salutations, I learned, are physically and mentally challenging. Of course we could take a break or rest in child's pose but I'd set the intention beforehand to do all one hundred and eight of them in honor of Mami and in gratitude for the opportunity to learn and practice alongside so many like-minded souls.

Throughout the day there were several auctions happening, raffling off some valuable prizes including the retreat to India in January of which I still dreamed. The only way I could see being able to afford this trip of a lifetime was to win a bid for it.

Somehow the day passed by. I got so busy that, by the time everything was shutting down, I'd completely forgotten to put in a bid. I couldn't believe myself. How could I have missed the opportunity? There was nothing I could do about it. It was too late now.

My stomach started growling so I grabbed Nicole and said, "Let's go for a bite right here on Lincoln!"

She was game. We chose a table on the sidewalk, which is what you want to do when on Lincoln Road. It's quite entertaining watching the colorful locals and tourists stroll by on this pedestrian-only street filled with stores, restaurants and dance clubs.

While sitting out there, Michelle, one of our fellow teachers in training passed by and stopped to chat with us. She'd mentioned that she had bid for the retreat in India and had won it. She'd gotten it for about one fifth the cost, which was astounding. I was genuinely excited for her. I mentioned to her that I'd wanted to go to India as well and had completely forgotten to bid. In that moment, I knew I was going to figure out a way to pool my resources and go. I told her how much fun it would be to go together. Michelle then confessed that, with some of her own life transitions, she wasn't sure if she'd be able to go during that time. She suggested that maybe she could sell it to me for what she'd bought it for. She'd ask Terri if that would be ok. I was floored. Wow, how generous of her!

I thanked her and silently thanked God and then let it go. Even though I felt Terri would approve the transfer, I didn't yet have the confirmation that any of this would actually happen.

Since that day, time—as it always does—went on. I hadn't heard from Michelle. I didn't want to reach out and ask her what happened to the ticket she was going to sell me because I was afraid to come across as pushy or with expectation. So I let it go. I started preparing for the trip anyway as if I were going. Part of the retreat was for us to bring school supplies and clothing for the kids at a local school named Khushi. There would be some time planned to meet them, work with them on art projects and cook lunch for them at the school. This was what Karma Yoga was about: service. Giving of ourselves.

There is something about when we most need love given to us that giving it to others fulfills us even more. The trip, I knew, would be exactly what I needed and yet the trip would not really be about me.

I looked into how I could pool the money together for both the flight and the retreat. I'd already been researching flights and learned the best day of the week to purchase them. Next step was purchasing the retreat. A strong gut feeling overcame me to call Michelle right away. I didn't quite know how to politely ask her about the ticket she said she'd sell me but I picked up the phone anyway.

She answered almost immediately and was shocked to hear from me at that very moment. I asked her why. She told me she had just gotten off the phone with Terri to confirm she definitely couldn't make the trip. She went on to apologize for not reaching out to me sooner; she'd been out of pocket dealing with life. I completely understood. Michelle noted that Terri had agreed to transfer the raffle ticket. I was over the moon for the support I had in making my dream a reality. I thanked her and asked her to let me know the best way to give her a check for the amount. She said she'd sort it out and keep me posted.

I reached out to another one of my fellow teachers in training, Christina, whom I found out was also booked for the retreat. We decided that, if we were going to fly all that way anyway, we should stay longer to visit the Taj Mahal and a couple of other areas of interest. Fortuitously Christina worked with several people from India who offered helpful recommendations and connected us with a travel agent with whom she diligently worked to plan our itinerary. Promptly we booked the tickets and I did a little happy dance. Things were coming together.

Before long, the departure was only weeks away. I'd reached out to Michelle several times to see how I could get her the check but I still hadn't heard back from her. I knew she was busy and I felt bad not having given her the money yet. She eventually called me back to tell me that, with everything going on her life, she would like to keep the faith that all will be well and "pay it forward". She explained that she was gifting me the ticket. Her generosity rendered me momentarily speechless. She had given me a trip to India. I felt my heart and soul expand with gratitude. I thanked her and asked her if she wanted me to bring her back anything from India, anything at all. She said that a mala would be nice. I knew I would give her the most beautiful mala I could find; the cost wouldn't matter.

Papi was impressed that I had such amazing friends. I'd gushed about Michelle to him in the kitchen as we prepared dinner later that night. He shared with me about travel plans he'd made for visiting our family in Germany right before year's end. We both had realized how much we needed a "time out" from life as we'd known it over the past year.

For the time being, however, there was still much for us to do. Once Mami's things were cleared, Papi and I set about organizing the rest of the house. The holidays were right around the corner so Papi contacted a realtor to get the ball rolling.

The house hadn't even gone on the market and, forty-eight hours after his call, Papi received an offer for the asking price from another realtor who wanted to move in with her family in the beginning of the New Year. Given our upcoming travels (I wouldn't be returning from India until the last week of January) and our need to find our own apartments, Papi asked if she'd be willing to move in March and she kindly obliged. So that was it. Our house would be sold. Momentary panic jolted through my stomach. I think Papi may have felt it, too, but, at the same time, a sense of relief that we wouldn't be stuck together there in the memories of our past for much longer.

Our home had held so many of my fondest memories with Mami. . .nights out on the patio drinking wine, talking about love, God and the Universe. . .afternoons in the dining room, laughing and playing Rummikub, a favorite family game we grew up with...quiet mornings when I'd visit her in her bed to kiss her sweet face good morning. Her smile would light up the whole room when she saw me. I imagined mine did the same when seeing her. I remember dancing barefoot in the living room with her late nights, Lady Gaga pumping through the surround sound speakers and immersed in Mami's Bliss Light; it was as if we were dancing together within a universe of stars. Yeah, our Mami was pretty darn cool.

She had decorated each part of our home with different themes. The kitchen, with accents of yellow and white and a large rustic floor vase bursting with tall sunflowers (Mami's favorite), felt like a country kitchen. The dining room was Asian-inspired with a modern black and white floor rug and a triptych revealing scenes from a Zen garden painted with Samurai and Geishas. Venture into the living room and you'd have found yourself on an African safari as you step onto a tiger-striped rug and come face to face with a cheetah, mouth agape and lounging in the brush, a baby elephant huddled by his mother's legs and a lone giraffe towering over an acacia tree. Papi, with a penchant and talent for photography, had taken pictures of these animals himself when he and Mami had ventured on the trip of a lifetime to Kenya. The adjacent living room where Mami and I would sometimes dance together late nights was classical-inspired with a large periwinkle and powder blue Oriental-style rug and a white baby grand piano in the corner.

Mami and Papi, both with adventurous spirits, had traveled a lot together over the years and had brought a special keepsake back from each country to make our home the unique and eclectic temple it had become for us.

Our Sanctuary had served its purpose. So had Mami. It was time to start a new chapter. It was time to let go.

136

It felt sudden but I knew there would be many layers of shedding and letting go as we moved forward. Our home was only the first of one of those layers. There is no way to move forward without taking a step. Selling our home, we determined, was a necessary step for our future.

The India trip was coming up sooner than I'd have liked and there was so much going on. Between my yoga training and studies, sorting through all of Mami's belongings and organizing the entire house, the countless trips to Goodwill, trying to keep up with work and teaching dance, I then had to shop and pack for this trip. I decided finding an apartment for myself was going to have to wait until I returned from overseas. I was confident that I'd find my own place in time before we had to vacate our home.

Papi was on a mission and had soon found a pied-a-terre for himself within walking distance to our home. It was so different, the vibe of the new apartment compared to the vibe of The Sanctuary. Both were beautiful in their own way. It's just that the new place felt so foreign. His apartment needed renovations, which would take a substantial amount of time so we planned for him to temporarily move in with me into whichever apartment I had yet to find for myself. It was so much, so fast. We were both aware we'd have to gain our bearings as we navigated through this odd journey together. And I couldn't have asked for a better dad to fumble through it all.

CHAPTER 25

Messages From Heaven

"When you believe, signs turn up everywhere."
~*Lyn Rogan*

The first Christmas without Mami was soon approaching. There was a slight chill in the Florida air, a hint of the upcoming season. Christmas had always been Mami's favorite holiday and it is mine too.

I remember every year she'd deck our home with garlands and wreaths and her beloved pinecones. Together we'd decorate a Christmas tree with jewel-toned ornaments, many of which had been in our family for decades. Mami had always been into real Christmas trees; that familiar scent of pine, to me, is addictive. But the year I'd turned nine, our vibrant tree had gone from glorious to limp well before Christmas Eve. I'd never seen anything look so forlorn—at least in my nine years of life. It had veritably bent forward, the top of it hanging low as if it were moping in our living room, burdened by the weight of the ornaments. It was so sad looking, it was kind of funny. It became the family Christmas joke. From that point forward, Mami stuck with artificial trees for the holidays. And while we'd lost that divine scent of fresh pine, Mami didn't sacrifice the festive feast for the eyes she'd create in deep hues of reds and greens and everything in between.

Mami was big into recycling and saving things. The longest lasting decoration we'd kept in our home never ceased to amaze me. It was tinsel from old-world Germany that, back in the days, was originally made from gunmetal. Every year, for decades, Mami would take it out of the packaging she'd made to hold and protect it (empty paper towel rolls slit down the side) and painstakingly iron every piece of tinsel before hanging it on the tree branches. After so many decades of use and reuse, it had become very delicate. The slightest tug on it would rip it apart so she would go through them one by one by one with a colossal amount of patience I didn't know was possible for a human being.

It would take weeks to decorate the house in full and, by the time we were done (Mami being the most involved in the process), every nook and cranny had something Christmas-y about it. A hand-stitched tablecloth on an end table, a wreath with bows on the door, garlands with bows wrapped around the stair banister, an angel statuette in a corner, a nativity scene with baby Jesus, Mary and Joseph surrounded by The Three Kings inside a papier-mâché barn filled with real hay, a homemade advent wreath with four candles on the coffee table. Our home was so replete with decorations that by the time the new year would come and we'd taken the decorations down it felt like we'd been robbed, the house would feel so bare. Inevitably those wide-open spaces would take some getting used to during the first couple of weeks of the New Year.

There had always been a sense of magic and hope around this time of year. Our lives had been so full in the immediate aftermath of Mami's death that we hadn't even given thought to decorating the house. Either way we couldn't have done it, even if we'd wanted to. The house had been staged to sell it. It would've been too much work on top of everything else to dig up the Christmas decorations and deck the halls. So that Christmas spirit, when I felt I needed it most, was gone.

The year before Mami's death in 2011, Lucas and I had gone up to St. Augustine during the holidays and I'd instantly fallen in love with the cobblestone streets and charming shops of the old city. Giant centuries-old trees with Spanish moss hanging from their branches stood on every corner. Every year the historic part of town hosts the Nights of Lights, a festival of twinkling lights that could charm even Scrooge into the Christmas spirit.

In the main park, large oak trees are strung with bands of light that spread out from near the top of the trunk to the outermost branches so that when you look up into them they appear as if they'd been dipped into spun sugar. Bushes and grand palm trees alike are also luminous with lights. Emerging from this incandescent sea of lights stands a large and colorfully decorated Christmas tree. Nearby storefronts and restaurants are just as dazzling adorned with icicle lights and lit-up garlands. It's like walking among thousands upon thousands of stars.

Quaint bed and breakfasts are decorated with wreaths and garlands and yet more festive lights. Inside their windows you can catch a glimpse of cozy fireplaces emitting a warm golden glow inviting you inside. It's right out of a picture book.

There are Christmas trolleys playing holiday jingles through loudspeakers and strangers wishing each other a Merry Christmas. When I first experienced St. Augustine in the jolly season, I'd felt like I'd slipped into another world in another time.

Lucas suggested we go again that year and it couldn't have come at a more perfect time. I was grateful that, even though we were falling apart in our relationship, he was still there for me and understood my desire for the holiday spirit to be sparked within me once again.

One week later we made the six-hour drive up to northern Florida. The afternoon following our arrival was a chilly one. Finally I got to wear my leather jacket! That is a novelty back in South Florida. In other words, the moment the temperature drops into the 60's, women across Miami are rocking their boots with the fur.

While we were strolling through the cobblestone streets of the old city (sans fur-lined boots), we passed a narrow alleyway where tiny stores were hidden. It didn't seem like much was going on down that path but, before I could think about it, I was walking in that direction. Or, rather, I was being moved inexplicably through the alley, lead by my gut feeling.

First we passed a quiet storefront with a needle-thin white Christmas tree adorned with candy apple red ornaments. Lucas stopped momentarily to peer inside the window and my intuition said to keep walking. The alley wasn't very long and we reached its end shortly where there was an art store. A painting in its window caught my eye. I stopped directly in front of it and stood there taking it in. It was landscape art on canvas and there was something about this landscape in particular that had drawn me to it.

It was a vision of rolling hills blanketed in pale autumn colors and in the forefront was a cottage that looked warm and inviting. The light in the painting was radiant and otherworldly. I had the distinct feeling that this was what Heaven is like for Mami. Just then it became apparent to me that there was music playing from a store somewhere distant. Its melody had me swaying.

Then it hit me what the song was. "On My Way Home" by Enya. I couldn't believe my ears. This was one of the songs Papi had added, upon my suggestion, to Mami's Celebration of Life DVD. Every time I'd listened to that song before, I'd envisioned how Mami went home when she died, how she went home to our Father.

Goosebumps rushed across my arms. Then followed a gust of wind. I turned in the direction from where the wind had blown and noticed a shop I hadn't seen before, tucked away kitty-corner from the art store. Its glass doors were wide open and welcoming. I couldn't make out yet what was inside but I already liked the soothing colorscape in the windows.

I stood for a few extra moments to listen to the end of the Enya song and, with a smile, walked in with Lucas. My eyes grew wide when I stepped across the threshold at the entrance. There were dragonflies everywhere. Coffee mugs with dragonflies painted on them, dragonfly napkin rings, dragonfly artwork, dragonfly sculptures and dragonfly stationery to name but a few. I looked back at Lucas who had a grin on his face and I don't think I could lift my bottom jaw, it hung so low in awe of the spectacle.

The glass doors in the back of the store were open, too, so there was tons of fresh crisp air to breathe in. It smelled of new beginnings.

On a display table in the entrance, next to several candles with dragonfly ornaments, was a notecard titled "The Meaning of the Dragonfly". Intrigued, I picked it up to read it.

"The dragonfly has a beautiful, jewel-like coloring. The bright colors take time to develop, reflecting the idea that, with maturity, our own true colors come forth. It symbolizes new life and joy, positive force and the power of life in general. Dragonflies can also be a symbol of the sense of self that comes with maturity. As a creature of the wind, the dragonfly frequently represents change. Dragonflies remind us that we are light and can reflect the light in powerful ways if we choose to do so. Life is never quite the way it appears, but is always filled with light and color."

I smiled and put down the card, continuing to explore the shop as if in a reverie. Next to the table was a postcard carousel filled with cards with quotes imprinted upon them.

"First my Mother. Forever my Friend."
"A Mother's heart is always with her children."
"Mothers hold their children's hands for a short while, but their hearts forever."

I instantly grew emotional. My heart was replete with my love for Mami. I could feel her love for me, too, pouring down from Heaven.

While meandering around other trinkets and treasures, another gust of wind blew in through the backdoors all the way through the front of the store, knocking a card off a nearby table onto the floor at my feet.

Lucas picked it up and, without looking at it, handed it to me, as if he knew it was a message for me. I looked at him and then at the card. It was a 2x3" card, plain white, entitled "Angels" with a small drawing of a female angel with a white robe and wings and blonde hair, like Mami had. It read:

"Angels around us, angels beside us,
angels within us.
Angels are watching over you when times are good or stressed.
Their wings wrap gently around you,
Whispering you are loved and blessed."

Tears of joy welled in my eyes. It was far beyond my comprehension how this was possible. I hadn't anticipated or expected to receive any messages from Mami. I'd simply followed my intuition.

"Thank you, Mami, I love you so much," I whispered to the wind.

CHAPTER 26

Journey To India

"The best way to find yourself is to lose yourself in the service of others."

~*Mahatma Gandhi*

Christmas came and went. Marita had invited us for dinner on Christmas Eve at her home in Naples, recreating a couple of Mami's favorite treats like traditional German Rotkohl (red cabbage simmered in red wine and sweet and tangy seasonings) and Spekulatius cookies (thin, crisp cookies made with nine mouthwatering spices) using a decades-old recipe unique to our family. We tried to get in the spirit but it was the gap at the table where Mami would've normally sat that changed everything. Christmas would never be the same.

By the time New Year's Eve was upon us, life was still in upheaval back home. I thought about how drastically life had changed from one year to the next. I remembered how Mami had always loved the entire holiday season and dressing up for the fun and festivities. I had zero desire to do anything.

Papi was getting ready to go out with some of his and Mami's mutual friends. Lucas, feeling bad that I would be home alone, had offered to take me out but I only wanted to stay in. I told him he was welcome to come over if he didn't mind doing nothing on the celebratory night. He agreed and, once he was there, convinced me to go to a local restaurant within walking distance to grab a bite to eat. Walking through groups of people buzzing happily around the outdoor restaurant, I didn't dare make eye contact with anyone. I didn't want to celebrate the New Year at all. There was nothing to celebrate. I knew this was not the case but that's how I felt. I couldn't fake it. So I averted my eyes from everyone. Lucas and I found a corner on our own and went through the motions of ordering martinis and meals. Everything was tasteless to me. There was no life in any of it. I knew it was me.

As soon as we'd finished eating, I encouraged him for us to head back. I sighed gratefully when back home on the couch and putting on a movie so I wouldn't have to think about my life the way it was.

Before I knew it, it was a brand new year. But it didn't feel like it. It didn't have that same sense of magic it held last year and every year before that. Papi emerged outside onto the pool deck where Lucas and I sat with Arco the following morning. He had a bottle of champagne and three glasses with him. How sweet. I smiled and blinked my eyes as the sun began to filter through the day. It was the love in our family that made everything alright. Things were definitely different. But there was still so much love there. We toasted to Mami and to life and sat there together, allowing the morning silence to fill us.

Those first couple of days flew by and, before I knew it, I was boarding a plane to New York, my first of two layovers to get to New Delhi. It was going to be a long journey. I was excited and overwrought at the same time. Flying on my own the whole way didn't bother me. It was that I'd be arriving in New Delhi and have to make the trek from the airport to my hotel alone. During the weeks leading up to the trip, news reports had leaked of several rapes around New Delhi in broad daylight and it was declared that women were unsafe there. I was slightly terrified to be on my own in a country whose culture and customs I did not yet understand.

For good measure, I pre-arranged a shuttle from the hotel to pick me up from the airport. Christina would already be at the hotel by the time I arrived. She too had pre-booked a shuttle; it was our safest option. I'd prayed for her safe arrival and for the protection of our entire group, all women, as I embarked on the first leg of the journey.

I flew from Miami to New York, from New York to Munich, and from Munich to New Delhi. In Munich I had a thirteen-hour layover. It was the longest layover I'd ever planned but it was one of the best ways to get there on time to meet the group and within my flight budget. I immediately found a bathroom, then a deli counter to pick up some takeout food and find a place to sit down and unload my carry-on baggage. The Munich airport offered napcabs, sleeping cabins and a large roomy area with rows of lounge chairs.

146

They really make it rather comfortable there. Among the lounge chairs were a few select mini couches with a big cushion surrounded by three padded walls to create a personal nook of privacy in which to read or curl up and rest. There weren't many and they were all full but one…I managed to find one open and was elated at my luck. (Ahem, what we call luck is really God's blessings on us). This little couch with three walls would now be my home for the next thirteen hours.

On the couch adjacent to mine sat a young Indian girl with kind eyes and a pretty smile. She must've been in her twenties. We smiled at each other and struck up a conversation. Her name was Prisha. She was traveling back home to New Delhi where she lived with her family. We happened to be booked on the same flight. There was an instant sense of trust between us and we agreed to watch each other's bags if either of us needed to go to the bathroom, get something to eat or walk around the airport and stretch our legs. We were both thrilled to have found each other. I felt safe, like I had guardian angels watching over me on this trip.

Shortly thereafter I dozed off while reading a book and later awoke to the same radiating glow of the fluorescent lights overhead in the terminal. I didn't know what time of day it was. My body was still on Eastern Standard Time and I had to think for a moment to remember that I was in Munich, six hours ahead. There was still another three and a half hours time difference between Munich and New Delhi and—I checked my phone—nine hours before our flight to New Delhi departed. Both the time difference and not knowing what time it was when I awoke on a couch in the middle of an airport, felt entirely disconcerting. But I looked over to see Prisha napping on her couch and I felt relieved. When she awoke sometime thereafter we made plans to take turns finding something to eat. It felt so liberating walking around the airport without my bulky backpack laden with books and toiletries, heavy sweater and shawl.

The rest of those nine hours were spent eating, reading, sleeping, then eating, reading and sleeping some more. I was bleary-eyed by the time they called our flight and Prisha and I began to collect our things. Before boarding we asked to be seated together and were grateful to be easily accommodated. Both of us had to move much further back from our original seats in the plane but at least we got to sit together. We talked for hours. She was in love with a boy her family didn't approve of. She talked about arranged marriage in her culture and I asked her questions about her life. She asked me what brought me to India and I shared with her about Mami and yoga. She taught me some Hindu words and offered that if I had extra time in New Delhi, she would take me shopping or wherever I would like to go. Even though I wouldn't have the time to take her up on it, I was touched by her immense kindness to someone who was, up until only several hours ago, a complete stranger. I quickly learned that this kindness of spirit is a staple of Indian culture. There would be many smiles and gentle faces greeting me along this journey in this part of the world.

Prisha and I exchanged contact info before she pointed me in the right direction for shuttle pickup where my driver was waiting. He took me right out to the car; there were no other pickups at the time so we headed to the hotel. Leaving the airport perimeters I noticed surrounding lookout points where guards stood pointing their rifles at exiting cars as they eyed them for suspicious activity. When spying one of those rifles pointed right in our direction, I fidgeted in the backseat, growing uncomfortable at the sight. Once we passed the lookout points, I let out a sigh of relief.

And then came the real excitement. The drive to the hotel. This was not for the lily-livered. The roads came at you from all sides, some without traffic lights, and travelers were not just allocated to cars. There were pedestrians, donkeys, elephants and tuk tuks all together, weaving in and out of one another on the dusty streets. Along the sidewalks were locals warming up by manmade fires in large metal drums, the thick smell of smoke wafting and penetrating the car windows. It would be a smell I'd grow accustomed to and eventually find comfort in. I'd soon discover this was the most popular heating system in India. Fires along the sidewalk meant people could gather together and share in the warmth.

A driver in a tuk tuk honked as he zoomed by on our left and to our right, merely inches from our car, passed an elephant, massive and majestic. I was mesmerized. I also realized I was white knuckle gripping the inside car door handle as my driver expertly zipped right then left then a sharp right again, evading obstacles with the greatest of ease.

It must've been about 3 PM India Standard Time when we arrived. The entrance of our hotel was quite literally a fortress. The giant twenty-something foot walls looked impenetrable and before we could come to a complete halt at the locked down entrance, several guards had approached us banging on the doors of our car, requesting that we open everything, including the hood of the car as they checked for bombs. We passed the first point of entry. Then there was getting into the lobby, where I had to go through another security check with a luggage and body scan.

Eventually, puffy eyed and bleary, I made it to the hotel room Christina had booked for us. I'd never been happier to see her there. We'd both made it! We were both equally exhausted so we napped for the rest of the afternoon before grabbing dinner downstairs in the hotel restaurant. We were to meet the rest of our group in the lobby at 11 PM to depart for our final destination, Rishikesh. Rishikesh, we were told, would be an eight to twelve-hour ride through the mountains, depending on fog. Well, that was comforting. At this point it didn't matter; we were zombies.

An hour before midnight our group convened, half asleep, in the hotel lobby and split into two vans that took us for a ride through the city and deep into rural northern India. In the wee morning hours, we stopped in a small village where an elderly woman came out and invited us to walk through her tiny abode made of stone, hay and cardboard boxes. She introduced us to her son and their prized calf. It was frigid and it was late. Despite our odd visiting hours, they greeted us with warm smiles before giving us their blessings as we took off on the road again.

Somewhere along the bumpy ride, between changing lanes in the city filled with back-to-back auto rickshaws, freight trucks and cars and then the potholes and donkeys on the rural roads, I fell asleep with my head flopped to one side and bobbing up and down with the van. You might've thought I was head nodding with the Punjabi music our driver had been playing all through the night.

I next awoke in the first moments of daylight as the van slowed to a halt on the banks across the Ganges River from Rishikesh, the birthplace of yoga. People have been traversing the globe for centuries to come here on spiritual quests and transformational journeys. We were being dropped off here to cross the river on the Laxman Jhula, a pedestrian-only suspension bridge that gives access to the town. Everyone in our group was tired and disoriented but the excitement of what lay on the other side of Mother Ganga was too great.

The roads were dusty. There were rhesus monkeys congregating and analyzing our every move with discerning eyes. And the sun was beginning to peak from beyond the horizon, casting a soft pink glow of the day to come. We all had heavy luggage, having also carried the additional items we'd brought for the school kids. And we were told it would be symbolic, the crossing of that bridge as we left behind our past, carrying all our luggage and our troubles alongside us…knowing we would be traveling lighter, without all our baggage, once we crossed that bridge back at the end of our time in Rishikesh.

The air was crisp here at the foothills of the Himalayas, I instantly felt clarity in my breath when I first stepped out of the van. I watched my breath rise up like a billowing cloud, as if reminding me of the life I still had left in me. It was chilly. But the thrill of the commencement of our journey plus the weight of the luggage we carried kept us warm. Once we got to the entrance of the bridge, we all stood there in a moment of silence. I think it finally hit us the magnitude of this moment. For each of us I imagine it meant something significant and meaningful. For me it meant crossing over from the grief of losing Mami. Little did I know at the time, this was only the beginning of an emotionally tumultuous path. But we were still connected by our very own bridge, Mami and me. No matter how much my heart hurt, it would always hold Mami's love for me and my love for her.

The heart, I thought to myself, is an incredibly resilient organ, pumping our blood—our life—through our veins and arteries enabling us to live and breathe life. The heart can be shattered from heartbreak and loss. It can shrivel and grow hardened from the pain of life and loss that we experience. And somehow it can love again and again and again.

I stood there at the edge of the bridge. The only early morning sounds were the rush of the gurgling river and the beat of my heart, which I could feel beneath my winter coat and multiple layers of clothing. The group started to cross the bridge and I hung behind to have a few moments for myself and take it all in.

Mother Ganga was powerful here, a continuous rush of water moving rapidly seventy feet below. When I set my foot on the bridge, I could feel her power, a rush of energy up my leg and then my other as I took the next step. My lungs expanded taking in the mountain air as I looked out over the horizon partially cloaked in a low haze rising from the surrounding foothills. The raw morning sun filtered through the haze. I was in a completely different world. Thousands of miles away. I had arrived.

Once we'd crossed the bridge Terri and our retreat organizer, Heather, greeted us with big hugs, a necklace of multicolored marigolds and a wool blanket wrapped around our shoulders. It was a warm welcome indeed. They guided us into our hotel, which was steps away from the bridge, where we were given fresh cups of piping hot chai tea. It is so much richer and fuller than the chai tea I've tried in America. The bold flavor and warmth was like an elixir for my soul.

We unloaded our bags, changed for breakfast and then made our way out into the town to explore. Shop after shop of colorful silks, saris, jewelry, and handbags beckoned alongside "daily needs" stores selling toiletries and cigarettes. There was the stir of locals and tourists alike. But it was the cows that ruled the streets. They are revered in India as a symbol of divine bounty of the earth. So it was not unusual for cows to come right up to us, as they were used to people's deference.

Every couple of hundred feet there was a small gathering around a fire and the commotion of kids running around and playing with each other. Some warmed up with tea or coffee by coffee stands. Every step brought something new and exciting to the eyes. It was within the vibrant buzz of India where I found my stillness.

We started each day with meditation and yoga and, in the afternoons, would explore Rishikesh and the adjacent banks of the Ganges River, rich in culture and history. One afternoon our group joined with another group from the Sattva Yoga Academy, a local school founded by world-renowned visionary and master, Anand Mehrotra, who guided us deep into the foothills of the Himalayas. To get to a path within the mountains only known by a handful of locals we had to climb giant boulders, at times holding hands and hoisting one another. It was a team effort and reminded me how Marita had been saying over the past few months when caring for Mami that "it takes a village".

Somewhere along the hike as we ascended to the highest point, a small river crossed our path, flowing and gurgling over rocks and stones. I grabbed onto low hanging tree branches and nearby boulders to help me gain my footing. Some of us, myself included, had taken off our shoes. The water was frigid as I stepped into the river's edge. Before I knew it I noticed one of my LOVE-JOY bracelets had snapped and flung out into the water. Everyday, since shortly after Mami died, I'd worn these bracelets to keep her close. Frantically I tried to collect the beads that were rolling off the rocks, trying to save it but the letters "J", "O" and "Y" had already been swept away by the river's current. It was a losing battle, trying to pick up the pieces.

I stood there and felt the familiar sense of loss rise up within me. I wanted to cry. I felt like the breaking of this bracelet was symbolic but all I could see was the loss. The bracelet was gone. The L-O-V-E and the J-O-Y were gone. Literally. I watched them disperse and float downstream.

The group witnessed what had happened and were aware of what it meant to me. Terri suggested that I hadn't lost the love and joy; rather, I was leaving some of it here in India. I was sharing a part of my mom's legacy here. That brought me comfort as I closed my eyes, standing in the cold river with bare feet, to honor the gift in that moment. When I reopened them, I was touched to see that several others had stopped to stand with me in the moment of silence. Seeing them stand there with me was the reminder I needed that I wasn't alone in this.

None of us are ever alone. We are all dealing with our own battles, our own stories and emotions. We have people who love us and care for us. There is also the kindness and generosity, as I'd seen, from complete strangers. And, above all, there's always the unending love and companionship of God.

After acknowledging the moment in silence, I left the site together with our group, never looking back. Mami's legacy of love and joy had reached the hills in Northern India.

Our hike had stretched long and night was soon approaching. We still had a ways to go. Several people reached for pocket flashlights to help see the rocky path in the rapidly fading light. I didn't have one with me so I stayed close to anyone who did. But I was always one who liked to be alone in nature. It is a way I commune with God and I soon noticed myself naturally trailing behind the group a bit. Even though night had fallen by then and I could barely make out the path, I had never felt more surefooted in my life. I felt my breath calm and deep, in an almost meditative state, as I took step after step across the rocky slopes. It was as if I'd absorbed the energy of the mountain and became a part of it.

The following day we visited the Khushi school kids. The Khushi Charitable Society founded this school for local underprivileged kids to provide them with education, vocational training, medical assistance and supplemental nutrition. Interestingly Khushi, I learned, is the Hindi word for "joy".

When we arrived, the kids there were just that—full of joy to see us. We were as excited to meet them. The school headmaster had a full day of activities planned for us, starting with helping the kids with art projects. Our group dispersed among the three hundred kids and spent time cutting construction paper, arranging stickers, drawing with markers and getting to know each other. There was something about the simplicity of drawing with children, seeing their imagination come to life that brought me serenity.

The kids later returned to their classes while the school headmaster recruited us for cooking duty in the outdoor kitchen. We met with the ladies responsible for cooking meals from scratch everyday for the entire school. These were strong women. I noticed their incredible posture, lifting and carrying gargantuan pots almost as wide as the full span of their arms and brimming with vegetables. It must be all that yoga. We sat on the ground chopping mountains of cabbage, cauliflower, daikon and red peppers. Then came the naan, a type of leavened bread traditional to Indian cuisine. The school cooks prepared the dough then passed it on for us to knead it. It was tough to manipulate it the way they'd initially demonstrated. Amused, the women smiled at as they watched us fight with the dough. I felt so proud when I finally got my first one into the right shape and thickness, then was given three more balls of dough followed by another three and so forth and so on, we went on kneading and rolling on the ground. My back was aching and my hands hurt. I couldn't believe these women do this by hand everyday, not only for the hundreds of school kids but again back home for their own families. I've eaten naan many times before but now I certainly have a new appreciation for it.

It was lunchtime that impressed me the most. They'd separated the kids first by grade then into smaller groups of about thirty. They lined up in two straight lines across from each other and filed in to sit down in the cafeteria, which was on the ground right next to the outdoor kitchen. Two kids would run down the center of the rows, one attending to each side serving food and water. As soon as the first group was done eating, they filed out, cleared the dishes, set another two rows of plates and cutlery as the next group would file in and sit down to eat. This continued with such precision and efficiency until everyone was fed. The entire time, those who served, whether cooking, cleaning or serving the food and water, were smiling with joy.

That's something I observed about Indian culture. It is an honor and a pleasure for them to serve. It struck me how people who have so little by American standards could give so much. Seva is the Sanskrit word for selfless service. In India it is believed that seva not only helps the community but it contributes to one's spiritual growth.

I felt fulfilled knowing that we had in some small way contributed to feeding these wonderful children. Our farewells were met with smiles, thank yous and big hugs. I felt tired and my body was aching but I was happy. Giving and serving, I learned there firsthand, are key elements of joy. I had spent an entire day not thinking about my broken heart and how much I missed my mom.

CROSSROADS

After our time in Rishikesh with the group, Christina and I embarked, the two of us with a guide, to traverse India's Golden Triangle—Delhi, Agra and Jaipur. We were thankful we had the foresight that there'd have been no way we'd travel this far to India and not see the Taj Mahal in all her majesty. The image of her shrouded silhouette in the fog of the first morning's light will forever be imprinted in my memories. But there was another city along the way where we opted to stay that particularly struck a chord in my heart. This…was Varanasi.

The streets were dirty and bustling, lined with busy shops decorated with strings of lights and large colorful signs. Men stood behind hand-built stands in front of these shops also selling anything from clothing and pashminas to jewelry and electronics. Some men sat stationary in a squat on the street selling marigolds and incense used for offerings to the holy Mother Ganga. Small natural wood sticks and twigs doused in neem, a natural oil touted for its benefits to teeth and gums, were spread out across old newspapers on the ground, also for sale. Heaps of trash and mounds of cow dung forced one to be mindful of their steps.

Scores of mopeds, tuk tuks, bicycles and cars continuously honked at one another, which to an untrained ear may have sounded chaotic but, after ten days of yoga, meditation and dharma (wisdom) talks, felt disturbingly peaceful to me.

Left and right lepers slouched on the street, either asleep or constantly shifting in visible pain. Stray dogs yapped and circled around cows that were also resting in the road. Beggars, mostly small children with big round brown eyes, unrelentingly pleaded for money. "Please help," they chimed together asking over and over again, sometimes following tourists for long distances. Around every corner people called out to us, trying to entice us to buy something. Outstretched arms and hands wanting help reached through the sea of people. I didn't know how to process all this; it was so much to take in all at once. It was heartbreaking to witness so much pain and suffering all around us. Despite the dilapidation of this ancient city, however, there was so much hope that lay within its borders.

We'd arrived in the early evening right after sunset, heading straight to the banks of the Ganges River, lined with ghats, flights of steps leading down to the water where devotees pray, worship and ritualistically bathe. Much of the traffic around us, pedestrian or otherwise, headed towards the main ghat, Dasaswamedh, where a nightly aarti (worship) ceremony is held.

The sound of bells accompanied by live music emanated into the smoky night air. Seven priests, dressed in red and gold, stood at the top of the riverside steps and, in complete synchrony, artfully waved large peacock feathers, swung pots of burning incense and camphor, blew into conch shells, and waved fans made of yak tails. Each of these gestures was executed in unison, turning to face each of the four cardinal directions. Every part of the ceremony was meaningful. The burning camphor symbolizes the destruction of the ego. Both the material and the spiritual world are honored in this daily tradition. It is a fundamental Hindu belief, I learned, that every human being has God within. I, too, believe this to be true.

That night I could feel the joy and celebration of life in the hearts of the hundreds of people that had come together on the banks of Mother Ganga. People clapped and hummed, swaying with the music. We were not just observers; we were participants. The haunting voice of a singer chanting devotional hymns echoed through his microphone into the night and, for the next hour, I was completely transported by the sounds, sights and smells of this historic ritual.

The following morning Christina and I returned to the ghats with our guide for a sunrise boat ride on the revered river. Even in the darkness before the dawn, the streets were full of life. On the riverbanks aartis were already well under way since 4 AM. Men, stripped down to their underwear, were bathing in the cold water and women were washing and wielding laundry. Scattered trash and thousands of rotting flowers from past offerings dotted the shoreline.

A thick layer of mist hung low barely above the water, veiling the ashrams (spiritual centers) on the riverbanks where spiritual seekers come to learn and grow. Amidst the motion of life was a sense of stillness as the magenta sun began to ascend into the sky. It is something we see everyday, the sun, but today as it broke through the veil of mist, its pink light shimmering across the ancient city and its devoted inhabitants, it was transcendent.

We glided across the still water in our small wooden boat. All other sounds faded in the distance so only the sound of the oars dipping in and out of the water as our guide rowed us downstream came into focus. In the sun's growing light I watched the kaleidoscope of colors on the shoreline before noticing the heavily rising plumes of smoke. The source of this, I knew, could not be incense. Our guide explained to us the Hindu belief that if a deceased's ashes are strewn into the Ganges here in sacred Varanasi, it is said they will receive moksha, the release from the continuous cycle of death and rebirth. I looked more closely. So those were bodies I smelled burning there.

We were going to get a closer look, we were told, after the boat ride. I was both nervous and curious—nervous that it would bring up anguish over Mami and curious about the local customs of death and cremation.

156

Later on our way on foot through the narrow cobblestone lanes leading towards Manikarnika Ghat, one of the main cremation locations, we heard chanting from a distance growing closer and closer. Our guide asked us to step aside just as I noticed several men march forward carrying a bamboo platform with a body covered in orange and gold cloth decorated with garlands of flowers. Christina and I both flattened ourselves against the wall and bowed our heads in respect of the funeral procession. Minutes later came more chanting and another body. Hundreds of bodies are burned here daily, our guide told us, and the pyres burn twenty-four hours a day, seven days a week. The smell of fire grew thicker in the air the closer we approached. It became apparent that we were walking along the passage of death.

Initially we felt trepidation when allowed to enter this consecrated ghat. We didn't want to be disrespectful in any way by viewing the cremation of those surrounded by their loved ones. Dogs roamed the property and sea gulls circled overhead. A man who worked there poked a long stick into a fire to move a body into position for most efficient incineration. Our guide respectfully nodded his head in the direction of the bonfire and divulged to us how men's bodies were burned down to the chest and ribs while women's bodies were burned down to the hip bones. These remaining body parts were then released into the river for eternal rest. So it's not uncommon to see dead bodies or parts of them floating downstream in the Ganges.

It surprised me to see that no one shed tears around their loved ones. It was a celebration and a blessing to be able to be cremated here and escape the endless cycle of rebirth in a world full of struggle.

Several fires were blazing at once, endless plumes of smoke rising into the sky. My eyes stung. The crackling and hissing of flesh and flame was overwhelming. I thought about the funeral director back home sliding Mami's dead body into the metal cremation chamber and fought back the tears.

Death was so out in the open here. From ashes to ashes and dust to dust, we breathed in the essence of so many lives that had come to an end. Gazing across a smoke-filled sky I felt like I was standing in the intersection between life and death.

The nature, culture and history of Northern India left an indelible mark in my soul. What may appear as chaos and cacophony had given me a feeling of peace. It reconnected me with myself and I felt grounded and grateful at the end of our time there. It was not a trip for the fainthearted yet already I longed to return to India for the way she made me see life so unapologetically raw.

When it was time to return home, I knew I'd have to face my own reality again. The reality that Mami is gone. The reality that Lucas and I had broken up. The reality that I was starting over again in my career. The reality that I would be moving out of the home I'd known and loved for years and have to find a new one. It was a lot all at once but India had been exactly the break I needed and God continued to carry me through day by day.

CHAPTER 27

Dragonflies In The Lobby

"I lift my eyes to the hills. From where does my help come?
My help comes from the Lord who made heaven and earth."
~Psalm 121: 1-2

When getting ready to buy something major or even if just for a printer, for instance, I do my research. So I scoured sites and skimmed local listings, honing down on where I wanted to live. I found an area I liked but when actually viewing apartments and seeing the limited options I had with a forty-eight pound dog in tow (many of the pet friendly buildings I'd found only allowed pets that were twenty pounds or less), I had to regroup.

Nicole, from my yoga teacher training, and I had decided we wanted to continue our training to become yoga therapists. Yoga had become such an important part of our lives that we wanted to share it with those who might not otherwise have found it possible. She and I both envisioned ourselves working with people who couldn't easily participate in group classes at a studio such as those undergoing cancer treatments or with limited capabilities because of injury.

Part of my apartment search criteria was being close to our yoga therapy mentor, Allaine Stricklen of Gentle Therapeutics Yoga, as we'd be training in her home over the next year. She lived in a gorgeous area, an island actually, that was connected to the Miami mainland via causeway. The neighborhood boasted mid-century American apartments filled with charm and vibrant personality and was surrounded by the turquoise blue intra-coastal waters. When scouting it out, it immediately resonated with me.

I found a new listing there that looked exciting so I called the realtor who'd advertised it. Jane was friendly and professional on the phone and I agreed to meet her at her office to discuss what I was looking for. When reviewing everything I wanted along with my budget, she noted the apartment I was interested in had just been put on the market and that, with that coveted neighborhood, it probably wouldn't be available long. I was just as ready to get going as she was so she took me to see the place. The neighborhood, I noticed, was safe, family-oriented and pet-friendly. Driving onto the island dotted with palm trees and surrounded by the ocean felt like I was going on vacation. The building was small and older but the apartment itself was big with more closet space than I knew what to do with. It had beautiful cherry wood floors with small crystal chandeliers in the kitchen and dining room, which overlooked the bay. The water outside was a dazzling mint green mixed with hues of turquoise and I couldn't take my eyes off of it! The bedroom overlooked the same view. The bathroom was big, too, designed in all white. The apartment had lots of sunlight pouring in. I fell in love with it. The price was right too. I thought it was perfect. I rejoiced in seeing the light at the end of this dark tunnel I'd been scrabbling through the previous eight months. Jane took me back to her office to discuss the lease terms. I expressed my interest and shared with her how much it meant to me to have this opportunity for a new home after losing my mom months earlier. She commiserated with me and said she was happy to help me with such a meaningful move.

I took home the paperwork to review everything, signed it and returned the next day with a deposit plus first and last month's rent as stipulated in the contract. Handing it over, I felt a sense of elation and accomplishment. Jane and I had discussed that the place needed a fresh coat of paint and, because I'd had an idea of the color I wanted, I'd offered to buy the paint and drop it off there for the contractors that the landlady planned to have come in prior to the move-in date, Friday, March 1st, 2013.

Going through the color swatches at Home Depot was a bit intimidating (how are there so many shades of white?) but then I found the perfect one, a natural light, soft yellowish shade that looked like the rays of the sun shining. I knew it'd look perfect with those dark wood floors and that spectacular bay view. I felt joyful when envisioning it. I bought enough gallons of paint for the whole apartment and coordinated with Jane for her to unlock the apartment so I can drop them off the following afternoon for the contractors.

Walking into the apartment for the second time, I'd left the paint cans in the living room and looked around again. I was floored by its spaciousness and bright light. Plenty of room for all the furniture Papi had offered to give me from our house plus plenty of room to practice yoga. I looked around one last time and walked out with a satisfied smile.

Then it was back to going through everything back at the house. This had been a long, ongoing and sometimes painful process. It blew me away how much stuff builds up in a house. You never realize it until you have to move. Moving is the ultimate spring cleaning. Moving, after the loss of a loved one, is the ultimate heart cleaning. At times my heart felt like it was breaking even more, if that were even possible, going through a multitude of memories that were so attached to Mami. Other times it felt liberating when I was able to let go of things and realizing I was going to be just fine.

We had two weeks left before the move into my place. I'd booked the moving company to pack up the furniture I'd take and Papi had already begun moving the furniture he'd planned to keep to a storage unit while the renovations at his place were under way. He was back and forth between keeping an eye on the work at his new place, his storage unit and the house. And I was home juggling my yoga studies, work and going through everything in the house with a fine-toothed comb. I didn't even have the time or the energy to cry, there were just too many other things that we had to take care of. At the end of the day, either Papi or I would whip up something simple for us for dinner and, one way or another, we made it through.

The day before our move-in to my new place I awoke with an intense gut feeling that something was not right. I couldn't put my finger on it but something told me I needed to go up to my apartment immediately. As busy as we were, I followed my gut and drove the forty-five minutes up there to the building and, to my surprise, walked right into the lobby, which was supposedly locked at all times for the safety of the residents. Hmm...intent on figuring out why I was being led up to the apartment, I began to question whether or not I should've called Jane first. I mean, duh, how was I going to get into the apartment? Other than the landlord who had been sick two weeks ago, Jane had told me, she was the only one with the key. I went up

161

anyway. When arriving at the front door, I noticed the lockbox on the door was gone. I placed my hand on the doorknob and suddenly felt sick to my stomach. I turned the knob and the door opened right up. I walked in to find a scene that until this day I still can't explain.

The paint cans were still lying on the floor where I'd left them two weeks ago. My eyes were drawn to the walls, however, which had, no exaggeration, close to one hundred nails driven into them randomly up and down and all across from end to end. There were nails hammered into the walls everywhere, from the entrance all the way through the living and dining rooms. What the hell happened? Who had done this? And why would they have done this? I suddenly became aware that I might not be alone in the apartment and straightened my posture, standing taller. As if that would help anything. I grabbed a can of paint, figuring I could swing it and knock someone out before checking out the rest of the apartment. Okay, nothing else had changed including the minor tile repairs that were supposed to have been made in the bathroom. But those walls! Even more baffling was the jar of half-eaten peanuts I found on the floor in the living room. I didn't know whether to scream in anger or to cry. There was no way the move into this apartment was happening the following day. In fact, given this bizarre turn of circumstances, I wanted nothing to do with this place ever again.

I called Jane, trying my hardest to compose myself. I recounted to her what had happened and demanded to talk to the landlady myself. The landlady, she explained, was now traveling in Paris.

"Oh, yeah?" I thought, "With my deposit money, I'm sure!"

I asked her why none of the work she'd promised in the contract was done. She had no answers for me and began to push it back on me that I should've been on top of this. Well obviously I should've been but then what was the point of me going through her to help me as a realtor? I told her there was no way now I'd be able to move in. Even if I still wanted to, the place had been vandalized and was in no state to be lived in. I requested my money back. She fired back that there was no way I'd get my full deposit back, saying that I'd taken her apartment off the market for two weeks, essentially making her lose money.

"You shrew, I just lost my mom!" I wanted to yell at her.

She knew this already too. She'd known everything I was going through since we talked together in the car ride we'd taken to first see the place. I wondered how someone could be so heartless. I wanted to scream at her. I wanted to choke her. I wanted to fight to get the money back that was rightfully mine. I just didn't have it in me. It was too much. I had to immediately figure out what Papi, Arco and I would do because, as of the next day, we would have nowhere to live. The moving truck was scheduled and the new residents would be moving into The Sanctuary right after. I knew that, even if I had the energy to fight back, it would be a losing battle. Jane, who'd seemed so friendly and nice, had turned into a rabid dog that sank her teeth into me when it came down to money.

With nothing else left in me I told her, "You know, Jane, take the two weeks out of the deposit for yourself and give me back the rest."

If that's what it took to never have to deal with her again, so be it. She agreed. I could almost hear her on the end of the line grinning like the Grinch.

I wanted to slam the phone down when ending the call to demonstrate my infuriation with her but that's an unfortunate impossibility with cell phones. I pounded the "End" button repeatedly on my phone's screen with emphasis as if that would've made a difference.

I called Papi right after to let him know our sudden change of plans. I think he was just as shocked as I was. But we had to keep moving. We had to be out of the house. The clock kept ticking. Thankfully he had a solution in mind; a nearby Marriott Residence Inn that allowed dogs so he booked us a room and then he called the storage company where his unit was and requested another larger space. We would still keep the moving truck as planned for the next morning but have them move everything to storage. We carried whatever boxes, toiletries and clothing we'd need over the next few weeks to the hotel, which took several trips. By the end of the day, I felt exhausted and defeated. I don't remember falling asleep and the next morning when I awoke the moving truck was on its way and it was time to go. So that's what we did. We just kept going. We kept moving. One foot in front of the other.

After five months caring for Mami at home, thirteen days in the hospital with her, the cremation, the spreading of her ashes, the holidays without her, the countless trips to Goodwill, my trip to India, my search for a new apartment, my yoga studies and transitioning career, teaching dance, my breakup with Lucas, I really have no idea how I made it through that time. Somehow you just make it through things.

God surely gives us some superhuman strength because looking back at it all, it seemed close to impossible, physically, mentally and emotionally, to do what I did. God must've given me the spiritual energy to make it through. It also definitely helped to have the family we do. Papi, Marita and I stayed strong, loving and supportive of each other. This made a huge difference. We cannot rely solely on ourselves to walk through the darkness. God, first and foremost, carries us through our toughest times. Then the people we choose to surround ourselves with help carry us through. This is when you realize you've got miracles happening for you every single day. This is when you begin to see the light.

Even though I was stuffed into a chair only inches between a small dinette table and the wall inside a hotel room crammed with stacked boxes and plastic bags full of our stuff, I found reprieve in simply sitting down. It was Friday night and Papi, Arco and I were settling into our hotel room. Arco was pacing back and forth nervously in the narrow spaces left between our things. I couldn't even begin to imagine how he'd been feeling through all of this. He'd just lost his mommy and was forced to leave the only home he'd ever known and now the three of us were cramped into a hotel room full of our messy boxes and heaps of clothes and a variety of new scents he'd never smelled before. I beckoned him to my side at the table and, after skirting around a couple of boxes, he tentatively sat down next to me. His face and ears softened when I stroked my hand over his head.

I looked at him and thought, "Yeah, sometimes I wish someone would just pet me often too."

That night I cried in my side room within our tiny suite, got down on my knees by the bedside and began to pray to Mami.

"Mami, I don't want to get into the habit of praying to you and asking you for things but we really need your help. I need to find a home for Arco and me. I'm going to find a new realtor first thing tomorrow morning and look again at places. Please, just give me a sign when I've found the right place. I no longer trust my own ability after what happened with the previous apartment I thought was so perfect. Please, Mami, just give me a sign," I beseeched.

I almost fell asleep on my knees, with tears streaming down my cheeks. I shook awoke and barely climbed up into the bed, falling into a dreamless sleep.

The next morning, with renewed gumption, I found a new realtor, Gloria, and asked Papi to come with me for support. I hated leaving Arco alone in the hotel room but we had to take care of this. We looked at several apartments, some of which were lovely but still left me feeling uncertain. Finally, Gloria mentioned that she did have one apartment in mind but that it was a little over budget. I didn't like the sound of that but Papi suggested we give it a try. I thought, ok, let's be open. The place was on the same island where the previous apartment had been, a few blocks northwest of it.

When we pulled around the block and the building came into view, I said to Papi, "Wow, that looks really nice."

He nodded in agreement as we passed through a gated entryway with blooming hibiscus plants. When I first stepped through the front door of the building, I felt a sense of lightness, openness and airiness. I couldn't quite explain it but it felt good. That was a good indicator I was on the right path. The apartment had a lovely street view of the island with sliding glass doors leading onto a patio. The living room and bedroom were big and the open floor plan had a spacious kitchen, which was separated from the living room by a long bar. It even had an extra office space, which I could convert into my yoga room.

I couldn't believe it but this was far better than the previous apartment. And it wasn't much over budget; it was doable. Then Gloria took us outside to the terrace overlooking the pool with tiki huts and a dock on the bay. I kept getting drawn to that mint green and turquoise water. This was beyond beautiful. I must've danced on our way back into the lobby, or at least in my mind I did, before I stopped at the front desk to say hello and introduce myself to the front desk assistant. She was young with short blonde hair and big blue eyes. She smiled and welcomed me. I reached out my hand and introduced myself.

She responded, "Nice to meet you, my name's Christa."

Goosebumps rushed across my arms like wildfire. That was Mami's name. Papi had caught up to me and was standing by my side listening to the conversation.

He gently nudged me and whispered, "That's a sign."

He hadn't known I'd prayed to Mami the night before in our hotel suite. This was the one. I knew it. I smiled and thanked Mami in my mind for having answered my prayers—with God's help, of course.

Then came the paperwork. The landlord turned out to be a company that buys apartments that had gone into foreclosure and then rents them out. This posed some challenges, the biggest one being getting approved as a renter. I'd rented places before but the fact that I'd most recently been living back home with my parents, quit my job and was in the middle of a career change with no big guaranteed and immediate income, did not incentivize the company to take me on as a renter. This delayed the process of our move but I was determined to make this my home and did everything I could to show them I'd be a responsible tenant, showing my bank statements and good credit history.

In the meantime, Papi and I were still living in the overloaded hotel suite with Arco. We shared one bathroom, waiting and taking turns with each other. It was almost funny coming home to this. Almost. Well, yeah, it was kind of funny at times. Sometimes. It was also uncomfortable and inconvenient. We were both dealing with some heavy emotions in our own ways and in very close living quarters with each other. But Papi and I learned to take it in stride and make do. In many ways, it brought us closer together. Literally, the dining table was one tiny square propped against the wall, enough to seat two people with their knees touching. But in all seriousness, it did improve our relationship. Papi and I had clashed at times before. It's because we're so much alike in many ways.

Now living in such small quarters in close proximity with each other while grieving the loss of our Mami, I could feel Papi's heart softening. I felt mine too. Even though our lives had unexpectedly been ripped apart, we were healing. Together.

We ended up living in that hotel for one week and, once Papi's apartment was move-in ready, we both packed up our stuff again and moved everything into his place. It would end up taking the landlord company in my building six weeks to approve me so I continued living out of bags and a suitcase in Papi's guestroom.

While we continued living together, this time we each had our own full bedroom and bathroom and some more space in which to walk around. Arco was so nervous in yet another new space that he often slid across the floors, his legs giving out from underneath him. He'd plop to the ground on his belly but got right back up, wagging his tail. He must've been so confused about everything. Still he remained such a good boy, ever loving, ever patient, ever sweet. He slept with me in the guestroom each night.

His presence and Papi's presence in my life at that time was a gift. It was kind of like a buffer before I'd be back on my own, with Arco in tow, facing my grief and creating my new life. Papi had boxes lined up the walls throughout the apartment for weeks. He'd unpacked the basics and retrieved the sofas and coffee tables from the storage unit. But the boxes sat there. I didn't know how he does it. I would've been unpacked with everything in its place within the first twenty-four hours. You can say I'm a little OCD. How did he remain so relaxed about all the unpacked boxes? Some of them, granted, were to be unpacked in the guest room, in which I was living so he had to leave them out there for the time being. I would've put them somewhere out of sight, regardless. But that was my incessant need to have things be a certain way.

We went on living nestled in piles of boxes like this until the big day arrived. It was finally time to move into my new apartment! The move was blessedly uneventful. Papi had generously given me his and Mami's furniture, as he intended to make a fresh start with everything. I was so grateful to not have to go furniture shopping, not to mention how nice the pieces were that Papi was donating to me. He even gave me a set of four bar stools that fit perfectly with the open bar in the kitchen. It was fun arranging everything in my new home to the way I'd best like it. Last but not least I went back for Arco who must've really been scratching his head in bewilderment by then with yet another move.

That first night alone with Arco in the new apartment was a strange feeling. It wasn't good or bad. It was just…different. I was so tired that I showed Arco to his bed next to my dresser, kissed him goodnight, and crawled into my bed, letting out a gratifying sigh. It sure felt good to be lying down. Arco, too, seemed wiped out. He and I were both asleep within minutes.

I was thrilled to be living in a new home of my own. Arco was excited, too, but not the same way I was. He was anxious. Every time I left the place to run an errand or go back to work, he'd cry and howl. How could I be mad at him for it? He was scared. Scared that his original Mami never came home when he'd waited by her bedside for almost two weeks. Now what if I didn't come back home to him? He'd been moved around several times, now settling into another new place he'd never been before, not sure if we were staying or moving again. Not sure if I'd come back home to him.

But I had to go to work. I had to go to my yoga therapy training classes. I had to run errands. So Arco and I were both going to have to get comfortable in our new routine. This was so novel for us both. I called a school for dog trainers thinking I should hire a canine counselor to help us work together in making Arco feel comfortable. I was also afraid with all his barking and crying every time I'd leave, we'd get kicked out of the apartment. That's all we needed—another move! Whenever I'd leave, I'd wait in the hallways to see how long he'd cry and he'd go on and on howling through the walls. It pained me to hear him like this. Since Arco was eight years old, the counselor advised not to spend the money on retraining an older dog. He did give me some helpful advice, though, which I immediately employed.

Every time I'd leave, I'd hide a cookie in my purse, lock up and quietly wait outside until I heard a lull between his barking and crying. Sometimes that would take awhile. I could see the shadow of his legs skittishly pacing back and forth from beneath the crack of the front door. When there finally came a moment of quiet from behind the door, I'd come back in and give him the cookie, reassuring him what a good boy he was. I bought him a Thundershirt, which is supposed to act like a swaddler does for babies to help calm frightened dogs. He was supposed to wear it whenever I left the house but I couldn't have him associate putting it on with me leaving the house or it would only increase his anxiety. So when I was home with him, I'd bring it out and place a cookie on it, making a big deal about how special it was that he got to wear his Thundershirt. He'd scarf down the cookie (I'm not sure he ever really chewed them) and I'd swaddle him with the gentle compression shirt and stay home and play with him or sit by his side until he began to think of it as a good thing. Then I'd put it on him at least one hour before I'd have to leave our home so when it was time to go, I noticed how much calmer he'd become.

It took about two months before I could leave the house without a single bark or whimper from Arco. We had started to get into our rhythm, even though my life itself was still lacking structure. I had my training. I taught classes at various times and various locations during the week and I also picked up some temp jobs, so my hours were constantly changing. Then I had to make time to walk Arco three times everyday. I was undeniably blessed that Mami had raised him on no particular set schedule. She'd usually let him out whenever she was ready to get up and do so. So I did not end up with a dog that would stare at me like clockwork every morning at 7 AM or every afternoon at 1 PM. In fact, many mornings I'd wake up for work and he'd shoot me the stank eye—but in the cutest way that only a dog can do—as if asking me why I'd wake him up so early to go out. He liked to sleep in. He always patiently waited for when I was available to take him out. He never once peed in the apartment. I wouldn't have been mad at him if he did. This was just his way. Always accepting, accommodating and agreeable.

Whenever I was home, he'd follow me around the apartment so closely that if I stopped in my tracks he'd walk right into the back of my legs. Wherever I'd sit, he'd come lay by my side. Sometimes he'd just sit in the living room staring at me for what seemed like hours when I was working on my computer, watching TV or reading a book. It wasn't that look that he needed to go out. It was more a sort of knowing look. Like he knew the pain I was feeling while getting acclimated to this new life. He could, of course, very well relate to it. But it didn't faze him. Every day we'd start anew, his tail wagging and ready to play, as if this had been his life all along. I was definitely not that strong. Looking back, I realized Mami knew exactly what she was doing by insisting I eventually become Arco's caretaker after she died, not Papi. She'd specifically instructed Papi to take care of him the first three months (in which we were all still living together anyway), so by the time I moved into my place Arco had become my responsibility. He also became my saving grace.

Many times after trying to hold it together through work and training, I'd come home and break down into tears and there he'd be, saddling up to me as I cried on his furry shoulder and held him close. He knew my every tear. He knew my every breakdown. And, without fail, he was always there by my side.

It had been almost six months since Mami passed away and we were beginning to find our groove. To make it more of a home, I went to Home Depot to pick out some plants for the living room and balcony. I found a vivid green Massa Cane for the balcony and added a garden stake with a decorative purple dragonfly. I'd gotten into this whole kick of buying things with dragonflies on them, including a set of bathroom towels with a dragonfly emblem on them and dragonfly nightlights for the kitchen and bathroom. Anything that would remind me of Mami and that her spirit was still with me.

When I unloaded the plants onto a cart in front of the lobby of my building, the front desk assistant on duty that day, Wendy, looked at it and commented what a pretty dragonfly ornament with the plant. That led me to share the story with her about what dragonflies meant to me. She had this smile on her face while I recounted it to her, which by story's end had become a grin, as if she knew something. She then asked me when I'd moved into the building. I thought it was strange but told her I'd moved here in April.

"And when did you start looking for a place?" she continued.

I thought back to the first apartment I'd put a deposit on that went bust and the long process with getting approved for this one.

"Hmm, it was back in February," I surmised.

She responded, "That's the strangest thing because back in February we had an issue with an influx of dragonflies that were continuously flying in and out of the lobby. We couldn't figure out where they'd suddenly come from, they kept flying around the front desk and our seating area, and it continued like that for a couple of months…yeah, up until right around April…then they just stopped coming. Nobody could explain it."

I stood there, motionless. She also shared with me that Christa even had a picture of one that had landed on her finger while she was working at the front desk. She immediately texted Christa to ask for it. Next time Christa was on her shift she showed me the picture she'd taken of the dragonfly perched on her fingertip. So Mami had been scoping out this building during those months, it couldn't be more obvious. For whatever reason, my apartment wasn't ready for Arco and me in February but Mami knew this would be the right place for us and, so, it was worth the wait and the struggle to get here. Mami had chosen our new home.

CHAPTER 28

It Comes In Waves

*"Grief is like the ocean, it comes in waves, ebbing and flowing.
Sometimes the water is calm, and sometimes it is overwhelming.
All we can do is learn to swim."*

~Vicki Harrison

Life after Mami's death kept moving forward and there was so much keeping me busy as Arco and I acclimated to our new lives in our new home.

"Michelle, you're so strong," my friends commended me.

I appreciated their encouragement and support. But I was tired of being strong. I felt physically, mentally and emotionally drained.

One morning I awoke feeling as if I were buried beneath a ton of bricks. I couldn't move. I couldn't bear to see the light of day. I lay there under my covers breathing laboriously, wishing I'd stop breathing altogether. My heart screamed at me in despair.

"Mami, come back to me. I need you. What am I supposed to do here without you in this life?" I wondered forlornly.

As I was wailing into my pillow, I felt something push into the covers by my arm. It was Arco's snout. He'd gotten up from his bed and was standing there looking at me as if he were telling me that he was there for me.

When I was growing up we'd never allowed any of our dogs into our beds. While we'd loved our babies, it was part of our house rules. I didn't care anymore. I pushed my covers to the side and patted my hand on the mattress next to me, inviting him in. He hopped in and curled up by my side as I hugged him close, his fur wet with the river of my tears.

I'm sure he had to go out for a walk to relieve himself but he never let on. He lay there with me letting me cry and cry and cry.

He was the only thing that got me to leave the house over the next five days. I couldn't bear to work, teach, study or anything else I was supposed to do. All I could do was take him downstairs to a grass patch next to our building and head straight back up. I wore big dark sunglasses on those brief trips outside with Arco, even when it wasn't sunny. Everything around me was too bright and I didn't want anyone to see my swollen, puffy eyes not out of vanity but because I didn't want people's pity, as it would've only made me feel worse.

I kept the curtains in my bedroom drawn and closed the ones in the living room so that my entire apartment was immersed in darkness. If I wasn't hiding under my covers in bed, I was lying under a blanket on the couch. I barely ate anything. I cried most of the time for five days on end.

Arco loyally stayed by my side and we grieved together in the perpetual night that blanketed our home.

On the sixth day I awoke and felt like I could open the curtains again. The sun and a cloudless blue sky greeted me. I stood there at the window feeling the weirdness of it.

It was a beautiful day in paradise and I couldn't get excited about it but I did think to myself, "Ok, I can do this."

I wasn't happy. I wasn't sad. I just was. So I went about my day, taking care of Arco and playing with him on a field across the street, going food shopping, studying and heading back to work. It was like a normal day again, only I was numb.

Getting back into the rhythm of things, I slowly began to find joy again. I was able to laugh again and smile. I was making progress with my yoga therapy training. And life felt pretty ok.

There wasn't a day that passed when I didn't think about Mami and often I found pennies or spotted dragonflies when out walking with Arco. Those special moments kept me going.

About two months later I awoke one morning as if in a déjà vu. I needed to be in the darkness again. I needed to cry for days on end. So I let myself. I didn't want to bottle it up inside only to have it explode from within me years later. It was the only way I knew how to get through it.

This time it lasted about four days and on the fifth day I was able to open the curtains and let the light back in.

It went on like this, an ebb and flow over the course of the next year. A period of "normalcy" (meaning I was able to accomplish what I needed to in life) was inevitably followed by a period of deep mourning and retreating into my self-made cave of gloom. Every time a wave hit me, and it would hit me at random times, it felt a little less. So I figured by some point it would completely subside and I would be ok.

CHAPTER 29

First Mother's Day Without Mami

"In the garden of memory, in the palace of dreams. . .
That is where you and I shall meet."
~Alice Through The Looking Glass

INT. KITCHEN – DAY

A large nondescript white kitchen with gray accents. A pregnant mother and five year-old girl are standing in front of a standalone countertop preparing pinwheels with Publix mayonnaise and other select ingredients. Both are smiling as they help each other in the kitchen. The mother suddenly scrunches her face in surprise and places her hand on her belly.

MOTHER

Ooh, the baby's kicking!

The daughter automatically places her small hand on her mom's belly and her mom lovingly places her hand over it.

DAUGHTER

(excitedly)

I can feel it! Can the baby hear me?

The mother proceeds to share with her daughter how she used to feel her kick and that, when she was restless in there, the one thing that would work was that she'd tell her secrets. The mother whips out fresh red bell peppers and the daughter dutifully rolls the dough for the pinwheel.

MOTHER

Do you wanna tell her a secret?

DAUGHTER

(with furrowed brows)

What would I say?

As they spoon out Publix yogurt into a dessert dish, the mother suggests telling her little sister about herself or perhaps what a good soccer player she is and, when that is met with thoughtful consideration, she offers the idea to tell her what a great sister she'll be. The daughter suddenly jumps off the kitchen stool she was sitting on and steps right up to her mom's belly, placing her hand on it. Her mom looks down at her in surprise.

DAUGHTER
You're really going to love mom.

The mother smiles as the daughter hugs her, placing her head on her belly. The music crescendos. Scene fades to black before the next scene boasts, "HAPPY MOTHER'S DAY".

NARRATOR
Publix. Where shopping is a pleasure.

END SCENE. START TEARS.

Why is it that Publix commercials make me cry every time I see them? And didn't they know I'd just lost my mom? How cruel was that?

My tears peaked around my first Mother's Day without my Mami. The commercials, the Hallmark movies, the holiday card aisle at Walgreens… anything and everything set off the waterworks. I developed a close relationship with my Kleenex box.

And part of me felt angry at the world that everybody else had their moms except me. Of course I knew this to be a fallacy but I felt like I was the only one who didn't have a mother to give roses and a sappy card to on Mother's Day.

I managed to find the bright side in acknowledging my friends who are mothers for all their hard work and dedication and wished them a wonderful day.

At day's end, however, I'd held in my despair so long that I longed to crawl into bed and be over with it all already. I dropped to my knees in front of my bed and cried out to my mom.

"Mami, I wish I could hug you right now. I'd give anything to be able to hold you close again." I murmured.

I wept as I burrowed under the covers, pulling a big pillow close to my heart and hopelessly clinging to it for comfort. I don't remember when I fell asleep.

I awoke to a verdant green meadow with tall silky stalks of grass resplendent in the sun's light. Hundreds of trees dotted the field and flowers blossomed with colors so vibrant, I couldn't even put a name to them. The air had an ethereal quality to it, shimmery and sparkling with light.

Delightedly I caught sight of several humming birds and was drawn to their beauty, so much so that I'd wished I could take a picture of them and show them to Mami. They were so sprightly and quick, though; I couldn't quite capture a photo. It was then that it dawned on me that it wasn't about me trying to show Mami all this splendor. It was Mami trying to show me. She was showing me where she is. She was showing me Heaven.

Basking in its glow, I looked up to a bright white light above and noticed a small white butterfly circling in front of it as if had emerged from the light itself. The butterfly gradually descended towards me, her wings growing bigger and bigger. I watched in awe until she touched the soft grass at my feet and wrapped her enormous white wings around me, enveloping me in her love. I fell into her wings and, ohhh, how I could feel her warmth and love.

When I actually did wake up I could still feel her warm, velvety touch. I could feel her there holding me.

I lay there, basking in her embrace, not daring to move an inch so I could feel her touch for as long as possible. Every fleeting moment that passed, though, she softly faded but her love still lingered on my skin. I flung myself from my bed and fell to my knees once more, this time in joyful tears, thanking my mom for holding me close as I'd wished for.

Not even death can separate us. We will always be together.

CHAPTER 30

Earth Angels

*I don't see how I possibly could have come from where I entered
the planet to where I am now if there had not been angels
along the way.*

~Della Reese

Right after the one-year anniversary of Mami's passing, I had an opportunity to volunteer for a bereavement camp for kids who are grieving the loss of a loved one. As much as I was hurting inside I couldn't begin to imagine what it would be like for a young child to mourn the loss of their mom. I felt called to help so I trained to become a cabin buddy and stay with a group of five to ten-year-old girls through the entire weekend of the camp.

Witnessing the range of emotions these small kids felt and were figuring out how to express tested the limits of my own shattered heart. First I thought maybe it was too soon to do something like this. At one point I had to excuse myself from helping out with an art project after a seven-year-old next to me had a breakdown, throwing a stool, screaming and wailing that she wanted her mom back. I couldn't keep it together.

"I want my Mami back too," I cried quietly to myself after I'd stepped outside alone and slumped down onto the ground.

Then there were other moments like when a five year-old girl reached her arms around me, seeking comfort, and I was so filled with love. I wanted nothing more than to take her pain away from her. My own pain was forgotten. It was no longer even important. What was important was that I was helping others.

By the end of the weekend when our group of girls hugged me and the other cabin buddies goodbye with smiles and tears in their eyes, I felt so grateful for the way God had used me as His vessel to be an emotional support for these children. Right when we think we're hurting and heartbroken, we realize there are so many other broken hearts out there that need love and mending. We are not alone and when we help others, we effectively help ourselves.

Slowly but surely I was picking up the pieces of my heart and restoring it.

Just after the camp, the Yoga Journal Conference was scheduled to come into town. This annual conference unites master teachers, spiritual leaders and yogis for multiple days to deepen their learning and yoga practice. I'd signed up for several sessions over the course of two days and was excited for the upcoming experience.

The night before the conference I'd prepped my snacks and lunch for the day. I woke up early that morning and put on my favorite hot pink and blue galaxy leggings with a hot pink tank top and Mami's Jesus necklace. A bright colored fashion sense was certainly a trait I'd inherited from her.

I got to the convention center early and learned my way around, finding the room where my first session would be held. There were a couple of auditorium sized conference rooms in the center but this one was small with several tables and chairs positioned in six neat rows. No seat was yet taken so I made my way close to the front, settling in with my bags and notebook.

Just as the room was slowly filling up with fellow conference participants, there, at the entrance, stood a beautiful Filipino girl, about my age. Our eyes met and we smiled at each other. She made her way to the table where I sat and asked if she may join me. She struck me as a kind, spirited person. Immediately I felt a kinship with her and said, "Sure!"

We introduced ourselves to each other and our conversation naturally led into sharing stories about who we are and where we're from. Anne taught yoga, like me, and was very involved with her church back in the Philippines. She told me about Citichurch Cebu and the wonderful kids she got to work with in their Christian youth ministry. We were both believers. I admired her involvement with her church and the children and respected her faith.

When we broke from the session around noon, we both found a bench in the corner of the convention center foyer and continued talking while nibbling on sandwiches. Anne then admitted that she'd sat next to me because she'd spotted the Jesus necklace around my neck and said she felt compelled to come over. I shared with her my story and she shared with me my sorrow.

She then sat up tall and asked me, "Have you accepted Christ?"

When she saw my perplexed look she explained, "I see that you've received a lovely Jesus necklace from your mom but have you received the Lord in your life?"

I realized that I hadn't. Not officially. Mami had never baptized me as a child. She'd wanted me to make the choice for myself when I was ready. I hadn't yet made that choice.

I'd certainly felt God's presence during the past year more so than ever. Yes, I wanted to accept Him! Our relationship, it felt to me, was only just beginning.

Here was Anne asking me if I'd accepted Christ but I knew it was really God, Himself, asking me. He was holding His hand out to me. Anne looked at me, reaching for my hands and I clasped hers.

I felt my heart heave and said, "Yes, I accept Christ into my life."

When I burst into tears from the swell of emotion within me in that moment, Anne put her arms around me and we hugged each other for several moments. In her arms—in God's arms—I felt something heavy release from within me. We'd been sitting amidst a crowd of people and I really have no idea what was going on around us during that time. Nothing else mattered. I'd accepted Christ.

I breathed deeply, smiled and thanked Anne for being God's vessel. She asked me if I'd be willing to write and send her a testimonial about receiving the Lord and I told her yes.

Until this day, over four years later, I have yet to write that letter. At this point writing a letter is not enough. At this point, I'm sharing it here in my book.

Why had I not yet written that testimonial for her? Because I'd let fears creep back in. I'd accepted Christ on a Friday afternoon and on the Saturday night thereafter, while I was asleep, there began dripping water inside my apartment. It was dark and I was long gone in a dream. In the middle of the night, the sound of rain awoke me.

"It sounds so heavy…" I thought to myself, bleary-eyed, "whoa, what a storm!" and rolled back over.

Several minutes later the sound awoke me again. I recalled that sometimes during heavy rain, I'd hear my pipes behind the stackable washer/dryer set start to tremble and make gurgling sounds. I got up from bed and walked out to that area, fumbling through the dark. I knelt down and felt around on the floor around the washer to check if there was any moisture. Nothing. I zombie-walked back to my bed and promptly fell asleep.

In the morning, I blinked open my eyes and could tell from behind the curtains the sun was out.

"Good, the storm is over", I thought to myself as I stretched my arms towards the sky.

I swung my feet over the edge of the bed and, when getting up, they sunk into wet carpet. Sopping wet carpet. What??? I stood up into the wetness, pulled my pajama legs up, and squished my way to the window to pull the curtains. I looked around me and saw the carpet was darker in almost three quarters of my bedroom, the wetness extended all the way to the window and around most of the bed. I noticed the sun glistening on the wall across from my bed. Oh my gosh, the walls were wet!! What was going on? I squish-squish-squished out of the bedroom and when I rounded the corner, I discovered my living room had turned into a lake overnight. I rubbed my eyes, thinking there must still be sleep in them but when I reopened them, the lake was still there. Literally, a large pool of water had congregated in the center of my apartment. The wall that divided the living room and bedroom was wet on that side too. The floorboards had lifted off.

I felt sick to my stomach. Then it hit me. This must've been the deluge of "rain" I'd heard last night. It was water pouring down from an upstairs neighbor through the walls of my home. Since it happened in the middle of the night, nobody could have known to stop it.

Since my apartment was owned by a corporation, the landlord's office was closed on Sunday. I called and left a voicemail anyway and then called my building maintenance for help. After almost an hour and several bucketfuls later, they were able to get the majority of the water soaked up and move the heavy sopping wet living room rug onto my balcony to dry. As far as the damage of the walls, the floorboards and the carpet, I'd have to take that up with my landlord. I dried off the walls with large towels and then patted them with a bleach solution in hopes that the Floridian humidity would not cause mold to grow.

I'd Googled what to do when your apartment floods and learned from FEMA that mold can grow within twenty-four to forty-eight hours if not taken care of immediately. I turned the A/C very low in temperature and put it on blast. Interestingly enough, the water had pooled into the center of the living room, missing the couch against the wall and the TV with all its cables on the opposite wall. The rug could be taken for a professional cleaning so, really, nothing other than the bedroom carpet was damaged. It was a miracle but it shook me up.

How is it that I'd just asked the Lord to come into my life and my apartment gets flooded? Why would He do that? I'd been through so much with losing Mami. Everything seemed so much more dramatic and monumental since she was gone. Everything seemed that much harder.

I made it through the day, albeit feeling disturbed about the whole incident, and went to sleep huddled with Arco that night inside my cold wet bedroom.

The next morning when I opened my eyes, they stung from contact with the air. Something was not right. My skin felt weird. I got up to check myself in the bathroom mirror only to find that my skin was flushed bright red. Mold. I knew it'd begun to form.

It was Monday so I called the landlord's office again; I tried several times before I got someone to talk with me. The company owns thousands of apartments all over South Florida, so as a tenant, you're just a number and they'll get to you when they get to you.

Despite there having been a flood the day before and a strong likelihood that mold was forming in the walls as we spoke, they put me in a queue and told me they'll get back to me. I expressed the urgency of getting a professional company out there to clean out the walls and properly dry the place. They said they'll have someone from their company come out first and give it a look, letting me know that one of their representatives could come sometime in the following couple of days.

My skin and eyes began to feel like they were on fire. I was living in an unlivable apartment. I couldn't believe that nobody was going to help.

Well I'd have to call a restoration company for myself to get someone to assess the damage and give me an estimate on professional flood and mold remediation.

I ended up paying for an assessment and estimate, then submitting it to my landlord who subsequently decided not to help. I was angry. They didn't seem to care. They didn't care that my home—their own property—had flooded. They didn't care that my mom had died and that I felt like I couldn't handle any more problems.

I had to take matters into my own hands. Otherwise I didn't think my eyes and skin would survive. The restoration bill came out to be hundreds of dollars more than my monthly rent. I felt flushed all over again when I saw the bill. So instead of a rent check that month, I sent a letter with a copy of the bill I paid explaining I was deducting it from the rent. Given that the bill was more than one month's rent, I'd be deducting the remaining fraction from next month's rent as well.

It was two weeks later when I received a late rent notice with a late fee stamped on it in the mail from my landlord. My mouth was momentarily agape.

"Are you kidding me?" I thought to myself, "Why does everything feel like an uphill battle?"

"Christ, where are you now?" I wondered aloud.

The truth is He was there all along. He always is and always will be. He is unchanging. Unconditional.

Looking back, I've learned that when we accept Christ into our lives, our faith may be tested. New challenges will arise. This is our time to rise to the challenge through our faith.

Remember, faith the size of a mustard seed can move a mountain.

I wish I could've gone back to remind myself of that in that moment. Instead I let myself get caught in fear over faith. Immediately grabbing the phone to call my landlord and set things straight, I already felt defeated inside. It ended up taking another couple of weeks for the landlord to pardon the rent to cover my out-of-pocket expenses but, in the end, it all worked out. It always does, one way or another, even when we can't see how it ever will.

The second year after losing Mami was harder than the first. In the first year, friends, family and loved ones were reaching out and checking in on me. They were actively there for me, asking how I was doing, sending their love and prayers, coming over to give me a shoulder to cry on. Everyone was more loving, understanding and sensitive to my needs.

In the second year, that all died off. It's not that people stopped caring. It's just that life goes on. As everyone around me continued living their lives, I was dreadfully aware that it was time for me to get back into living my life too. I wasn't sure how so I kept muddling through, putting one foot in front of another.

Later that year during my yoga therapy training, I took on a temp job at a commercial real estate office to supplement my income. I was not thrilled about being back in a corporate environment but God has a purpose for everything. I was to support the building manager with various office duties.

On my drive there one of the mornings, I was unexpectedly overcome with missing Mami. I wanted so badly to get over that hump of grieving her that I'd gotten to a point where it was hurting me rather than healing me. I didn't want to show up to the office in tears so I swallowed it down and focused on the beauty of downtown Miami's skyline as I approached the office building.

When I'd first met Renee, I instantly felt at peace. She had a warm, loving energy, which was reflected in the way she'd decorated her welcoming office. When handing her some paperwork that afternoon, I felt so comfortable in her presence that I began to open up to her. I divulged about losing Mami and how deeply it had cut me. I'd fumbled through the past year as best as I could but I still felt so lost without her.

It turned out that, like me, Renee had been best friends with her mom and she, too, had lost her mom around the same age I had. She was devastated after her death and was forced to grow up in ways she couldn't have imagined.

I felt like she was the first person who had really listened to me and understood exactly what I was feeling. Renee was very gentle and sensitive with how she spoke with me. I also sensed her intuitiveness, so much so that it was as if Mami was standing by her side, whispering in her ear, and she was relaying Mami's words back to me.

Renee commended me on how well I'd done over the past year and that everyday I was doing things to honor and celebrate Mami, like through my yoga, through a dragonfly tattoo I'd gotten on my shoulder just before the one year anniversary of her passing and through sharing my mom's legacy with others.

Putting her hand in front of her face in demonstration Renee said, "You've been walking through life with your mom in front of your eyes, which is limiting your ability to see all the amazing opportunities in life before you."

"It's not about you 'getting over her' or 'getting rid of her' in any way," she continued, "it's about moving your mom next to you." She moved her hand from in front of her face to the side of her cheek.

"This way, your mom will always be by your side but you'll be able to see clearly ahead of you and, therefore, be able to take on your new role in life," Renee explained.

"This would be the greatest honor of all to her," she concluded.

So my temp job, I suspected, hadn't been so much about me coming in to assist Renee. It was about Renee assisting me through the grief and confusion that had been brewing inside of me.

CHAPTER 31

A Beautiful Life

"We therefore buried with him through baptism into death in order that, just as Christ was raised from the dead through the glory of the Father, we too may live a new life."

~Romans 6:4

The year that followed that one, then three years after Mami died, I'd since graduated as a yoga therapist and was working with people with various injuries or ailments. I found it to be fulfilling work; God provided me with wonderful clients and I was learning a lot about running my own business. Arco and I had also moved into the apartment directly across the hallway from us and we loved our new home with a view of the bay. Arco was a constant source of love and I cuddled with him any chance I could get. I was moving forward with my life.

But there was something deep within me that still felt unnerved. I couldn't figure it out. Hellbent on making changes, I embarked on a nine-month journey of personal transformational courses, hoping to find the love, success and happiness I'd been dreaming of for my life. Upon completion of the courses, I'd broken through a lot of my own walls that I'd put up, not just after Mami's death but also throughout my entire life.

I was on such a roll and it was during that time that I'd recalled Anne's question to me, whether I'd accepted Christ. While I'd said yes at the time of her question, I wanted to make it official. I declared to myself the choice to be baptized.

When we have a genuine desire and make a resolute choice for something in our lives, God moves swiftly.

The day after I'd made the choice that I wanted to be baptized I got together with a dear friend of mine, Emily, whom I hadn't seen in over a year. She came over to my place and I was intrigued to see that she'd grown in many ways since we'd last seen each other. She attributed the positive changes to her involvement with a church beginning several months prior. Emily gushed about the events she was participating in, including getting baptized the very next day.

"How often do they offer baptisms at your church?" I asked her.

"They do it every six months so the next one would be in April," she replied.

"Perfect, the next one's right around my birthday! I decided yesterday I want to be baptized so how symbolic would it be to be reborn for my birthday?" I suggested.

"Why wait 'til then? Why not come with me tomorrow?" she questioned.

Was God testing me? She was right. What was I waiting for? I'd already made the choice. It was time to act.

"Ok, I'll go with you tomorrow!" I exclaimed.

She shrieked excitedly and we embraced in my kitchen.

Baptism is a public declaration of one's faith in Jesus Christ. The act of it symbolizes Christ's burial and resurrection. Entering the water is identified with Christ's death on the cross and His burial in the tomb while emerging from the water symbolizes His resurrection and new life.

Standing with Emily in a line of fellow believers in front of the pool for submersion at her church the following day, I was filled with emotion. We reached for each other's hands in prayer and leaned our heads in towards each other. I felt the excitement of embarking on a new journey, on letting go of my old ways of thinking and emerging restored—mind, body and spirit— with my faith in the protection and guidance of God for the rest of my life.

As luck would have it, there were four ministers in the pool and, so, they were submerging two people at a time in baptism (two ministers to one person). Emily and I got to step in together, still holding hands, before we each paired off with a duo of ministers.

Before my submersion I was overcome with tears as I thought about how Mami had saved this choice for me to make on my own and everything it had taken for me to get there. When I rose up from beneath the depths of the water, I raised my hands to the sky to thank God for the chance at a new life after a time when I thought life wasn't worth living without Mami.

CHAPTER 32

Earth Angels (Continued)

"We never need feel we are alone or unloved in the Lord's
service because we never are. The Savior has promised angels
on our left and on our right to bear us up, and He always keeps
His word."

~Henry B. Eyring

Being baptized does not ward off life's challenges. However, it does equip one with the faith to get through them—if one remembers their faith. Over the course of the next year I stumbled in my faith more often than I could've anticipated. Enter Earl.

I was teaching yoga classes on the rooftop of a Miami Beach hotel. One morning a Polish couple new to yoga came for the class. They spoke no English so it made for an interesting session trying to explain the correct alignment and fundamentals in a sort of visual sign language to keep them safe. Just after we'd started the class, I noticed a gentleman walking onto the terrace to join us. He spoke English. I was grateful at least someone would understand my words!

After class we struck up a conversation. Earl was visiting from Oklahoma and had been taking his regular morning walk on the beach before he felt a calling to head to the rooftop of the hotel to see about yoga. He mentioned that once he'd arrived he'd noticed the Jesus necklace I was wearing and thought that to be a good sign to go ahead and try the class.

It seems that Jesus has become my calling card these days. He has connected me with so many people through this necklace that Mami left me.

Earl was a sweet-natured man of strong faith. We must've talked on the rooftop for about an hour. I found myself sharing with him some of my struggles and fears, as if we'd been friends for years. He offered to mail me some booklets from Kenneth Hagin Ministries that had helped him through tough times. Normally I would've never given my personal address to someone I'd only just met, especially a man I don't know, but my gut said to accept his kind offer and so I did.

A couple of weeks later I received several booklets on faith, finances and the power of our words and thoughts with a letter from Earl that displayed so much care and thoughtfulness in the literature he had chosen and why. He also included his suggestions for the best order in which to read them. I was touched by human kindness like this that was unmistakably directed by God.

Reading those booklets was like receiving a beacon of light. I felt a newfound strength in my faith. Earl and I continued communication via email spanning out over a period of months, sharing more about our lives, our fears and our faith—me more so about fears and Earl more so about faith. His knowledge in God's word was vast; he had studied at Rhema Bible Training Center. He shared with me stories and verses from scripture right when I needed to hear the message. Earl soon became my brother-in-Christ.

But it would be months before we communicated again. Life grew busy and time ticked on. He often remained in my good thoughts and prayers.

CHAPTER 33

God's Movie Theater

"Thunderstorms are as much our friends as the sunshine."

~Criss Jami

On the day that it would've been Mami's seventy-fourth birthday, inclement weather struck. In a fantastical storm, which I watched from my balcony, the rain was tap-tap-tapping against the pavement below, casting a wet glow in the fading daylight.

Bolts of lightning shot down towards the dark clear water in the bay. They were so powerful I could feel their energy—the electricity—heavy in the air. I breathed in deeply. The air was fresh and cool with a hint of wet earth and salt in it.

The lightning bolts were followed by thunderous claps so gut shattering I imagined that's what Mach3 jets sound like when breaking the sound barrier.

All the while I was teetering on the edge of my seat, watching this with wide eyes like a child as if it were the coolest movie I'd ever seen.

It was like sitting in God's movie theater with IMAX and Dolby surround sound.

When I was a young kid I was frightened of thunderstorms and I'd retreat into my bedroom for refuge. One afternoon, when a storm loomed overhead, Mami led me by the hand towards the patio door to show me there was nothing to be scared of. Still uncertain, I hid behind her leg, wrapping my little arms around it. With a rumble of thunder I cowered.

She had one hand on my shoulder and, with the other, pointed at the darkening sky on the other side of the windowpane and explained, "You know, those are angels bowling in Heaven. That's the sound of thunder you hear."

"And those streaks of lightning you see," she continued, "are the angels cheering each other on with flashlights."

Ever since that day I've been drawn like a magnet to my window with my eyes on the sky when a thunderstorm passed, imagining those angels up there playing in the clouds.

As I watched the magnificent storm on Mami's birthday, I knew she was now up there playing with them too.

Like An Angel Passing Through My Room

"For He will order his angels to protect you wherever you go."

~Psalm 91:11

March 17, 2016

The sun had dipped below the horizon and the sky was progressively darkening into night. There was a gentle breeze wafting across the ocean and, so, I was tempted to open the door and welcome it in. Little did I know I'd be welcoming Mami in too.

I live several floors up with a balcony overlooking the water. It can get pretty breezy and windy up here yet somehow dragonflies find their way up to my balcony.

I cracked open the door and there she was, waiting just outside—this tiny, rail-thin dragonfly—and she darted right in. She glided up to the ceiling inside my living room. I was so moved to see that it was like she'd been out there all along waiting for me to open my door and let her in. At the same time, I was worried the dragonfly would die if she couldn't find her way back out again. I've found a dead dragonfly in my apartment before and I'd feel awful if I'd let her perish in here with me.

So I followed her flight, trying to reach my hands up to her to guide her back towards the open patio door. But she wasn't having it. She kept flying further and further inside my place, first dancing around the hanging kitchen lights then heading towards my dragonfly nightlight by the stove. How cute that she'd found the other "dragonflies" in my home. She hovered there and then ascended to the ceiling once more.

Jumping up and down with my arms flailing in the air proved to be futile. She did not want to leave. It was almost endearing and for just a moment I felt bad that I was trying to kick her back out.

She must've been amused because she took flight again only to land on my dance pole. Yes, you read that correctly. I have one in my apartment from when I'd taught pole fitness. I still love to dance and choreograph. Apparently now Mami wanted to do the same. I couldn't help but laugh and remember when she came to support me at one of my public performances for the anniversary event of the fitness studio where I'd taught. She'd looked at me proudly with slight tears rimming her eyes and told me how beautiful I dance, how I tell a story filled with such emotion. That's pole dance for me. It was never about shaking my booty. It was about telling a story. Poetry in motion. My mom was one of a few who really got it.

It was like she was telling me that again tonight as she sat on the pole, fluttering her wings. Now I was the one looking proudly at her with slight tears rimming my eyes.

"Thank you," I whispered to her.

There is so much I still regularly thank her for. Sometimes I laugh to myself that she already knows the love and gratitude in my heart for her; there is no need for my words. But I say them, regardless, probably more for me than for her.

Surrendering my failed attempts to direct her back outside, I plopped to the couch watching this tiny dragonfly make herself at home with me. I'd received bad news earlier that day that was going to seriously and suddenly affect my income. I felt like Mami was telling me that everything would be ok.

I sat there with Mami the way we used to sit together on the patio at The Sanctuary and pretended for a moment we were having one of our Girls Nights. I pulled out the Bliss Light and turned it on in her honor, watching the pinpoints of green light travel across the deep blue sky projected onto the ceiling.

Mami left the pole and followed the lights spiraling across the ceiling, eventually getting close to the patio door. I breathed a deep sigh and opened it wider, beckoning her out to save her. She landed on a wall nearby at about the height of my heart. I reached out to her and she climbed onto my hand, as if trusting me the way I'd trusted her my whole life.

I stepped past the threshold of the living room onto the balcony and still she stayed on my hand with me. As I walked towards the plants in the corner, I lowered my hand so she could easily step onto one of the leaves. But she insisted on staying with me. I gazed at her with love-filled eyes and eventually she took my cue and fluttered off my hand, landing on the wall just above the plant.

I backed up until I was back inside, closing the patio door so she wouldn't fly back in again. Sitting on the edge of the couch, I could still make out her silhouette on the wall above the plants. She must've stayed there for a while.

It became apparent to me that there was a message in all this. Any time I see a penny or dragonfly, I stop to catch my thoughts and actions to see if I can understand a particular message. Sometimes it's just to let me know that she loves me and sometimes I've felt deep down inside there was something more to it.

Today there was something more. Today she was saying I need to let go of her a little more in order to keep growing and living my life. And also to let her soul flourish how it needs to. I didn't want to keep holding her back by holding on. But, really, I was holding myself back.

There was part of me when she first died that was afraid if I "let her go", I'd stop receiving her signs and messages. I no longer believe that to be true. Over the years, I've been able to let go more and more and, if anything, I'm receiving more messages now than ever.

Later tonight I randomly turned to PBS to check out a program about health and wellbeing only the program wasn't playing as advertised. Instead, there was a woman singing a rendition of Abba's song, "Like An Angel Passing Through My Room":

Long awaited darkness falls
Casting shadows on the walls
In the twilight hour I am alone
Sitting near the fireplace, dying embers warm my face

In this peaceful solitude
All the outside world subdued
Everything comes back to me again
In the gloom
Like an angel passing through my room

Half awake and half in dreams
Seeing long forgotten scenes
So the present runs into the past
Now and then become entwined, playing games within my mind
Like the embers as they die
Love was one prolonged good-bye
And it all comes back to me tonight
In the gloom
Like an angel passing through my room

I close my eyes
And my twilight images go by
All too soon
Like an angel passing through my room.

As I heard her hauntingly beautiful voice belt out these touching words, I cried. That is exactly what had happened to me tonight with the dragonfly visit. It was like an angel passing through my room.

CHAPTER 35

Stuck

"Do not cling to events of the past or dwell on what happened long ago. Watch for the new thing I am going to do. It is happening already—you can see it now! I will make a road through the wilderness and give you streams of water there."

~Isaiah 43:18-19

November 7, 2016

We'll never have what we once had, but if we keep looking back and crying over those closed doors behind us, we'll never be able to see the new doors opening in front of us. It's a balance. We must let ourselves acknowledge the past, the pain, the heartbreak and whatever feelings come up. Someone we love dies. Someone we love breaks up with us. But life keeps going and it will move around you the way water moves around rocks in a river.

We can't stay stuck there. It's like being stuck in a prison of our mental construct, this endless waiting. But waiting for what? Things to get better? How can we see them getting better when we're still wiping our eyes from all the tears that keep pouring out? And isn't there some sort of allotment to how many tears we can humanly cry in one lifetime? Because it doesn't seem to be the case. I've cried when I thought I couldn't cry anymore. And then I cried again when I thought I was finally ok.

It makes me wonder have I really processed the grief for my mom all that well? I thought I was doing so well by letting myself feel everything as it came up and giving myself permission to sit and cry for days on end as the waves of grief pounded into my soul. I thought I was doing so well by coming out of those dark days when the sun called me back into its light. I thought I was thriving by talking about Mami's legacy and her death so openly with others. So how come I'm still crying so hard four years later? Because my life hasn't worked out the way I'd dreamed it would. Because I can't call Mami for advice when the going gets rough.

I feel so lost. I don't know what steps to take next. I don't have the answers. I talk to God everyday and, while I believe He hears me, for whatever reason I'm not hearing His response. There are moments when I feel like giving up. I wonder what's the point? Why am I here? I'm still not married nor do I have kids nor is my business where I'd envisioned it to be. All things I've dreamed of for years yet nothing seems to be moving forward. I'm stuck in my own purgatory. Waiting. Waiting for it to get better but I don't know how to make it better myself.

Life goes on. People forget. They forget the loss you've been through. They forget that deep down life has broken you. They, themselves, are broken too. We all carry such pain in our hearts. Some of us carry it like a badge of honor. Others bury it so deep they're not even aware it's still lurking beneath. That might be me. This emotional pain manifests into physical pain and we wonder why we have the persistent back or neck pain or why we get injured or get cancer. It's all born out of emotional pain that we stuff deep into the recesses of our being hoping to never have to face such heartache again. Because it would be too much. It would cut too deep, threatening our very existence.

How did I get here with this giant gaping hole within? It's like a black hole, sucking the life force out of me. This past month especially I've felt this heavy energy weighing me down and draining me. I can't explain where it came from but it's palpable. I could feel it when I walked into my apartment.

Coming home after a client one evening, I was greeted by Arco at the door. I put my stuff down and sat on the floor with him to hug and kiss him. He rolled onto his back with his paws dangling in the air so I'd pet his belly. These were the moments I'd live for. It had been years since I'd been in a relationship, I still missed Mami and living alone was becoming lonely.

As I rubbed my hands in Arco's warm fur, I wondered what the hell had happened to my life. I'd had many moments of happiness and laughter since Mami's death but whenever something challenging happened, it shook me to my core. I knew that Marita and Papi were always there for me and loved me deeply but it didn't feel the same as my Mami's love. I found myself crying often. I was mildly depressed but didn't realize it.

The Pillow

"Clutter is not just the stuff on your floor—it's anything that
stands between you and the life you want to be living."
~Peter Walsh

November 19, 2016

I clutched the pillow in my hands, feeling a weight in my heart. It was faded royal blue and square shaped with two penguins on one side—a mother and child. The baby penguin, with her wing, is reaching out to her mommy.

The way that her mother looks at her reminds me of the way Mami had always looked at me, like I was the most exceptional, beautiful soul in the world. I've never known anyone else to look at me in that special way. It's been over four years now since she's been gone. I yearned for that look again. Beholding this timeworn pillow that Mami had given me as a kid, I could see that I've been attached to how she perceived me. What about how I perceive myself? Can I not look at myself this way in the mirror everyday? Can I not love myself the way Mami loved me?

The penguins on the pillow are embossed; when I run my fingers across it, I feel the additional cushioning puffing up their wings and bellies. Their white bellies are no longer so white though. I must've had this pillow for over thirty years. But I haven't used it or had it out on display for probably the past eighteen years. The last place I'd most recently stored it was in the trunk of my car. My closets are already stuffed and I don't want to add any extra things in my apartment. But I just can't bear to let go of this pillow. So my car seemed the next logical place where I could still hold onto it.

"Out of sight, out mind," goes the saying. So I've effectively buried my feelings, keeping them hidden from my own view.

Unsurprisingly I recently read an article on feng shui that described cluttered closets to signify an unwillingness to examine one's emotions and the inability to move forward.

This was incentive enough for me to confront my closet and face my inner demons. This was how I got here, having removed the pillow from the trunk of my car and placing it next to all the other stuff I'd accumulated on the floor of my closet. Being that I'm rather OCD with cleanliness and organization throughout my apartment, my closet has become the dumping ground for things I tell myself I'll one day get to.

The edges of the pillow are frayed and the seam close to the baby penguin was ripped with some of its stuffing coming out, which I've kept trying to jam back in. That's how I've been feeling. Ripped open with my insides coming out. . .all my thoughts, all my fears. Yet I kept trying to stuff them back inside like I have with the pillow so it—so *I*—would look presentable on the outside.

I wonder why I've held on this long to that old dirty, ripped pillow. For me it represented the love between Mami and me, that's why.

I pulled out a giant box filled with old paperwork and cards that I'd saved over the years from birthdays and holidays. A lot of the cards were from Mami; I'd saved virtually every card she had ever given me. Opening one with Snoopy on it and several stickers of hearts and butterflies that she'd adhered to it, I began reading her familiar handwriting that was so distinctly hers.

"To my beloved daughter of my soul,
My first words to you were:
"Jesus loves you and I love you."
Those are my words to you always.
Keep them in your heart and receive their strength."

The tears began to fall as I cradled the card close to my heart. I thought about what happened when I walked into my yoga room last night. I'd stopped to admire the beauty I created in there. The walls I'd painted mint green, which reminded me of the dazzling green and turquoise water in the bay outside. I'd scanned the posters and pictures I'd hung in the room, which included a waterfall image from Peter Lik, macro shots of vibrant flowers that I'd taken in Costa Rica and India and then my eyes landed on Mami's picture hanging on the wall. It was a 30" x 20" poster board print of her that Papi had professionally made for her Celebration of Life party. In it, she was sitting in front of the ocean in the Florida Keys, sun shining bright and her smile even brighter. Her hair was swept over in a side ponytail and, paired with ripped jeans, she wore an off-the-shoulder top, revealing her rose tattoo. I'd kissed this picture goodnight every night since she died.

Last night it dawned on me that that picture wasn't actually her. I mean, duh, I know that but I was suddenly aware it was merely an image, a likeness, of her captured by a mechanical contraption. She, herself, wasn't there. So every night I'd been kissing a piece of cardboard. It seemed so absurd when I thought of it that way. I had been giving myself and my energy to false images.

I'd looked at Mami one last time looking back at me from her piece of cardboard and I smiled—for the first time not to her, but to myself. I realized I didn't need any physical item that Mami left me.

I put the Snoopy card in a separate box to save and then proceeded to read and get rid of most of the cards she'd written me over my lifetime. It was painful but I had so much gumption to discard them so I could clear out space to allow fresh life, new energy and abundance to flow in. I knew that she couldn't take the cards with her when she died and neither can I when it's my time. It took me hours and several Kleenex to read through everything and to sort through the mountain of old mail and papers I'd accrued over the years.

Just as I'd lifted the heavy garbage bag replete with happy memories to haul it to the trash chute, I hesitated and opened it back up, digging through the papers and cards, seeing if maybe, just maybe, there would be at least one or two more cards from Mami I might still want to keep. After wading through a heap of old journal entries and outdated paperwork and not being able to find them, I somberly closed tight the garbage bag reminding myself they are just cards. The words Mami had written in them to me were indelibly written into my soul. Nothing can change that. This is the thought that hit me. Mami was not around me in "things". Mami was *within* me.

I am an extension of her. Just me being me is how she lives through me. With this realization I could clear out all the extraneous clutter taking up space in my life. All the clutter that has been holding me back from moving forward and investing in myself. Mami had once told me that my heart's desires would come to fruition when I learn to love myself.

What a long roundabout way of coming to this epiphany. Many months—no, years—of self-inflicted mental anguish. On the outside, I looked ok. I'd even convinced myself that I was ok. I've thought of myself as so strong, the way I'd carried myself through her final months and the aftermath beyond.

And I *was* strong.

I *am* strong.

I was always stubborn and change, especially of big-picture things, can be a big battle for me, a sort of inside tug-of-war. But it doesn't have to be that way anymore. In fact, it can't be that way anymore. I can't go back to the way things used to be. I can't relive those moments of joy I had in my former life when Mami was still alive, beyond what I've stored inside my own mind as memories. I can't bring Mami back to my life. That chapter closed over four years ago.

I can, however, end that story that I've been living within my head and begin a new one. And I can create whatever new story—whatever new life—I choose.

I picked up the pillow noticing how much lighter my grip was now and how much lighter my heart had become. I looked once more at the mother and child penguins gazing lovingly at each other, the baby penguin with her wing reaching up towards her mom.

Every time in the past four years when I discarded a memento of Mami's, I had a moment where I would kiss it and say goodbye. It had become like a ceremony. There was no more need for that today. I'd said my goodbyes to her before she breathed her last breath in this life.

I opened up the big garbage bag one last time and slipped the pillow on top. No words. No tears. No goodbyes.

There was no more meaning to that. I'm throwing out the pillow because I'm throwing out the pillow. Nothing more. Nothing less.

And, like the baby penguin reaching up to her mommy, I now reach up to God.

CHAPTER 37

When The Lord Calls

"In the dark places, we prove to God what we're really made of.
You have to be faithful when things aren't going your way."
~Joel Osteen

We'd had a rough holiday season when Arco had an infected bump surgically removed from his head. The night before Christmas Eve the vet called to tell me they discovered it was a cancerous tumor. It was like a stab in my heart amidst what should be a joyous time of year. My sweet baby had to wear a cone for almost eight weeks through the whole process. He lost his spatial awareness stuck within the confines of the cone and repeatedly walked into walls and furniture. I felt so bad for him. Yet he still licked me with his kisses even when I was cleaning out his tender sutures daily.

Once the cone came off, he rebounded to his normal self, back to playing fetch with me in the field across the street. It was as if nothing had happened. In the meantime I was hustling to get a leg up in my business, having had a difficult season with numerous cancellations from clients who were traveling or with family. This meant shorter walks for Arco but I made a point to still get him out relatively regularly on the field to play.

X-rays following the removal of his cone showed no metastasis of the cancer and that everything had been completely cut out during the surgery. What a relief. The doctor even pointed out on the x-rays that his heart looked strong. Arco was healthy and happy again. We had our lives back. And I rejoiced.

Several weeks later, I noticed Arco began slowing down. He no longer pulled on the leash during our walks. Sometimes he even lagged behind a bit. He displayed no other changes in behavior. He was eating and drinking normally. So I figured it must be old age setting in that's slowing him down.

It wasn't until the day after Valentine's Day, on a Wednesday just after Arco's twelfth birthday, that I came home to find him barely able to walk, his legs shaking and face contorted in pain. Horrified, I immediately called the vet and took him in. He was subjected to a battery of tests over the course of the following week.

Within that one week alone I noticed his belly had become distended, his scapula, spine and hip bones started to jut out and he'd lost almost all the muscle mass in his normally powerful hind legs. The changes in his body happened right before my eyes, they were so precipitous. What was happening to my baby?

The first discovery the vet made was that Arco's red blood cell count dropped twenty-one percent over the past month, a significant decrease. I had a suspicion the cancer had returned. Looking at the rapid changes in Arco's body, I wondered if there was hope for him. I believe there is always hope and that miracles happen but, when it's one's time, nothing can change that. It's just that we never know when exactly our time is. Perhaps Mami had known it was her time and that God was calling her back, which is why, after so many years and so many battles with cancer, she gave up the fight. Did Arco know whether God was calling him back too?

Over the weekend Arco stopped eating. I pulled out his favorite cookies that he would habitually inhale but now he spit them back out. He was back on Rimadyl, an anti-inflammatory medication, which I'd squeeze into a pocket of peanut butter for him. He'd animatedly lick and swallow and lick again until he'd get all the peanut butter clean from his lips and the roof of his mouth. This time, however, he seemed disgusted by the smooth creamy taste as he pulled his snout away. I tried every which flavorful way to disguise the anti-inflammatory tablet but he just didn't want to taste anything anymore. My heart sank.

At one point he stopped resting in his bed and began circling around in the corner of the bedroom until he stopped to lay down there. I thought about how I'd heard that animals tend to go into corners or closets when they're about to die. I feared the worst. I spent the night with him on the floor in the corner of my bedroom, holding him close so he'd feel warm and loved.

212

The next morning he jumped up, tail wagging, when he heard me suggesting a cookie. I was perplexed. Hmm, he seemed like he could be dying last night and today he's following me around the house at my heels again like he always does.

When I brought Arco back to the vet for the next tests including x-rays, I wondered again if he knew whether or not it was his time. I didn't want to think this was it. Yes, so he had cancer a couple of months ago but they'd cut it out completely and he was totally fine afterwards. This had to be a fluke!

The x-rays later revealed his heart was enlarged and that something was pressing on his stomach. Further tests indicated that he was internally bleeding. The vet called Arco a "ticking time bomb".

When he said that, it felt like the bomb had dropped on us both. I felt sick to my stomach. Given these circumstances, I had the sinking feeling that I would have to put him down. It was a Tuesday morning and I began planning in my mind to do this on Friday so we could at least enjoy the rest of our week together. I'd invite Papi and Marita to be here as a family for him, as we had been there together for Mami.

The vet wanted to run more tests, including an ultrasound to determine what exactly it was that was causing the pressure on his stomach. There was still a sliver of hope that maybe we figure out exactly what it is, remove it and get Arco back to himself like he did after the previous cancer scare. I mean, Mami had gone through it a number of times. Not that I wished this upon Arco but if she was able to rebound, so could Arco. Right...?

We scheduled the ultrasound for the following morning, a Wednesday. I brought him home and we collapsed together in his bed while I held and rocked him, tears welling in my eyes. I knew I should find a vet for euthanasia, preferably one that would come to the house because I didn't want him to have to die in a vet's office. It was too much for him and I felt he would be most comfortable at home, in his sanctuary with his family. I didn't have the heart to call the vet in front of Arco to discuss options for ending his life so, once he was relaxed and sleeping, I left the house for an errand and made the call from the car. While sitting in the Whole Foods parking lot, I Googled local at-home pet euthanasia and was drawn to one particular site. Upon calling I was connected to a Dr. Amoros. Like with Mami's hospice nurses, I made the connection to the name. The root of her name "Amoros" was "amor" meaning "love". And she was just as kindhearted as her name sounded when I asked her several questions about the process and how we go about scheduling it.

We scheduled it for Friday in case Wednesday's ultrasound shows no hope left for him. Deep down, I already had the feeling that the hope was gone. Once it was scheduled, I messaged Marita and Papi to coordinate all of us coming together. I wanted to cry right there in the parking lot inside my car but, instead, I focused on taking care of everything. I beelined into the store, grabbed the items I needed, then made my way home. When I pulled back into my parking space in my building's garage, I sat there for a moment, frozen. I wanted to run back up to Arco so I could spend every waking second with him. I was also scared of seeing him in this condition. I questioned if I'd done the right thing by waiting until Friday. I questioned if I should even bother with the ultrasound tomorrow. I questioned whether I was being a good mommy to my baby boy. The tears came and I finally let myself cry inside my car, gripping the steering wheel as if it would help me feel some semblance of control. It only reminded me that I had no control over any of these circumstances. I cried even harder.

Then I took a deep breath, wiped the tears from my eyes, and ventured back up to my apartment. Arco was still in his bed where I'd left him an hour earlier. I narrowed my eyes to look at his belly. It rose slowly and then deflated before rising again. Ok, I sighed with relief; he was still breathing. I approached him quietly and ever so softly lay my hand on his head. His eyes gently blinked open, just a crack, as he looked up at me and I smiled. "My little baby," I thought. He is so helpless and it's up to me to make sure I do what's best for him.

That night I spread a towel across my bed and invited him in with me. He hopped onto it and then plopped down beside me, his head at the foot of the bed. I swiveled around so that my head would face the foot of the bed, too, and so that I could spoon him. I tucked my feet under my pillow at the head of my bed and wrapped the covers around us before we both fell asleep.

At some point in the middle of the night, I awoke from a deep sleep. It was still dark out. I held my breath as I gently placed my hand on his belly to feel for his. He was fine. Still alive. My brain still felt like it was mostly asleep but there, in the quiet of the night, the realization struck me that this would be Arco's last night here. I hugged him closer and eventually fell back asleep.

Wednesday, February 22, 2017:

This morning he was in the same exact spot as he was when he'd climbed into bed the night before. Normally he would've moved or hopped off the bed during the night. But there was no more normal. Things were changing. And they were changing at breakneck speed. He was still breathing. Thankfully. We lay there and snuggled before I persuaded him out of bed for a walk.

I never take my phone with me when walking Arco but this morning I did. And I'm glad I did. We went for a short and very slow walk around our building stopping several times while Arco just stood there looking around him. He was visibly having trouble walking, even though I could tell he wanted to. Would we make it back?

Eventually we made it around the dock in the back of our building and sat down on the bench where we'd sat together almost every night looking out over the ocean. I took out my phone and must've snapped almost one hundred photos of him. I felt the memories slipping away fast and I wanted to keep them as close to me as possible.

It was cloudy and gray out. A breeze caught Arco's ears blowing them back and he sniffed the air, looking out across the bay. The water, usually a light mint green, had turned into a dark opaque emerald color. Arco stood up at once and walked to the edge of the dock. Strange…a bright lemon yellow ball, the size of a basketball, out of nowhere it seemed, floated across the water towards the dock where Arco now stood. The wind blew it closer and Arco's eyes were intent on this ball making its way over to him.

I don't know why but there was something about the sudden appearance of this seemingly random yellow ball coming to Arco that felt like a sign. The ball floated all the way towards the edge of the dock where he lowered his head to sniff at it. He looked back at me and I smiled before he turned to look back at it. For a moment it hovered in place, slowly spinning, before it floated away across the water to be claimed by the ocean once again.

I felt like that yellow ball was sent by the Lord to let Arco know He is claiming him back to His Kingdom. And the color yellow symbolizes joy and fresh beginnings. It felt like a happy sign being sent for us, assuring us that everything's going to be alright. And it will. In my heart, I know this. During a time of fears, attachments and sadness, however, it can help to be encouraged by such signs and messages.

When our time out there felt complete, I got up from the bench to take him back upstairs. He put two paws in front of the others and then again, slowly stepping forward, until we made it to the elevator. But when the elevator doors opened he just stood there. I started to walk and coax him inside with me but he continued to stand, frozen in place, looking up at me. He couldn't take another step. His fuel had run out. Fear rushed into my veins like it was adrenaline. This was it. We couldn't wait until Friday to put him down. It was going to have to be today. My premonition in the middle of the night had been true.

I stepped back out of the elevator and knelt down before him. We looked at each other for what seemed like a long time. His eyes gave away the pain he held inside. His face suddenly seemed so much older, his fur more gray and dull, as if he'd aged in fast forward motion right before my eyes. The elevator door had long since closed again and I pushed my tears back down inside. I tried again to coax him to walk. Nothing. Finally I picked him up and carried him the rest of the way home. He weighed almost fifty pounds. It never ceases to amaze me the amount of super human strength we magically gain in times of distress.

We made it back and, once I settled him into his bed, I called Dr. Amoros who was thankfully able to move our original appointment from Friday afternoon to today at 5 pm. Today. I knew this time would come but not this fast. Immediately I messaged Papi and Marita. It was late morning already and I knew they were busy; I had no idea how it would be possible for them to be here on such short notice, especially with Marita currently working in her office in Naples, two hours away. Papi responded that he would be there later this afternoon and Marita said she was wrapping up a meeting and would go home, pack up and drive over right after. It was a miracle.

It started to rain outside and Arco looked at me with those big expecting doggy eyes—you know, the kind that dig down deep and reach into your soul. I wanted to give him a nice last meal. Chicken, steak or sausage... something that would get him licking his chops the way he used to, something that would leave him feeling satisfied. I'd originally planned to go supermarket shopping tomorrow, not knowing this would be suddenly so…sudden. While, for the large part, I eat vegan I generally have salmon and tuna in the house but an empty bin in the fridge stared back at me when I checked. I looked back at Arco and felt awful. I was torn. Should I run to the supermarket and pick up a ready-made chicken for him to devour or do I stay with him, making sure he has me by his side every moment until his final one?

I chose to stay by his side. I gave him several Pupperoni treats, one after another, which he wolfed down before retreating to his bed. Then I fixed up a vegan burger for myself. I'd only just realized how hungry I was. I'd forgotten to eat lunch. I didn't know if he'd go for vegan. With the piping hot meatless burger smushed between two pieces of sprouted bread with spinach, mustard and avocado, I went to Arco's bedside and sat down on the floor next to him. His head perked up as I took a hefty bite of the sandwich. I looked at him, looked back at my sandwich, and tore out half the burger and started ripping it into smaller pieces, feeding Arco as I ate the other half with the rest of the bread. He looked so happy. I couldn't help but laugh. So this was my dog's last meal. A previously frozen vegan burger patty. "Poor guy," I'd thought to myself.

I remembered Mami's last meal. It seemed so meager but, like Arco, she'd really enjoyed it. Of course at the time I didn't know it would be her last meal. This time with Arco I was certain.

When things are unquestionably final they automatically seem so much more important. I sat there and watched his every move and kept close enough to him that we were touching at all times. I'd scarfed down the rest of the sandwich so that I could cuddle him—I felt like I couldn't get close enough. His back was warm against my stomach as I spooned him in my arms. I wanted so badly to extend every possible minute we had left together but the time flew by too fast. It always does when you know the end is approaching.

Before I knew it Marita had arrived from Naples and, with her knock at the door, Arco was up rather quickly and wagging his tail. The swiftness in which he'd gotten up to greet her made me question my decision. He seemed ok again in this very moment; I had to remind myself to look at his protruding bones and that he was internally bleeding. This back and forth really messes with your head. Is he ok? Not ok? Am I making the right decision for him? Yes. No. Maybe. I just don't know.

I was grateful to see Marita. I felt relieved and comforted to have the support of the people I love when looking into the face of death. I needed it now more than ever.

It was past 3 o'clock and time was slipping away. It had been raining off and on most of the day so when it dialed down to merely a slight drizzle, I suggested we try getting Arco out for a bathroom break. He managed to walk with us to the elevator and then a nearby grass patch next to the building. He kept stopping and looking around, wiggling his snout as he breathed in the cool, wet air. He looked like he was already somewhere else, not fully here with his mental capacity.

By the time we returned, the rain had gotten heavier and Marita and I curled up with Arco on the bedroom floor, petting him and loving on him. Inside I wanted to cry so hard but I refused to let him see it. I didn't want his last memories to be of his mommy in tears. I wanted him to remember love—the kind of love he'd given me relentlessly and unconditionally over the years.

This was the hardest thing for me to do, to not let him see me cry. As if saved by the bell, Papi knocked at the door and we all embraced when he came in. In a way I felt as if we'd rewound back four and half years ago, all of us pulling together to be there for Mami in her final days.

I silently thanked God for having the kind of family that is here for each other when we need it most. I couldn't imagine having to go through this alone.

Papi suggested taking some pictures of us together with Arco, which I thought was a great idea (I couldn't collect enough memories of him that day) so we had a mini photoshoot on the living room floor with him. He sat up tall and let us kiss and hug him while snapping photos and trying our best to smile. I didn't realize until days later when looking back at the pictures how tired and sick he'd really looked. He appeared to be holding on by a thread.

Once we had plenty of photos, Papi brought out a special poem called "The Rainbow Bridge", which he'd printed and put in a silver and gold frame to give to me. I was so touched by his thoughtfulness and felt it would be nice to read it to Arco and our little family. So there we sat together on the living room floor, my one hand on Arco and the other hand holding up the frame while I read aloud:

"There is a bridge connecting Heaven and Earth.
It is called the Rainbow Bridge because of all its
beautiful colors.
Just this side of the Rainbow Bridge there is a land of meadows,
hills and valleys with lush green grass.
When a beloved pet dies, the pet goes to this place.
There is always food and water and warm spring weather.
The old and frail animals are young again.
Those who were sick, hurt or in pain are made whole again.
There is only one thing missing,
they are not with their special person who loved them so
much on earth.
So each day they run and play until the day comes
when one suddenly stops playing and looks up!
The nose twitches! The ears are up!
The eyes are staring and this one runs from the group!
You have been seen and when you and your special friend meet,
you take him in your arms and hug him.
He licks and kisses your face again and again -
and you look once more into the eyes of your best friend and
trusting pet.
Then you cross the Rainbow Bridge together never again to
be apart."

It was silent when I finished reading it. Again I was fighting back the tears. I looked up at Arco, then at Marita and Papi. No words were needed.

And as quickly at that moment came, it passed, and there was another knock on the door. It was 5 PM already. A wave of panic swept over me. She was here. This was it. There would be no turning back after this.

I reluctantly got up to open the door. Dr. Amoros was young, petite and very kind. I could only imagine how difficult her work must be, going to people's homes to help them euthanize their pets when they're sick and dying. She is helping so many animals by relieving them from their pain but seeing the families left behind must be gut-wrenching at times. I commend her for what she does.

She knelt down to say hello to Arco and stroked him behind his ears. He was really soaking up a lot of love today and for that I was grateful. When she stood back up, she pulled out some paperwork for me to fill out, authorizing her to euthanize Arco. Oh, boy. It was realer than real now. I had to sit down for this.

We each pulled out a chair from the kitchen table and the four of us sat down together. As I began writing Arco's name, age and weight in the form, Arco jumped up and walked around the table to where I sat and put his head in my lap. I looked down at him and he gazed back up at me with his tail wagging. There I was signing his assisted death waiver; it took everything in me in that moment not to lose it.

I got confused again. Was I really making the right choice? He now looked so limber and happy. I turned to Dr. Amoros and, without being asked, she let us know it's common in the end for pets to have moments of renewed vigor and energy. They want to be strong for their families. Meanwhile, I was trying to be strong for him too. I blinked away the tears as she gave me time to process this. I remembered the time with Mami that it had been up and down, spiked with moments of false hope. There was no denying reality however.

I signed the paper and handed it to her, then kissed Arco on his head.

Marita comforted me by saying that perhaps this was Arco's way of telling me I was doing the right thing for him and he was happy that he'd be relieved of his physical ailments in such a humane way.

Dr. Amoros went on to explain that she would first give him a shot that would put him to sleep. For larger dogs like Arco, it could take up to ten minutes. Once he was unconscious, she would administer the final shot that would end his life. I nodded my head in understanding so she then asked where we wanted to do it.

I hadn't even thought about it to that extent but, in a moment, I decided to bring his bed out into the living room for him and surround him with his stuffed animals and favorite rope toy and, of course, us. The sun, I noticed, had emerged for the first time all day. Another sign. It would all be perfect and beautiful for him.

We set everything up while Arco curiously watched everyone and everything, then coaxed him into his bed one last time.

I was scared. I was scared of all the emotions threatening to erupt from inside of me…the sadness, the fear, the uncertainty, and the finality. It was all, quite literally, one breath away. Dr. Amoros turned to the door and said she'll step out to give us whatever time we need before beginning the procedure. She closed the door behind her on her way out.

I sat there, completely unnerved. Goodbyes to the ones we love are never easy. Arco had been nothing but a good dog, consistently loving, giving and wanting to please me. I told him that right there. I told him that his mommy loves him always and forever and that in just moments he would get to be with his original mommy, our Sweet Mami, waiting for him with open arms in Heaven. I thanked him for all the ways he'd been there for me over the years. I began to choke up while Marita, who was on the floor with us and already in tears, put her hand on mine. What else could I say?

I couldn't find any other words but I wanted to keep talking, if only so we could have more time together. I'd said what I needed to say (anything else might've ripped open the floodgates on my tears) but I wasn't ready for that final moment so I sat there kissing and petting him.

There are moments in life when I wish I could freeze time and be in that moment forever. This was one of those moments. Like with Mami, I wanted to keep Arco forever. He was a living, breathing link to her. I still didn't feel ready. When Marita gently asked if I wanted her to get Dr. Amoros, I realized I would never be ready. It was now or never. I let out a heavy sigh as I nodded my head.

I wrapped my arms around Arco whispering sweet nothings so that he'd keep looking at me while Dr. Amoros walked back in and knelt down to give him the first injection. He winced as the needle went in and I held him closer.

"It's ok, baby," I kept whispering to him. "It's ok…"

I think I was saying it more for me than I was for him. He knew what was going on and he seemed to have accepted his fate.

Dr. Amoros then excused herself out the front door to give us some privacy again, asking us to let her know when he was unconscious. She'd been right. It took about ten minutes. In some ways it felt like ten years. Yet, at the same time, it felt like ten seconds. Time has a funny way of warping when our emotions are maxed out.

Arco's head began to nod back a couple of times while Marita and I continuously petted him and reminded him how loved he is. Before I knew it, his eyes had rolled back in his head and he slumped down, his snout to the floor. Only then did I become aware that I'd been holding my breath much of that time. His belly continued to slowly expand and contract, his breath still there even though he'd checked out. Tears began to rim my eyes but, still, I pushed them down. I knew even though he was unconscious he could still be aware of the sounds around him.

I thought back to how I'd sang for Mami on her last night on earth.

"Wait, I want him back! Can we get him back still at this point?" I thought in a panic.

Sadly I knew it would've only prolonged his pain. Marita was crying and checked back in with me if I was ready for her to get the doctor for the final shot. Deep breath. No, not really. But…yes, I had to be. For Arco. Dr. Amoros returned and announced she was going to administer the shot. When she did, every muscle within his body went completely limp. It's like everything that was holding him together let go all at once. Within seconds she pronounced him dead. And the tears, the fears, the pain—all of it burst out of me at once.

I dropped down to lay on my belly so I could be face to face with him and I kept stroking his head and body, noticing how different he felt. Only the shell of his body now remained. Arco was gone.

Then it was time to take him away. Dr. Amoros would need our help to get Arco into her SUV with which she'd take his body away for cremation. I'd opted for him to have group cremation and no urn of his personal ashes. I understand how, if opting for cremation, having an urn of a loved one's remains can bring so much comfort to those left behind but I knew, after losing Mami, it was no longer really him and so I didn't feel the need to have his ashes. I decided for him to go with his bed and one of his stuffed animals. Keeping his bed here for myself, I think, might've torn me up even more than not saving it.

Papi went down to the lobby to grab a cart to make things easier on us. When we first picked up Arco in his bed all together, his head flopped over the side like a ragdoll. This was completely opposite to the memory I have of seeing Mami's dead body, which had been frozen by then and was hard as a rock. It almost shocked me to see how limp and flaccid he was. So fragile. I tucked his head, which hung heavy, inside the bed and we hoisted him onto the cart outside my door.

It was time to wheel him down to the doctor's car. We rolled the cart down the hallway to the service elevator, all the while I was looking at my baby's lifeless body, my cheeks wet with tears. As we waited for the elevator, I prayed that we wouldn't run into anybody. I didn't want to scare anyone spotting us wheeling a dead dog through my building.

Of course when we got downstairs and started to push him out the door, one of my neighbors who was pregnant and walking her puppy passed by us. There was mascara smudged under my eyes, my face was red from sobbing and I couldn't bear to make eye contact with her. I felt awful she had to catch a glimpse of the whole scene.

Dr. Amoros brought her car around and we finally hoisted Arco's body into the back, closing the door behind him. She expressed her sincere condolences before driving off. And, just like that, another chapter in my life had closed. The three of us stood there in the parking lot, holding hands and looking out into the setting sun.

The bench where Arco and I would sit together every night was nearby and I asked Papi and Marita if we could sit there. They lovingly obliged.

We must've sat on the bench for half an hour or more, as the sky changed colors and night slowly fell upon us. A cold breeze blew in and Marita then asked if it'd be ok for us to go back inside.

It was the first time I walked into my apartment without Arco there. Thankfully with Papi and Marita with me I didn't feel the sting so much. In Meier family tradition, Papi suggested opening a bottle of bubbly to celebrate Arco's life.

Once we'd made a toast in his honor, Papi turned to me and asked me what I was doing to attain more clients for my business. Instantly I felt hurt and angry at what I interpreted as his lack of sensitivity that my baby had literally just died and he was questioning me about my business affairs. I had to stop for a moment to think before reacting.

Everyone has their own way of processing grief. I recognized that, while I need to sit and be with it and cry and rejoice and feel all the emotions that are coming up, some people need to change the subject and come to it on their own terms. Arco's death, of course, affected me far more than it did Papi, since I was the one who'd inherited him and had been taking care of him for the past four and half years. But, still, I'd thought that maybe Papi would've stopped to think about that before posing the question. He only wanted to know if I was doing ok financially because he loves me, I reminded myself before answering him.

Once the three of us finished the bottle of bubbly, Papi hugged us goodbye, leaving Marita and me on our own. She'd thankfully planned on spending the night with me so I wouldn't have to be alone. I was even more grateful when she suggested ordering pizza. There is something about comfort food—warm, cheesy goodness in particular—that seems to feed the soul in times of despair. When we'd devoured the last of the slices, Marita got ready for bed.

I stayed up writing in my journal, then slipped a note on a red heart-shaped piece of paper in her overnight bag thanking her for being here for me, for our family.

If there's one thing I've learned through the hardest times in our lives is that we are really always here for each other. We've always come together as a family.

Thursday, February 23, 2017:

I couldn't have imagined being alone after all this. I was wide awake most of the night listening to the silence of the room, Marita being the quietest sleeper I know. But just her presence alone was reassuring. In the muted darkness I was haunted by treasured memories of Arco that now seemed so far away from my reach.

Marita got up before dawn and, in the darkness of the room, quietly got ready to make the trip back to Naples. I was awake but tired and buried myself under the covers. I got up when she was ready to leave to help her carry her stuff downstairs and hug her goodbye.

When I walked back up to my place, I opened the door, half asleep and fully expecting to see Arco lying on the floor mat in the kitchen. It hit me. I looked around. My apartment looked exactly the same. But it was not. All of it felt different. It felt empty. . .my home, my heart. . .all of it, empty. I forced myself back to bed, pulling the covers over me, then sneaking a peek over at the space next to my dresser where Arco would sleep in his bed, if he weren't snuggling with me in mine. It was like staring into a gaping hole. I burrowed myself back under the covers, pulling them over my eyes and enveloping myself in my own private darkness.

Hours later I awoke after a dreamless sleep. From the moment I opened my eyes, all the hurt and pain flooded back in. I didn't want to get out of bed. I lay there, as if frozen in time, scared to step out of bed and scared to be in it. There was nowhere safe from it. The pain was there. Arco's gone. It is real.

Staying in bed seemed like the lesser of the two evils so I did so up until a business-related call came in and I answered. It was a new client wanting to start with me. Even though I felt incredibly grateful, I could not feel excited in that moment. It wasn't until later that it dawned on me this was another one of God's blessings that would keep me busy with something purposeful. By the time we got off the phone, I had to start getting ready to meet with another one of my clients.

Part of me wanted to cancel (she would've been understanding) but the other part of me thought it'd be good for me to get out of the house. I would make time later to process my feelings. But there was one thing I didn't think about. That leaving the house would mean I'd be coming back to it. And when I did, it broke my heart all over again as I automatically waited for Arco to come to the front door, tail wagging, to give me kisses.

I was met only with silence.

The private session with my client had gone well. I'm thankful to have fulfilling work that is also therapeutic to me. I didn't mention anything about Arco to her because I didn't want to upset her; she is a rather tenderhearted soul. I'm learning over and over again that helping someone else when you're in pain can be so helpful in healing your own heart.

Then I came home to the emptiness and yearned to crawl back into bed again. I'd still had the curtains drawn, sealing in the comforting darkness, which lulled me into a restful nap. Waking up from it was just like before. Reality kicking in as fast as Arco had left mine.

"Dear God," I prayed, "please continue to guide me because I can't do this without You. In an incessantly changing world, You really are the only constant in my life. You really are the only one who always comes through."

And He did. The outpouring of love from my neighbors and friends, who had found out the news so far, was touching.

Friday, February 24, 2017:

But there's been something gnawing at me. I needed to speak with Arco. Things that I wish I would've told him on his deathbed were swimming in my mind. Since writing helps me sort through my feelings I decided to pen a letter and read it aloud to him so it reaches him in Heaven.

My dear Arco,

You were the sweetest, most loving doggie ever. I think of the many nicknames I had for you…"Patient Poodle", "Bark-o", "Loverboy", my "Handsome Man", "Mr. Lickie Pants" and it makes me smile thinking of all the awesome memories we shared together.

I'm so proud of you for how well you acclimated to condo living and learned your "apartment voice" after moving out of the house and grieving the loss of our Mami together over four years ago.

I hated leaving you to go to work those first couple of months, hearing you cry on the other side of the door. But you eventually understood that I was always coming back home to you. And there you'd be—every time—to greet me at the door, giving me kisses and flashing your big round eyes at me, hopeful for treats.

You never got cranky or antsy when I couldn't take you out on a walk immediately. You always waited so patiently for me. I really would not have minded had you ever peed on our floors.

I sometimes wondered whether I was a good mother to you. I know I worked a lot and sometimes rushed you on our walks to make it to the next class or client.

But your love remained unconditional. You were quick to forgive and quick to love. You were also quick to rebound after we had that cancerous tumor removed from your head. You were back to playing fetch shortly thereafter like nothing had ever happened. Humans can learn so much from you.

When your health deteriorated so suddenly, I was scared. I was scared that you were in pain. I was scared that I could lose you. You were my saving grace when Mami died. What will be my saving grace now that you're gone?

It was the hardest decision of my life to end yours. But I know in my heart that I did right by you and that I gave you the best departure possible, surrounded by our family, kissing and loving on you like the special soul that you are.

You stayed so brave through to the end, right until your last few minutes on this earth when you came up to us sitting at the table while I was signing the euthanization release waiver. You looked at me, your tail wagging. And that utterly killed me inside. I know you were in pain though. You tried so hard to be strong for your mommy. But I could see it in your face and in the sudden and noticeable change in your body that you were struggling.

I tried so hard to be strong for you too. I didn't want to cry when I knew we were sharing our final hours together. I didn't want for you to feel stressed. When your eyes began to fade in those final moments of life, I couldn't hold it in anymore. The tears burst forth until I felt I'd lost my breath too.

It broke my heart even more to see you leave this earth but I'm so happy I could be there with you and for you, to remind you that you're safe and loved. And now you're reunited with our Mami in Heaven.

Everything here now reminds me of you. When I'm sitting on the couch, I keep looking down thinking you're laying where you usually are on the rug right beside me. Every time I walk into the bedroom, I expect to see you snuggling in your bed but all that's there now is a big, glaring empty hole. No bed. No Arco...my little "Snuggle Bunny".

Your food and water bowls I've still left out along with the placemat that has your name on it. I can't bear to look at them. Yet I can't bear to get rid of them.

Whenever I open the balcony door to sit outside, I think of your hurried footsteps, your nails tapping across the tiled floor, wanting to see what's going on in the world outside our windows. And, of course, to stay close to your mommy as you always did.

You were always right behind me, following me wherever I went around the house. When I turned around, I'd stumble over you. Sometimes I'd get annoyed and tell you to sit. But, really, I was touched by your commitment to staying by my side through everything.

I remember how your ears would perk up all cute when you spotted a boat speeding across the bay outside and I could hear the bark you'd try to stifle to honor your "apartment voice." And then sometimes you'd just let it rip—sudden, loud barking—and send me jumping out of my skin.

You always wanted to be close to "the party". Whenever I had friends over, you just had to be a part of the action. And everyone adored you. They said you were like a human inside a dog's body. A truly one-of-a-kind dog.

I wondered why you'd sit up tall and stare at me for hours sometimes when I was working from home or watching TV. You had this sort of "knowing" about you.

You filled my heart with so much joy over the years and I thank you for being such a good boy. You fulfilled your mission of being here when I needed you most. Now without you in my life, my heart is broken in a million pieces. My schedule feels off. It's time to walk you now. I keep forgetting you're not here. My "Baby Boy".

It is so weird coming home now without you here. Our home and my heart feel empty.

But having gone through losing Mami, I know I'll make it through this. I know we'll be one day reunited. I want you to know that I'm ok. I'm just letting myself cry a lot for you now because I love you so darn much.

Always and forever,
Your mommy

Monday, February 27, 2017:

It is so tempting to shift those negative thoughts to positive thoughts too early on in the grieving process. We must first acknowledge the pain in order to let it go.

I remember a couple of years ago moving into the apartment directly across the hallway from the one Arco and I had first moved into after Mami died. It was the same exact layout as our first apartment, except it was flipped. When you walked into the first place, the kitchen was on the right; whereas in the new place I'm in now, the kitchen is on the left. For over two months after I'd moved into the new apartment, every time I walked into my yoga room, I reached for the light switch on the right side past the doorway, whereas here it is on the left. My hand was on autopilot. I'd created a habit through repetitive action. It's the same here now. Every time I walk past the bedroom door, I go in to pet Arco who was often lying in his bed. Then I see that blank space where he and his bed used to be.

Grief changes us. We realize life will never be the same after we lose the people we love. But we so desperately don't want things to change. We try to go back into our routines but things are different. We become hyper aware that it can't go back to being the same. So how do we move forward?

I've been teaching my classes as usual, until tonight, five days later, I had to ask for a sub for my beach yoga class. I'd crawled back into bed after my morning class and only got out to go to the bathroom. I've lost my appetite and have probably only eaten once a day since he's been gone and that one meal has been cereal. It's all I can stomach.

I find we go to extremes during major life changes like this. Either we overindulge in food and eat everything in sight or we lose our appetite completely. I wonder if there's a middle ground. I wonder how can a middle ground be found when we're not anywhere near a sense of "normalcy" within our own lives?

Suddenly I'm pacing inside my apartment. Aimlessly pacing. I don't know what to do. I don't know where to go. I don't want to do anything. I don't want to go anywhere. But here…this…now…it hurts. I don't want to be here. But there is no escape.

Even though I had a full night's sleep, I have no energy to do anything. The physical body expresses the energy of the emotional body. And my emotional body feels like it's drowning, suffocating, dying…

I finally opened the blinds in my bedroom after the whole day in bed in the darkness. I felt maybe I should let some light in. As I swiped the big, billowy white curtains to the side, there was the familiar sound of the metal grommets sliding across the brass rod and from there my tears began to fall as I looked out across the bay. The sun was setting; another day had slipped away. Time has this way of swallowing us up.

With the little energy I had left I plopped down on the floor where Arco's bed used to be, the carpet lighter and cleaner there because his bed had always been in that spot over the years. It made it even more obvious now that he was gone. I curled up right there, thinking of how Arco used to curl up in his cuddler bed. I'd come lay beside him and he'd put his head in my lap as he lay there with me. The tears just wouldn't stop. It was that loud kind of crying, where you're gasping for air and sporting the ugly cry face. It's not a good look. But I found it helpful to make the faces and to let the sounds come out of me. I felt as if there were trapped emotions inside of me that I was releasing. I reached out for one of his fuzzy soft toys, a big yellow duck that squeaks when you squeeze it and held it close to my heart, stroking its soft head and imagining it was Arco I was petting.

I thought back to the times I'd gotten upset with him during the rare times he didn't listen to me. I remember smacking him, never hard, but enough to get him to listen. But remembering it now, now that he's gone, made it feel a hundred times worse.

"I'm so sorry, Arco, for ever hurting you or getting mad at you, I'm so, so sorry," I cried out.

"You were always just trying to be a good boy. And you were the best boy ever."

We have this way of thinking back to the times we hurt the ones we love who are now gone. And we beat ourselves up for it. We have to remind ourselves that we're always doing the best we can in any given moment. There will be times when we get hurt or upset and act out. We are human. I have to remind myself who I am and where my heart is. Then I remind myself of all the times I loved him, each and every day, cuddling with and

231

caring for him, walking him and feeding him. Then I'm back to how much I miss doing that for him and with him and how much I wish I could be there for him again. It can be a vicious cycle.

Allow yourself to entertain this, just don't let yourself get lost in that loop or overly attached to your feelings around it because it will play over and over and over if you let it.

As life all around us moves forward, it feels like there is no other choice but to move forward. But the truth is we always have a choice. You can choose to let this take you so far down until you self implode and become incapable of living a fulfilling, joyful life. And there are so many escapes to help pave the way down that path. Drugs. Alcohol. TV. Work. Sometimes you throw yourself more deeply into your work so you don't have to deal with life around it. Even self-help courses and therapy can keep you trapped. You feel like you're making progress by working on yourself and working through the pain but until you enter back into real life, emerged as that new person and using the tools you've learned through therapy, you stay stuck. The therapy itself can become a crutch. At some point, you have to assimilate back into real life.

The question is, "But at what time?" How long do you take to "grieve"? There is no right answer to this.

There is no ruling that decrees, "You will be set free from the grief in __X__ amount of days/weeks/months/years".

Nor are there specific instructions on how to cope. Sure there are grief counselors and books and well-meaning friends but nobody can ever fully put themselves in your shoes. It is a terrain only you can navigate. No one else can do it for you.

The grief will always be there. It has now become a part of you. We simply learn to integrate it into our lives. I will always miss Mami when I think about her. But I won't always break down into tears anymore. One day you realize you're laughing and having fun again and this time you don't feel guilty about it. You're wholly in the moment, enjoying it for what it is.

The more you acknowledge your feelings now—all of them: sadness, hurt, pain, anger, guilt, fear, etc.—the sooner you can integrate the grief into your life and find the freedom to live your life as intended, with joy and fulfillment and an open heart.

Tuesday, February 28, 2017:

When I creaked open my eyelids this morning, the hushed morning light made its way through the spaces between the curtains and the wall. Immediately and unconsciously, tears formed in my eyes and I felt blanketed in a world of sadness.

"How many more days would I wake up to life like this?" I wondered.

I pulled my blanket, a puffy white down comforter, up around my head; it was as if I'd been swallowed within billowy clouds. I drifted back down below, nestled into my own cocoon. I didn't want to get out. I got a full night's sleep yet again I felt exhausted, drained. It was too much energy to try to sit upright, let alone swing my legs over the edge of the bed to stand up. Thankfully I had this morning free. My eyelids fell heavy, cutting off the tears, and I was lulled back into sleep.

Later upon waking and feeling no more restored from the additional sleep, I peeked over the covers and looked directly at the wall across from me. There it was. The emptiness. Glaring right at me. It was a prominent hole, a new space created since Arco's bed in it had departed along with Arco. From my view from underneath the covers, I could see as far down as just above the floorboards where the top edge of his bed would meet. I wanted to sit up and look further down to see where his bed used to be, to make sure it was real that he wasn't here.

I knew the answer. But they say seeing is believing. I regretted trying to see.

When I sat up and looked all the way down the wall to the floor, the emptiness opened up even wider—that giant, gaping mouth. Hungry to devour my broken heart. A moan escaped my throat. His bed was really gone. He…was really gone.

The words "nothing lasts forever" slammed into my mind like a guillotine. We want to hold onto things forever. There are those moments in life when we are filled with joy and laughter, falling in love, looking into the eyes of a loved one, laughing until our cheeks hurt…these are the moments when we feel free. These are the moments we wish to freeze and live in forever. We get attached to the seeming perfection of the moment. And somehow, in hindsight, things can become even sweeter. Especially if those memories included the loved ones we're grieving. Remembering and reminiscing is one thing. Getting attached to our past is another. Wishing for things to be the way they used to be keeps us stuck. It keeps us in the bondage of suffering. For things are never the same. Just as we get comfortable, just as we fulfill a big life goal, things change.

"Nothing lasts forever." Yet again those ominous words resounded in my mind like a thunderclap. It felt so final.

And it was.

The silence of the morning and the soft muted darkness enveloped me and I burrowed back under the covers. I slept some more.

It was time to get up and get ready for my early afternoon client and I thought to myself, "How the heck can I go there to help her when I feel so down, glum and lethargic?"

I began crying all over again. Geez, the cycle of one's thoughts can be so destructive.

I'd checked Instagram earlier while still in bed to keep my mind off things and saw a friend's post that spoke about grace.

It said, "We can't do everything on our own. I know you're a Super Hero! But seriously…sometimes you just need to take a deep breath, close your eyes and ask God for help. He will give you the grace and strength that you need in order to face life's challenges. He will give you the wisdom and guidance that you need, when you feel like you're all alone. You're not alone. We are all inter-connected in this world by love, grace, and compassion." (@heatherleebeasley)

As I stared at my tired reflection in the mirror, I thought back to Heather's post and asked God right there in front of the bathroom sink to give me the strength and grace to serve as His vessel and help my client this afternoon in the best way I can.

She was in such a good mood when I knocked on her door later. I had just enough gumption to get there in the nick of time. Her smile made me happy but at the same time sad because I didn't want my sadness to bring her down. This is why I generally become a hermit when I'm feeling low. I don't like being a Debbie Downer so, instead, I retreat.

But this time around losing someone I love—my Arco—I've been pushing myself to get out of the house, to continue teaching and working, to go bike riding and be in nature and to spend time with friends. I've had a genuinely good time in each of these activities. All the while, I've let myself cry and grieve and journal in between all these activities. And I've been gentler with myself.

This afternoon I looked over a pile of documents accruing on the bar countertop, all things pending for me to take care of. I just didn't have it in me this past week to address them. I'm telling myself next week I'll get back into my regime by going to bed on time, eating right, drinking more water, etc. Plus get back into checking off all those pending items that require my attention (taxes, creating a better money management tool for my growing business, renewing auto insurance, renewing yoga insurance, renewing my driver's license—this time in person at the DMV…you get the drift). For now, I'm just going with what I'm feeling. And if I feel happy, I let myself feel it. If I feel sad, I let myself feel it.

When I was with my client this afternoon she cheered me up and made me laugh. She had no idea how much I was hurting inside. I was happy and grateful to be laughing again. She ended up inviting me for a snack and chat in her kitchen after the session. I've always enjoyed her company. She's fun with a bold sense of humor and a very generous heart. We'd clicked since her first session with me.

As she dug her spoon into a cup of strawberry Greek yogurt topped with fresh strawberries, she cracked another joke sending me into laughter.

I thought to myself, "Thank you, God, for giving me the strength to be here. And thank you for bringing so much love into my life, especially during the tough times."

Saturday, March 4, 2017:

Tonight I'm alone in my place and finally getting used to the idea that Arco is not here with me. It still hurts but the bad days are less bad so I guess that means I'm doing better.

After dinner, I looked outside at the clouds that were turning from pink into grey as the sun disappeared beyond the horizon. I missed our walks together and decided why not go out for a walk anyway?

I put on the sneakers I'd always worn when walking Arco, the ones that didn't matter to me if I'd accidentally step in poop. They were clean and comfortable but old and worn. I walked out the usual way that I used to take with Arco, down the stairwell and out through to the grass patch next to my building reserved for dogs. Often we sprinted together right to this spot but this time I stopped at the ocean and stood there.

It was unusually windy. The wind whipped across the surface of the water in a sort of endless restlessness. I realize that I felt a little restless inside, too, like I didn't quite know what to do with myself.

I welcomed the fresh air as I turned to walk down the dog path from my building into the neighborhood, remembering how Arco used to pull on his leash because he couldn't wait to sniff all the outside smells. It felt weird walking along that path without him by my side. I felt his shadow with me as I crossed the street to the field in which he'd loved to run and play fetch. The field was empty tonight. Nobody else was out there walking any dogs. Just me in an empty field. And the forceful night air. In spite of the wind nipping at my cheeks, I kept walking.

"At least let me make it around the block once. At least let me give this a try," I pleaded with myself.

So off for the walk I went, stuffing my cold hands deep into the pockets of my sweatshirt and bracing myself from the relentless wind. After coming around the block I felt somewhat revived. Still lonely but with a sense of "I'm ok" hovering within.

Automatically I walked towards the bay. The sky had begun to darken significantly and quickly as it does after the sun sets. The ocean had turned black with churning waters being pummeled by the wind. Somehow I found comfort in the harshness of Mother Nature. It reminded me there's still life out here.

I plopped down on our favorite bench where Arco and I would regularly sit together, me meditatively focusing on my breath and staring out over the bay and into the night…Arco inhaling the various scents that carried across the water's surface. I used to wonder what he'd be thinking and what kinds of stories traveled across the ocean along with those smells.

Tonight I sat there alone and began to sniff the air but all I could detect was the faintest smell of salt. Everything else was muted by the heavy winds. There was this incredibly bright star out that I'd never noticed in our time together there before. It was big and twinkling and I imagined that it was Arco shining his light for me.

I looked to the moon hanging almost full in the night sky and the clouds blowing in around it. I noticed a cloud shaped like Arco. Really, I could see his head with his long snout followed by his body. He even had his signature "pom pom" poodle tail. I sat up and stared at this cloud sailing rapidly across the sky. Eventually he kissed the moon before his head began to separate from his body as the wind pushed through the clouds. Then he vanished into thin air.

Maybe I was really reaching to find something there, as if it were a message or a sign. It didn't matter. It comforted me.

March 7, 2017:

One day shy of the two-week anniversary of his death, Arco came to me in a dream. We were in this majestic forest with trees dotting rolling hills full of fall foliage. The fall-like colors were more vibrant than I'd ever seen anywhere on earth. Vivid jewel tones such as copper, topaz, ruby red and golden amber. Arco was with me. He looked stronger and healthier than ever. A black Range Rover was driving over a path through this forest and I knelt down to grab Arco's powerful hind legs so he wouldn't run out in front of the moving car. The SUV passed through the woods and then it was just the two of us alone together in the entire expanse of forest. I could feel Arco ready and reeling to run so I released my hands from his body as he bolted off. I ran after him and he turned around and we chased each other in circles. His tail was up and his tongue was hanging out of the side of his mouth. I could see the corners of his mouth turned up in joy. I felt elated. Arco was showing me that he is happy and free now.

He then led me to the edge of the forest where there was a school on a large property and near it stood a lone tree with a sad young man stooped under it. I looked at the man and wondered about him and turned to Arco but Arco was already turning around to leave. He had showed me what he needed to and then led me to where I was to go next.

I awoke with tears in my eyes. In that moment I learned it is actually possible to feel happy and sad at the same time.

Six days after he'd passed I'd made a mini video tribute for Arco, a compilation of pictures of him and of us together. We have this way of torturing ourselves when going through a hard time. I can't remember the number of times I replayed my tribute to Arco, watching the images of him flashing before my eyes coordinated to Mariah Carey's song "We Belong Together". Her words:

"When you left I lost a part of me,
It's still so hard to believe.
Come back, baby, please,
We belong together."

Looking at him makes me press my hand into my heart, for fear it will rupture from within my chest because the pain is too great for me to bear. I was in bed yet again. The depression seemed to overcome me most in the mornings, stalking in the night shadows and waiting to creep up on me when I'd first open my eyes to another day. As I reached my hands under the covers for my heart, it felt as if my body disappeared into the mattress. I felt like I'd shrunk. But my heart was engorged with the weight of my woes.

I thought to myself, "I am too small to carry this."

When Arco died, some people didn't really understand my pain. People who don't have pets or don't love animals were kind but indifferent. People who do have pets could greatly sympathize with the loss of a pet. It felt as if I'd lost my own child. Only a very few—less than a handful—understood what losing Arco really meant to me. How it stirred up all the emotions around watching Mami's condition deteriorate in her final months before seeing her lifeless body in the end, then facing the gaping emptiness of her absence from my life.

Arco's death had triggered the memories of Mami's and had unearthed more layers of grief and levels of understanding I wasn't aware of in the previous four and a half years.

Mami and Arco: the two who loved me the most in this world—absolutely and unconditionally—were now gone. Sometimes I wonder why am I here? What is it all for? The questions lingered upon my lips as I fell asleep yet again. It's the dreams that show me the answers; the dreams that show me what's real.

Since Arco passed away, I've felt tired everyday. Completely drained with little energy to animate my flesh. I needed to get moving. I signed up to take yoga classes for myself again. I hadn't practiced asana (the physical poses) in a couple of months. But I had to go easy on myself during those sometimes physically and mentally challenging yoga sessions.

The right side of my body had been "talking to me" since Arco died. My piriformis muscle and IT band felt locked up and sometimes I got sciatic pain, a dull sensation, shooting all the way down into my ankle. My right shoulder had limited mobility and ached from deep within. I had not recently worked out vigorously or moved in an awkward way that could've caused the pain and tightness. This was undoubtedly the grief manifesting in my body. Interestingly enough, the right side is said to represent the masculine and our past (while the left represents the feminine and our future). It's no wonder I felt the physical pain I did. I was emotionally unable to let go of Arco, to let go of my past.

CHAPTER 38

The Energy Of Emotion

"Unexpressed emotions tend to stay in the body like small ticking time bombs, they are illnesses in incubation."

~Marilyn Van Derbur

Everything is energy. Energy, as defined by physics, cannot be created or destroyed; it can only be converted in form. (This is another reason why I believe death is not an end). Our minds, bodies, emotions and breath are all a form of energy and are inextricably connected.

Grief, too, is a form of energy. And all energy needs to be moved. Otherwise it sits in the body, becoming heavier and heavier until we eventually sink or explode. When we push down our feelings or ignore them completely, they will only burst forth even stronger. The more we push our feelings away, the more they will push back at some point.

It's not that we should deny ourselves emotion. That would be like denying being human. The key is to step back into the consciousness within that is aware you're feeling sad, depressed, lost, angry, or whatever other emotions that come up for you while mourning your loved one. Don't try to resist it. Don't try to fight it. Worse, don't try to stuff it down and avoid it all together.

Because it will inevitably resurface.

The key is to recognize you're sad or whatever it is you're feeling and let the emotion move through you, no matter how impossible it may seem in the moment. When we stop fighting or resisting our emotions, they are able to pass freely through the mind, psyche and body and, therefore be more easily released.

This is important because grief is a weighty emotion. I felt it in my body like a colossal pit in my stomach; this can affect the digestive system as well as decision-making. The heart can feel like lead. My eyes were heavy and swollen from steady streams of tears. At times I felt like I was carrying the weight of the world on my shoulders and noticed how my upper back would want to hunch over in an effort to protect my broken heart. Hunched shoulders lead to back pain and shallow breathing because that defeated posture compresses the lungs. Sometimes I felt like I couldn't breathe.

Thankfully Mami taught me good posture and yoga taught me how to breathe. Most of us are already unconsciously shallow breathers, breathing only from the chest. Learning to use the diaphragm at its full capacity allowed me to go deep into my belly, the site of the solar plexus chakra (one of our seven major energy centers), which correlates with our self-esteem, willpower, taking responsibility for our choices and moving forward with them in confidence.

Practicing yoga helped me clear my feelings of helplessness in a time where I felt no control over my life. Of course control is just an illusion. And, with continued practice, everyday I learn to surrender a little more.

Tightness in the hips is another common side effect of grief. The psoas, a large deep muscle that connects the thoracic spine (mid back) to the femurs (thigh bones), helps us sit, stand and walk. It is also known as "the seat of the soul", as it's said it's where we store our emotions and fears. It was no wonder that all the heart-openers and hip-openers in yoga helped me access my emotions and release them.

My jaw was often clenched, as if sinking my teeth into the past in every effort to hold on. I could physically see how much I'd aged in a matter of a year from when we'd first received the news of Mami's imminent death. Now it was happening again with Arco's passing.

Mourning the dead figuratively creates a dead weight within us. Grief can either weigh us down or set us free. Everything for me felt cumbersome. At the same time, I felt all these gaping holes within me. The hole in my heart, the hole in my belly and the hole in my soul with both my soulmate and my baby now gone. It would seem that these holes would lift some of

242

the weight off of me. But it was just the opposite. Instead, they were like black holes, heavy and sucking everything into them.

Through yoga, I learned how our bodies are constantly communicating to us.

Physical pain is simply our bodies saying, "Hey! We've got to work on something. There's an emotional lesson we need to learn here. Won't you listen? I'm trying to help you through this."

We often only start to reevaluate the way we live and begin to work on ourselves after an illness arises or once we've been dealing with ongoing pain long enough that it forces us to stop and examine ourselves and the way we've been living.

Only then we might become aware that our thoughts form into matter. Look at the human brain; pictures of it alive are fascinating. It's like a major circuit—a hard drive—and it's far more complex than we can fully understand. It works in conjunction with the enteric nervous system, also known as our belly brain, which relates to our "gut" feelings and intuition (intuition can be linked back to the third eye, our seat of wisdom). I believe our heart completes the trinity of our capacity as spirit in human bodies. We are sparks of God, the Eternal Spirit, and we're already equipped with the tools for success. Most humans give up. Life is hard and it can get scary— the scariest part having to face our own egos, our own self-made fears. It's much easier to shut down and to let the obstacles overcome us.

I believe we have infinite power when we reunite with God. God, to me, is the Universe, Infinite Love, Source Energy, Truth…He is everything. He is that which is greater than us but, at the same time, that which makes up our very own chemistry. And even though we're living in finite bodies with generally finite thoughts, we can break through the walls we put up and live in the pure joy and bliss we're meant to be living in. Life is not meant to be a struggle. We only make it that way by attaching meaning to everything, making it good or bad. It simply is. It's in this space of energy that we can begin to feel bliss, love, peace and harmony within ourselves and with all others. It's within this space that our lives begin to transform.

CHAPTER 39

Cherry Blossoms

"The only thing we are dealing with is a thought and a thought can be changed."

~Louise Hay

I had to come back to loving myself. Despite feeling exhausted all the time, I'd incentivized myself to get out and enjoy my life.

It was a bumpy ride and God knew I needed support in this. Not only did He offer me the comfort of good friends but also, after months of no communication, Earl chimed in via email to see how I was doing. I recounted to him what had transpired in the past couple of months and confessed I wished there was a way I could take a "time out" from life. I needed everything to stop but it all kept moving forward without me.

About a week later I received a call from a local spa informing me I had two spa treatments of my choice and I could spend the day there enjoying the facilities, a gift from Earl. I was beside myself with gratitude over his generosity, thoughtfulness and understanding of my need for a break from everything. There is nothing like a spa day to soothe an aching soul. And God's gifts can come from the most unexpected places.

March 17, 2017

It was another one of God's blessings that my cousin and her husband had long ago booked a trip from Germany to visit Florida and they'd soon be staying with me for a few days. This gave me a good reason to spruce up my place, which meant a trip to Home Depot was in order for some new plants.

I'd had a true Floridian pine tree on my balcony, gifted to me by a thoughtful client who had remembered that we'd strewn Mami's ashes out in nature under the pine trees she so loved. I'd always been open with talking about Mami's death. He'd lost his mom about a year after Mami had passed away so we could greatly empathize with each other's grief. I was touched by this meaningful gift. So it dismayed me to discover that all of its needles had turned brown and the tree had died on the same day Arco died. I don't believe in coincidence. I was sad to have lost this tree too. It had reminded me everyday of Mami. The timeliness of the pine tree's death and its obvious need for replacement felt symbolic.

I thought to myself, "What will I replace it with?"

There's this urge to try to replace things of the past with the very same that once existed. But nothing can ever be replaced. And everything always changes.

So I dared to dream of all the possible plant ideas to create a new ambience on my balcony. Spring was in the air, a time for renewal. I thought of bromeliads bursting with fiery red and orange blooms and sunset-pink colored hibiscus plants that would add a pop of color to reflect the spring season in the paradise we live in.

That is how I've come to see it. God has given us paradise. It is hard seeing it this way with a broken heart. It's as if the shards of our broken hearts have somehow lodged themselves into the backs of our eyes. Our vision of life becomes distorted. We are more easily stirred to emotions. More abruptly angered. More suddenly saddened. Unmotivated to accomplish much. Things around us feel duller, gloomier and heavier. But when we let that heaviness go and come to be thankful for the love and grace in our lives, we begin to recognize the magnificence that has been surrounding us all along.

So today I was determined to surround myself with more of God's beauty. I drove up to Home Depot rather excited, as opposed to the usual annoyance I feel with some of Miami's most oblivious and reckless drivers barreling through its continuously busy parking lot. Once I got a parking spot, I sauntered towards the store in search of something new.

So many vibrant colors dotted my view as I strode into the outdoor garden area…deep purples, flashy reds and velvety violets sat alongside periwinkle blues and hues of soft light pink. Rows upon rows of blooming flowers greeted me; it was certainly a sign of revival. The sun peeked through the clouds and sent a ray of light down ahead in front of me, right upon a big, bright yellow sunflower blowing in the breeze. I thought of Mami and how she'd loved sunflowers. I was instantly drawn to this one, walking directly to it while staring at its lemon yellow petals and large velvety brown center. I strongly felt Mami's presence there.

I stooped down to the young flower and said, "Hello, Mami" as I gently and lovingly brushed my fingers across her petals.

It suddenly became apparent that, from an outsider's perspective, I might've looked a touch crazy petting and talking to sunflowers in Home Depot.

Well, whatever. I smiled, feeling her warmth, but at the same time began to choke up over her. I closed my eyes and took a few deep breaths before I turned the corner to walk down another aisle and there by the crotons stood a man with a blue Hawaiian shirt and blue-rimmed glasses. (Blue and green were Mami's favorite colors). And with this man was a stunning white standard poodle by his side. I lit up and, with my outreached hand involuntarily guiding me towards the dog, approached them and asked the man if it was ok to pet his dog. Her name was Gracie (as in "Amazing Grace") and she was snow white with a green bow on her right ear. The man explained how he'd lost his other standard poodle in January and Gracie, one year old now, was his new puppy. I shared with him about Arco and we chatted a bit. I was so delighted to pet this beautiful, sweet-tempered dog—the angel-white version of my baby. Then I thanked them both for letting me gawk over Gracie. When I walked off I noticed several colorful butterfly and hummingbird chimes twinkling in the sun. Hmmm, more signs from Mami. I stopped to admire them and silently thank her and Arco for being here with me in spirit.

Then I thought, "Wait, I should get a picture of this man's dog to remember Arco's visit!"

When I turned around they were nowhere to be seen. Not even a minute had passed. The man had a cart full of plants so I walked to the register to look for them and then around the entire garden section and they were gone. Just like that. I had to pinch myself and thought maybe I'd imagined it but, no, I'd seen someone else pet Gracie before I'd approached them.

I'd been wishing to feel Arco's presence and here it is. No doubt they came to show me that both he and Mami are right here with me by my side.

March 22, 2017

Even though my cousin and her husband had planned their trip last year, the timing couldn't have been more perfect. Their presence while staying with me at my place helped fill the void I'd felt with Arco gone this past month. The immediate bleak emptiness right after he died had begun to subside. And, really, it was being with my family and surrounded by love that gave me the boost.

We went out and had fun together. We jumped into the ocean, despite the unusual South Floridian cold front. I shrieked and then laughed while paddling around to keep myself warm. As I floated in the bay in front of the dock where Arco and I used to sit every night, I looked around at the blue sky, the water now mint green again, my cousin and her husband laughing and splashing, too, and I felt full of joy.

At the end of their stay, they packed up their things and we hugged goodbye. I thought about how empty my place looked again with them and their belongings gone and I cried. It was a blessing in disguise I had a busy schedule booked with clients so I had to collect myself to stay on task.

Later this evening when back home, I was drawn to the cupboard where I'd kept all of Arco's stuff—his monthly heartworm and flea medications, his treats, his handkerchiefs (he had different ones for special occasions), and most recently added were his cleaned out food and water bowls along with his leash. I'd given away one other set of his food and water bowls, all of his treats and all but one toy to some of my friends who have dogs. But I kept the rest and now I looked at them stuffed in this box inside the cupboard taking up space that I could make use for in my kitchen. I pulled the box out and began emptying it. Taking a fancy black and white paper shopping bag, I carefully packed every item of Arco's to keep for the time being. As I looked at how neatly I'd placed everything out of reverence, I began to cry again. I noticed it didn't cut as deeply to cry now as it had in the beginning. There was a light at the end of this tunnel; I could finally see it in the distance.

I tried to justify to myself that I was keeping the rest of his things in case I get another dog one day. I thought how wonderful it would be to have a loving family of my own with a dog as sweet as Arco. I smiled and thought of how much had changed over the past few years and how much would still change to manifest that vision in my heart.

When emptying out the remainder of his belongings, I found the bottle of Rimadyl and was curious if it was safe as an anti-inflammatory for human consumption so I looked it up online. I discovered several articles on the potential side effects of *death* for this drug. My heart sank.

Arco was given this after his surgery to remove the tumor on his head back in December and, again, when he started slowing down in February. Granted I'm aware that he started slowing down before the second time he was prescribed it. But what about the first time? I trembled to think that there was a possibility that Arco could have experienced liver toxicity after taking the drug post-surgery, which could have led to his death. Was I, in some way, responsible for this? I'd given it to Arco because the vet prescribed it but I never questioned it. I always look up information on my own prescriptions before taking them. How could I not think to do this for Arco? I looked at the bottle and noticed there were no side effects listed on it. Simply the drug name, dosage and instructions. I shuddered at the thought of whatever pain he'd gone through and how strong he'd tried to be for me. Just like Mami.

Instinctively I went to the console table where I've displayed my dearest family photos. I call it my "Happy Table" but now I didn't feel too happy anymore. There stood the picture of Arco and me with my arms around him in his final hour on earth.

I looked into his eyes in the picture, the tears falling from my own, and whispered, "Arco, I'm deeply sorry if I contributed in any way to your death. I wanted you here longer. You were so good to me—too much so—and I'm extremely blessed to have had you in my life."

In that instant I realized I had a choice. I could allow myself to be consumed by the guilt over the possibility that the prescription meds I'd given him from the vet could've caused his death. I'd never have a concrete answer. It was way too late for an autopsy now to determine that. In this sense, the guilt could haunt me forever if I let it. Or, instead, I could choose to accept that he had lived a good life and that this was his time.

April 8, 2017

Losing the ones we love makes us acutely aware of how different one moment from the next can be. One last breath can be taken in the blink of an eye. It may seem like the world's standing still when you discover such news. But, at some point, reality hits and you blink open your own eyes and see that everything is moving and changing all around you. Death speeds up our perception of reality. It makes things more final, more real. Our priorities shift. What was once important becomes trivial in the face of losing the ones we love or in the face of our own death. Today I found myself looking at pictures of both Mami and Arco. I don't know how I got there. I hadn't been feeling well and my energy had been running low again. But there I was sitting with all these pictures from my past. It's tempting to go down Memory Lane when things aren't feeling so good in the present. And I wasn't feeling so good in the present because I was focusing on what I missed about my past.

I looked at my smile in those pictures with my beloved ones and saw someone who was once so happy. Someone blissfully unaware that she would soon lose the ones whom she loves so deeply. I scrolled through dozens of pictures—each one, stopping and zooming in on each of our faces, remembering how I'd felt in the moment in time those pictures had captured us in action. Life is a series of moments and I began to feel like my happiest ones had been when Mami and Arco were around. What has happened to me? What has happened to my life?

There were so many beautiful pictures of Mami dressed up, with hair and makeup done, and a big smile to boot. But it was the picture of her in bed with her nightgown, her side ponytail with a curler in it and no makeup on during her final months that made me pause for a length of time. Placing my fingers on the screen to expand the image and zoom in on her face, I looked at her eyes. She was smiling in the picture but I could see the pain in them.

Tears streamed down my cheeks as I thought of all the pain she'd gone through while keeping a smile on her face. I wondered if she'd done it solely for us or if she'd found it helped to smile for herself, in spite of the circumstances she faced. I cried for all the anguish Mami had endured. I hated that she had to go through this slow, excruciating death. For us, the ones who were left behind, it was fast; the time kept slipping away like

250

sand in an hourglass. There was never enough time to be with her and to enjoy the limited period of life we had left together. But for her...for her, it must've felt like a long drawn out deterioration of her body with her bones gradually giving out from inside of her until she could no longer walk. Then lying for months in bed. It seemed like such a cruel death. Yet it wasn't. She filled it with her incredible, silly and fun-loving spirit because she chose to.

Arco was the same. I came across pictures of us together all the way through to the end. The last photo I had with him was one that Papi had snapped when Marita and I were petting Arco after he was injected with the sedative prior to euthanization. His eyes had begun to get heavy and he was looking out past us, his eyes slowly fading. I wondered what he had seen in those final moments. I wondered how he'd felt as life was so quickly expiring. I must've stared at that picture for a while. Every time the screen on my phone would begin to fade, I'd press on it to bring his face back. Eventually, after several times, I let the screen fade until I could only see the silhouette of his face. It was like I was watching him slip away all over again. Then the screen went black and he was gone.

Another deluge of tears overcame me as I stared at the black screen of my phone, only now seeing my own reflection in it with furrowed brows and cheeks glistening from my tears. It was the reflection of sadness. I wondered if I'd ever feel that kind of love and happiness again.

I keep thinking I'll be happy again when I have a family of my own, to feel that unconditional love that I've been so blessed to grow up with. This, of course, is a fallible notion, to think we can be happy from outside sources. We know this to be the truth but it's like we're hardwired to keep looking outside of ourselves anyway.

I've always known myself to be a happy person. Sure, I get moody at times and certain things tick me off but, generally, I was full of joy. This was one of the major components of the legacy Mami had left us—to live with love and joy. I fear that both have been missing from my life ever since she died and I'm not quite sure how to recover them. Mami had been so strong and courageous to choose to face her death with love and joy in her heart. And here I am—facing *life*—with fear and despair. It is up to me now to choose love. Nobody else can do this for me. Not Mami. Not Arco. Not my family nor my friends. No matter how much it feels like my default setting is a broken heart that can be glued back together but never made whole again, I must choose love. Life is too short not to.

I spent the afternoon wallowing in the hurt of missing them. What had come over me? It's been four and a half years since Mami passed. It's been almost two months since Arco returned home. There is no right amount of time; there is only the time I choose. While I'd assimilated the grief pretty well into my life, there were always the memories. Sometimes one memory brings you such joy yet other times you can think about the same memory with sorrow. I can't explain the trigger other than Arco's death setting off a domino effect of all those memories. The trigger doesn't matter though. It happens. Sometimes for no apparent reason. So I let myself feel it.

This is how I came to crying and falling asleep from a sharp and sudden lack of energy today. I just let it happen. I let myself scroll through those pictures. I let myself look into the eyes of love and let the tears fall from my own eyes too. I fell into a dreamless sleep, an abyss of nothingness, feeling no better when I awoke hours later.

I was scheduled to teach a yoga class and, while I didn't feel like doing it, I knew it would be good for me to get out, move my body and connect with my students. I also knew that sometimes I couldn't "fake it 'til I make it" and, so, I was honest with them when they asked me how I was doing before class. They were so compassionate in their response, hugging me and letting me know I'm not alone. I reminded myself that I didn't always have to be a hermit and carry everything inside. Sometimes it's good to share with others, even when you're afraid they'll see you as a complete mess. Every one of us is going through something. Every one of us has a story. No matter how lost and alone you might be feeling in this moment, you are never alone.

God sent me friends, neighbors and clients who showered me with love and hugs. And if there's one thing I learned, even when others aren't around, God is always here. He is the one, above all, that will never leave your side.

April 20, 2017

Lately I've been buying myself fresh flowers on a regular basis and always have a vase of calla lilies, tulips or roses standing on my kitchen table. I now think I understand why. Flowers teach me about beauty, about

252

the perfection in simply being and about the impermanence of life. They also teach me that there will always be more flowers.

Tonight I watched "The Last Samurai" with Tom Cruise and the life of the Samurai touched my soul. To live with such honor, integrity, respect and compassion—it moved me to see the human spirit so evolved. They are not ruled by their emotions. They have mastered their minds through meditation, discipline, honor and ethics. I cried in the end when Algren (Tom Cruise) helps Katsumoto (the last Samurai) kill himself with dignity on the battlefield. A Samurai must never live in the shame of defeat. Algren understood and respected his wishes. They looked into each other's eyes, flooded with all the memories that they had shared in battle against each other and then together fighting side by side after learning about each other's cultures. The brotherhood between them would remain eternal despite Katsumoto's imminent death. Algren would carry on his message through the man he had become, thanks to Katsumoto's teachings and influence.

When first getting to know one another, Katsumoto had touched the petals of a cherry blossom from a tree in his garden and told Algren, "The perfect blossom is a rare find. You could spend your life looking for one, and it would not be a wasted life."

Before Katsumoto took his final breath on the blood-soaked battlefield amidst the fallen soldiers, the last thing he saw were cherry blossoms blowing in the wind from nearby trees.

"Perfect. . ." he said, falling to the ground. "They're all perfect."

And his eyes filled with tears of joy before he slipped away. It was a beautiful death.

The culmination of love and sadness in that one moment was so intense I thought my heart would rupture.

When the movie had ended and I turned off the TV, I passed by my Happy Table. Inspired, I felt compelled to kneel before it, in honor of my loved ones. I looked to pictures of Mami and Arco. There was the close-up picture of Papi and me with the late afternoon sun on our faces after a day out boating with Mami, both of us cheek to cheek and with big smiles...I can see the resemblance between us when I look at this one...the slope of his chin...his nose...and his roundish cheeks when he smiles...I smiled... his features are similar to mine. Papi who loves me dearly and, even though he can be rough around the edges at times for me, he has my heart and my gratitude for his unending love and generous support throughout my life. He has been such a good father to me. And then there's Marita who is always so selfless, kind and giving. A tear rimmed my eye as I looked at each one of their faces held within the picture frames, held within my heart. I wondered what is the legacy they leave me? What legacy can I carry on in their honor? I thought about how much they've filled me up with love in this life, so much so that I am overflowing with love. It is my legacy to share that love. To trust that there is a reason for everything, even the life events that hit us like a tsunami. There is so much more to this life than meets the eye. For every death there is a rebirth. It is my legacy to not give into my emotions and fears and to live with courage, faith and, above all, love and joy in my heart for all things in life.

So I may have stumbled many times but God keeps revealing a higher path to me along the way. Each day I feel Him chipping away at the things that no longer serve me. And, so, I am free. Free from physical attachments, but never detached from my spiritual bond with Mami. Free from fear of what could go wrong and, instead, full of joy and gratitude for every life experience, for they are here to teach me, to help me grow.

What is the legacy my loved ones have left me?

When asked by the Emperor how Katsumoto died, Algren looked him in the eyes with a glimmer of joy in his own and said, "I will tell you how he lived."

So this is where death has brought me. Not the fear of it. Rather, the question of how will I *live* my legacy?

April 22, 2017

When I came home today to my empty apartment, without thinking, I made my way to where Arco used to lay in his bed. I sat on the floor hugging his floppy rabbit doll with the squeaky paws. I must've sat there like this for at least half an hour in an almost meditative silence. I noticed my thoughts running in all sorts of negative directions. I felt deflated. Depleted.

The sadness erupted and I thought, "Don't cry, Michelle, not today. You've cried enough for now and need a break from it."

I took a deep breath and realized they were tears that didn't impress upon me the need to release. I don't ever want to hold back because, when we do, we risk the possibility of manifesting our bottled emotions into our physical existence. But today it felt ok. There wasn't much there to cry out unless I repeatedly poked a stick at my feelings.

I stood up and stepped out onto the balcony to watch the sunset. I acknowledged that I was still saddened by thoughts of missing Arco.

Watching the sun slip away beyond the horizon, I thought, "This is it. What if this were my final moment on earth, what would I want my thoughts to be? What would I want my experience to be?"

I'd been harping all afternoon on negative and depressing thoughts. And then I wondered why I was having issues with skin inflammation lately. My thoughts were inflamed! I'd checked that with Louise Hay's "You Can Heal Your Life", one of my go-to-books to make sense of the messages my body tells me.

This was it? What if those were my last thoughts?

I gazed at the glowing citrus orange sky surrounding the sun and across the jade colored bay and told myself, "Wow, look at this…all this beauty all around me this whole time! What if I'd missed this? What if I didn't feel awe-inspired in my final moment of this life?"

I will never know what exactly Mami's last thoughts were as she took her last breath. But I can imagine. I imagined she beheld all the adventures she'd had in life, all the love she'd felt and was immersed in joy to return home to the Lord, our Savior.

I think of Katsumoto's last vision before he died on the battlefield… those delicate pink cherry blossoms blowing from an enormous tree and then floating, as if in slow motion, across the field. He'd deemed it all "perfect".

Isn't that the beautiful death? To go with beautiful thoughts? Katsumoto could've chosen to see all the dead and maimed bodies on the battlefield. But he chose to see the cherry blossoms. My body, with its inflammation, was telling me to change my thoughts.

It is time for me to see the cherry blossoms.

God has given me so much. And so much has changed over the years. Nothing has remained constant in my life. Nothing other than God, even though I've only come to Him in my most recent and trying years. And He has graced me so abundantly. Every time I've felt stripped away of something, like from my Mami and from Arco, He has increased the abundance in my life and surrounded me with so much love. I'm only seeing it now because I chose to shift my perspective. I could stay in my cocoon of pain, darkness and tears for the rest of my life or I could acknowledge all of it and choose to see the goodness anyway. I choose goodness.

Life is short and unpredictable. And, so, I'm stepping forward into my future by letting go of my heartache and creating the life I dream of. Life will always be changing. But every moment is a chance to start over, a chance to surrender and a chance to embrace it as a gift.

We can be buried beneath the ashes but choose, at any time, to rise from them like the Phoenix. It is but one thought away.

CHAPTER 40

Open Your Heart

"We can cling to hurt and let it destroy our day-to-day
happiness and poison our future, or we can choose to release the
hurt and trust God to make it up to us."

~ *Joel Osteen*

People come and go. It's like an ever-revolving door between Earth and Heaven. So the spirits of the loved ones we've lost return home and life, as we once knew it, continues. Except for one thing that's different. Your loved one is not in it. Suddenly everything feels different. Things you did together with your loved one once brought you joy. And now it can bring you pain when you do them alone. It can also keep you connected to your loved one, when you're ready to see it that way. Sometimes you want to share something with them and pick up the phone only to realize that you can't call them. At least not the way you're used to anymore. You can still call on them and have heartfelt conversations, spirit to spirit. They may respond to you in a dream. They may show up as a dragonfly or a songbird or may drop you a feather or a coin. They may suddenly fill your nose with their scent, as if they're standing right there beside you. They may leave with you the feeling of their warm, loving embrace.

These signs are all special and beautiful. And they are available for us all to experience.

I've stumbled many times over the years; sometimes I'd receive multiple signs and messages and other times, nothing. I learned in the silence that I didn't need the signs but I certainly welcomed them.

Many people have asked me, "How come you get to see so many signs from your mom?"

They struggle with the fact that they haven't seen anything or had any dreams while they're grieving. There is nothing particularly special about me. There was only the fact that I kept my heart as open as I could throughout the process.

I accepted my mom's death as a part of this life (it would've happened one day or another) and my family and I even managed to find humor during the hardest times. Finding humor kept us open. And because I looked for the magic and mystery of this world and beyond—that extend past my reasoning mind—I've been able to recognize so many signs. You have the ability to open your heart, too, even in the scariest, most vulnerable moments. And you will be amazed at what messages and signs are already all around you when you choose to stay open.

But in the direct aftermath of the death of someone you love, how do you find joy amidst so much pain? When you're right in the deepest, heaviest part of grief, how do you find love? How can you keep your heart open when it's been shattered into a million pieces?

As with everything, practice makes perfect. And this requires discipline, a word I don't particularly like. Discipline conjures images of me back in school slaving over hours of complex trigonometry homework for which I knew I'd have zero use in my life. Disciplining ourselves to keep our hearts open amidst our deepest pain, however, is of great use to our souls. But it can certainly feel daunting. We can take baby steps like smiling to a stranger when we feel like crying or noticing a nearby tree for its striking beauty. The heart is a muscle too and, so, we must exercise it.

There is no way to shut off the pain. Sure, there are many types of distractions and ways to avoid it or run away from it altogether. And it might feel good in the moment to do just that but it will only prolong it. The only way past the pain is *through* it.

This is where faith comes in. Faith that there is light beyond the darkness you're in right now if you're in the throes of grief. Faith that you will get through this—and you can and you will if you just let it happen. There is an incredible light on the other side of that pain. Whether you believe your loved one has crossed over to see the light, there is light in this life for you, too, once you cross over the pain.

CHAPTER 41

Letting Go

"How strange this fear of death is! We are never frightened at a sunset."

~George MacDonald

We were sitting on the Hollywood swing in the screened-in patio in The Sanctuary. It must've been over ten years ago. The sun was out but hanging low, as dusk was drawing near. Mami was wearing a loose black and white tiger-striped nylon dress, one of her favorites. Her feet were bare. So was her scalp. She'd lost her hair to chemo once again and it had only just started growing in. She was tired of wearing a wig in the muggy Miami heat so the moment she'd get home, she'd pull it off. Freedom.

She and I were animatedly engaged in a conversation about souls, the Universe and God. We often shared not only the same mental, emotional and spiritual interests but also the same life lessons at the same time.

Sometimes we'd sit with a bottle of wine and contemplate the infiniteness of the Universe. I loved moments like this. It reminded me I had a soulmate in this life.

There was one moment in particular when she began sharing some of her spiritual insights. She turned to me to ask me something I no longer remember and, although her hair was gone and she'd aged from the battery of chemo treatments, her eyes remained vibrant and full of joy and her skin was still aglow. She continued down the road of curious life questions and, as I gazed at her face even more pronounced by her pale scalp, I distinctly remember that all I could think about was how utterly beautiful she was.

When Mami died, I was scared of losing my memories of her. It was hard enough losing her physically. I didn't want to lose everything else

259

we'd shared together. With each passing day, I became aware that images of her that had once been so clear in my mind had begun to fade. As I grasped for them in vain, forcing myself to remember every precious detail, I felt frustrated when the fuzzy edges of my mind's impressions become a blur. The blurrier they became, the more I felt like it was all just some dream.

There are many times in life when I've seen something so magnificent, like a sunset or when Mami pondered life with her bare scalp, that I'd take a mental snapshot and tell myself I would remember that moment forever. Now I was feeling these memories slip through my fingers like infinitesimal grains of sand. The tighter we grasp onto things, the faster we lose our grip upon them.

Sometimes I sit on my balcony watching the world go by. . .the ever changing movement of the ocean, like a rippling piece of glass, the sway of the palm trees in the breeze, a flock of seagulls dipping in unison into the water and reemerging from it and I'm reminded again how everything is constantly changing. There are no two moments exactly alike. Every moment is a freeze frame of another moment that shall never exist quite like this one. Together those freeze frames become a moving picture. Together they become our lives. The challenge arises when we attach ourselves to one particular moment. When someone we love dies, we cling to those memories of the special moments we shared together. Death is the slap in the face that says we can never go back. It says we can never have that again.

Or, death is the loving teacher who reveals to us that true joy can only come from within. That nothing, not even death, can separate us from love and joy. Love never dies. Joy is already within.

The thing I feared most after losing Mami was letting go. I thought letting go of her meant that she'd be forever gone, just a memory—a prolonged moment in my life—fading into the background until it succumbed to complete nothingness.

When watching the sunset, first you see the large spherical shape of the fiery orb gradually descending towards the edge of the earth, then its convex edge dipping into the horizon. Notice how the moment the sun greets the horizon, the faster it disappears. Before you know it, it gets smaller and smaller and then it's gone. If you blink, you might miss it, that last little bit of sun left in our lives for today.

That's how it felt when losing Mami. She was radiant, always shining her light high in the sky of my life until she was given her six-month life sentence. The moment we knew for sure she was going to die was the moment the goodbye, like the sun touching the horizon, began to approach that much faster.

And then in its final moments, like in Mami's final days, it slipped so fast. It was gone before we knew it. She was gone.

I've tried to capture sunsets on camera and, while the pictures are gorgeous, they never quite come out the same as the actual sunset viewed by the naked eye. It's kind of like the memories of our loved ones—they never quite come out the same as actually being with our loved ones.

The work of letting go is really letting go of our attachment to the person we love and lost. We are attached to the way they felt to us when we hugged them. We are attached to the way they looked at us or the way they made us feel. We are attached to their smell, their touch. . .all the ways we had of connecting with them in the physical body.

It is our attachments that cause suffering, not the physical act of death of the ones we love. The physical act of death is natural and necessary. Imagine we kept on living and living and living in our bodies. At some point, I think we'd be ready for something different. Our souls crave something more, something beyond what we know with our five senses. Our souls yearn to return home.

Practicing non-attachment is one of the principles of yoga. It is not an easy practice. We base so much of our existence upon our physical experience of reality. We'd have to be robots to not get attached to the people we love and care about. Life wouldn't be worth living if we could not experience deep love, intimacy and connection. We are built for it. Which means we must also be built for processing loss and grief.

I remember many people telling me after my mom died that she wouldn't want me to cry for her. I know their intentions were well meaning but hearing this one, in particular, really got under my skin. Of course I know she wouldn't want me to be sad and miserable when she's gone! But that's where it gets dangerous. If we don't allow ourselves to cry and feel the pain, we're only stuffing it deeper down for it to unexpectedly explode one day. Deal with it now! This is probably some of the best advice I can give on basically any of the uncomfortable feelings that will inevitably surface throughout our lives, whether from grief or otherwise. Face them. Feel them. And when you feel complete, let them go.

There will be phases of letting go after the death of a loved one. In the beginning you might want to keep everything you can from that person, holding onto anything that reminds you of every detail of your loved one (their clothes, their favorite piece of jewelry, their signature perfume or cologne, a book they were reading, pictures of you together, etc.). Or you might want to get rid of as many things as possible because it is too painful a reminder of all the times you shared together.

Remember there is no right way to grieve. There is only what feels right for you and you need to honor that.

You will feel in your heart when you're ready to let go, knowing that it doesn't mean you are discarding your loved one by moving forward in life.

One thing that helped me was realizing that when we keep holding on to the past, we don't make the space to allow for new blessings and miracles to happen in our lives. If we're so focused on looking back at the closed door behind us, how will we ever walk through the open door right in front of us?

My fears of letting go came from not believing what's coming next would be as good as I once had it. How can we embrace God's abundance when we're focused on what we feel He took away from us? We can only receive His abundance in letting go of what's He's removed. Trust that He adds and removes everyone and everything in our lives for a purpose. He is preparing us for the next level of blessings.

Some may think that, after five years, I took too long to get over the grief of losing my mom. Some people are still holding onto the pain twenty, thirty years later. And some may feel that, after facing their emotions head on, they can move forward with integrating their loss into their lives within one year. There is no right amount of time. Only you can determine that. I think my journey of letting go has been exactly what it needs to be and the lessons that have come along the way are exactly what I needed to learn at the time I was ready to learn them. Trust this is the case for you too.

The fact that my mom's given me so many undeniable signs because I kept my heart open has helped me see that we are never really losing our loved ones. Like a dragonfly emerging from the muck below the water, our loved ones have shed their physical bodies and emerged above water in their pure spiritual form. I believe we are all connected in spirit so we can never really "lose" someone. We are all a part of each other. What you see in me is in yourself too. It is this spirit that is eternal and that binds us all together.

Somewhere along the way before she died my mom had come to terms with letting go. It wasn't until after she was gone that we discovered it. We found it in her journal. It was the last poem she'd written:

"At the end of my days
When I'm quiet and still
And gladly lay down
My own free will
In my Last final hour
With a heart so true
I'll whisper:
Come death embrace me,
I'm ready for you.
HOME."

CHAPTER 42

The Seed

"For a seed to achieve its greatest expression, it must come completely undone. The shell cracks, its insides come out and everything changes. To someone who doesn't understand growth, it would look like complete destruction."

~ Cynthia Occelli

December 31, 2016 (two months before Arco died)

On the last day of the New Year, I awoke to crisp blue skies and a refreshing chill in the Florida air.

That familiar spark of hope and light that comes around the New Year reemerged. I've decided this year not to make any New Year's Resolutions. They never really stick anyway. Instead I'm focusing on my dreams and vision for my life. Whatever I do and whomever I spend my time with, I'm going to make sure it all supports my dreams. Now's the time. No more sadness. No more excuses. If not now, when?

Looking back over the past year, there seemed to be one challenge after another. I'd been working through all the walls I've put up since childhood and the additional walls I put on top of the initial ones when Mami died. I witnessed my own shadow, my blind spots and my fears. And seeing these parts of myself really shook me up. Sometimes I wanted to run away from myself.

There were things I'd never thought to examine before Mami died. And Mami wasn't there for me to talk to while working through these new life lessons. I really battled with myself, even wishing that I could take the place of a young friend who recently died of cancer and give her my life. I saw no point in mine and I felt like I had no one to live for, not even myself. In my own life I was doing relatively well, from the outside looking in, but inside I'd emotionally hit rock bottom.

Nonetheless I'd been on a mission: try to discover what was holding me back from creating the life I dream of having and then go create it!

It's the pain that can make or break us. I believe it can make us stronger but it takes discipline, work and faith—a lot of faith. While I feel my faith is now relatively strong, I've struggled many times with it. I've had some choice words with God. I've questioned why things happen the way they do and isn't there a better way? Then I realize this is the best way. That doesn't mean I might necessarily like it but I can practice my faith and it becomes easier.

Life still throws its challenges. The difference is I'm not afraid to face my demons anymore. I've got God by my side. I'm willing to go into the pain, without getting attached to it.

So now I've been discovering my blocks and have been facing them head on. I feel like the seed that had come completely undone, cracked open in the darkness of the soil underground, now ready to burst through the surface and blossom in the sun's light.

January 1, 2017

Today on New Year's Day the sun dazzled the wide-open sky with its bright light, calling out to my soul. When I came home, I smiled as I looked all around me at the Winter Wonderland I'd created. I was so proud of my beautiful Christmas display. A flair for decorating was another trait I inherited from Mami. I'd strung a garland with pinecones, ornaments and twinkling lights around the bar. I'd also put together my own little Christmas village on my Happy Table including a church with carolers, a snow covered log cabin with a snowman donning a scarf and top hat, a mini LED Christmas tree and opalescent artificial snow dusted around these scenes. I'd put up my very first Christmas tree that I'd bought for my new apartment after Mami died. It was an artificial one, two and a half feet tall, bedecked in pinecones and lights and frosted with glittery snow. I'd saved and hung some of Mami's tinsel on this tree, remembering her patience and the joy with which she'd decorated every year. Having craved the scent of pine, I'd added a real tree this year, seven and a half feet tall, with both solid and twinkling warm white lights, ornaments in purple, teal, gold and silver along with peacock feathers that Mami had collected, which I used to complete my fantasy Christmas look. I'd successfully integrated our old traditions with new ones I was establishing.

It would soon be time to take the decorations down again to store away for next year and I thought, "Here I go again saying goodbye to something so special. But that's life—always cycling. There are always going to be "hellos" and "goodbyes"."

As I've been saying, we can choose to be sad. And it is necessary at times to allow sadness. But how long you're sad for can make all the difference in your life. The thing about darkness is that our eyes adjust to it. When we linger in sadness, we, too, adjust to it. We can begin to feel that this is how life is. We see life as living without the person we love rather than living with purpose and joy. We think and talk about our past like a broken record—we live in it, and for it, as opposed to living in the gift of this moment. We define ourselves by our loss, by our past stories.

Sadness has its purpose too. We just have to know when enough is enough. We have to be able to see there is a whole life still ahead of us, for however long that may be, and we can do anything we want with it. We can create a whole new story.

Don't let your eyes adjust to the darkness, when there is so much light here for you.

I've been sharing with people how Mami not only gave me life but she gave me death too. It was through her death that I was reborn.

Some of the lessons that have been revealed to me since, and because of, her passing are:

- Nobody—man, woman or child—can be your "everything". God is the only everything.
- Joy is a choice. So is sadness.
- Praise and thank God everyday; it creates so much more joy and abundance in life.
- Do not withhold a gift—giving opens the doors for receiving.
- Own who you are. God created you as you are for a reason.
- Speak your truth and do so with love.

Birth and death are one and the same. They are a part of life. They are new beginnings. When we see any difference between the two, we are losing our connection to Spirit, to God, to our Divine Energy. When we recognize the Great Eternal that resides within us, we are connecting with our hearts. We are remembering our essence and our purpose here.

What's important is what we do here and now. Not to be stuck in our past or worried about our future. As the Prayer of Abundance states, "I'm not burdened by thoughts of past or future. One is gone. The other is yet to come." Here and now—the Great Eternal—is all we have.

Focus on your relationship with yourself and your relationship with God. This is the basis for all that we are and all that we have in spirit. And spirit is the only lasting and continuous part of this thing we call "life".

Don't you forget
Who gives you
Life and Death.
Who gives you
The seas so blue.
Who gives you
A love so true.
As in Heaven,
So on Earth.
With every death
Comes rebirth.

I'd let my fears stop me so many times from finishing this book. It doesn't matter what your fears are. The fears actually point us in the right direction. What matters is following your heart and living your life with purpose.

I'm hoping that by finally stepping forward in sharing my story, it will help you see that there is a light at the end of the tunnel. Maybe I can even be God's vessel to help shorten its length for you as you walk this journey of grieving the loss of your loved one(s). I want you to have everything you dream of. You deserve it. Be sure you know that. Let this pain help you burst through your own walls and your own fears and ignite you to blossom into your best self. Your deepest pain can be your greatest gift.

Life is so short—really the blink of an eye—as you've seen when first embarking on the path through grief, so don't waste it by getting snagged by the shards of your broken heart. Pick up the pieces, look at them, acknowledge them, be with them, then discard them when you're ready, knowing that your heart is born anew...open to love, open to life, open to possibility. Don't be afraid to come completely undone like the seed before it breaks through the ground and into the light. Be willing to let yourself feel what you need to feel. And then be willing to let it go so you can grow into your greatest expression this world has ever seen.

CHAPTER 43

From The Ashes Springs New Life

"He makes beauty out of ashes."

~Isaiah 61:3

On the first anniversary of Mami's death, the three of us—Papi, Marita and me—got together and packed up a picnic lunch to visit her in her special spot. Despite it being October, it was another typical hot Florida sunny day. Only a few clouds dotted the skyline, the sky a cerulean blue.

I struggled with two different worlds of feelings that morning. I felt the heaviness of my heart from missing Mami so much. I wanted desperately to hug and kiss her, to look into her eyes and to see the way she used to look at me.

At the same time with my heart like a deadweight, I felt the lightness of Mami's spirit free from all the pain she'd endured in her final months. I felt her presence with a sense of delight and hope. She was often sending us messages, little reminders to tell us she's still here, watching over us.

I thought back to the very first message she'd given us with the pennies she'd left for Marita and me at the farmer's market when she, herself, left this world. Shortly thereafter, she'd left us her second message when she was being cremated. Inside the crematorium before Papi pressed the button to start the incineration process, the director had handed him a copy of the metal chip with which he'd tagged Mami's body. The chip had an identification number so we could later identify and pick up her ashes. Out of curiosity I'd asked to see it. Papi handed me the chip and, when looking at it, the fluorescent lights overhead glinted across its face, causing me to blink twice before I could make out the numbers engraved in it. "14354" were the numbers. Marita, looking over my shoulder at it, then looked at me and we grinned at each other. Mami's message to the three us couldn't have been more obvious.

In my junior year of high school I'd worked hard to get straight A's to earn a beeper that Mami had promised me, contingent upon my report card. It was all the rage back then to have a beeper. I was so excited when I got it and the first numeric message I'd learned to send on it was "143", which meant "I love you". The other numbers "54" on her chip were evident to Marita. "50" represented the fifty years of marriage Mami and Papi had just celebrated and the "4" represented the four pennies we'd found when she died—a reminder that the four of us will always be together.

It warmed my heart recalling these memories of communication from Mami after she'd left her body.

With the sun shining bright and Mami's smile shining down upon us, we packed into the car and headed south. It was a long car ride and we played music and chatted along the way.

When we turned onto the road to lead us towards Mami's resting place, we noticed several barricades with "No Entry" signs all around. It was amidst the government shutdown and there was to be no access to the surrounding parks and overall area.

It hit me that we would not be able to get to be with Mami on that important day. Thoughts of frustration raced across my mind.

"Why did we go through all this trouble to get here and now we can't pass through?....Marita drove two and a half hours from Naples and then we drove another hour altogether and now *nothing*!...Why can't we see our Mami?...How are we going to commune with her?"

These were all silly thoughts in hindsight because Mami, of course, had been sending us signs wherever we were throughout the year. But right in that moment it felt like an arrow piercing my heart. A huge letdown. I wondered if Papi and Marita had similar thoughts but, if they did, they didn't let it get the best of them. Papi had pulled over to the side of the road and, turning to face us, he suggested we head towards the Keys instead.

Now any mention of the Florida Keys at any other time would have lit me up beyond measure. Every time I've gone down to the Keys it's like a switch goes off and whatever worries or things that have been ailing me disappear and I'm in another world.

That day, however, it was a tough pill to swallow. I've always been a stubborn one so whenever things don't go as planned, I have to actively work on detaching myself from the outcome I'd expected. It's another part of learning to let go.

Marita was immediately on board with Papi's idea and they both looked to me. I halfheartedly agreed. As we drove off, the dust from the road rising in clouds trailed behind us and I must've stared back at it for another mile, looking in the direction of Mami's resting place. Eventually the dust dissipated and the tall trees I'd been looking at diminished to the size of ants until we rounded a bend and they were lost from my range of vision. I realized in that moment my neck ached from looking back so much. That's what happens. It's ok to look back but it starts to hurt when we become too attached to what's back there and can't stop looking at the past.

Papi's SUV continued along the road. The scene outside of my window danced and moved like an old silent film. Trees shifted. Bushes morphed. Restaurants and shopping plazas began to appear. The terrain was continuously changing as we drove further and further away. At the same time we were getting closer and closer to our new destination, even though at the time we didn't know where exactly that would be. We decided to let our intuition guide us.

We drove past The Last Chance Saloon, an old weathered bar and the final pit stop on the mainland, before the twenty-four-mile, two-lane road down to the Keys. The sky opened up and the sun hung high above as the Atlantic Ocean shimmered on the left side of the road and the Gulf of Mexico sparkled on our right. The colors of the water varied from teal to turquoise to sapphire blue. There was so much beauty there, I didn't know where to look. Left then right, then left again and back to right, my eyes darted back and forth, taking it all in. And to think I'd been stuck with my vision on those dust clouds on the old road far behind us.

"Ok, Mami," I'd thought, "What do you have in store for us now?"

She sure did have something planned for us. It was at The Caribbean Club in Key Largo where we felt like stopping. There was the customary Keys gift shop replete with seashells and t-shirts for sale along with boating gear and accessories. We walked past it down to the water to take in the feel of the place. We were on the Gulf side where the ocean is typically calmer.

Behind the Club was a lawn with trees and picnic tables dotting the area. Perfect! We were hungry and had our lunch packed up in the car so this was the place. Other than a small family sitting at another picnic table much further away, it was quiet and peaceful there. The water gently lapped upon the shore as if caressing the sand the way someone would lovingly pet a dog.

As we cleared off the table, Marita exclaimed, "Look at that cloud!"

Papi and I turned to where she was pointing in the sky and were amazed to see a perfectly heart-shaped cloud floating over a nearby tree. We looked at each other with our eyes wide in excitement, feeling Mami sending us her love and assuring us she liked this spot.

We dug into our sandwiches, chewing in silence and looking around at the greenery, the water and the sky. We took reprieve sitting in the shade of the trees as the sun peaked brightly through the leaves illuminating bright red and orange hibiscus flowers bursting forth from the bushes below. The day was utterly spectacular.

I thought again about the dusty roads we'd left behind with crickets abuzz; you could almost hear the heat fizzing in the air. Now we were refreshed by a tropical breeze wafting across the turquoise ocean and surrounded by colorful flowers. Had we been stuck on only going to Mami's resting place and turning back home otherwise, we'd never have enjoyed this beautiful afternoon with Mami's loving presence very much all around us.

To experience life's magic, we have to stay open to its possibilities. All too often we get stuck in what we think things should look like or how we think we're supposed to honor our loved ones. It dawned on me that it didn't really matter where we went each year on the anniversary of her passing. She is always with us, no matter where we were.

On the second anniversary of her passing we did, however, feel like we wanted to go back to her resting place. This time the roads were clear and we parked several hundred meters from the lake surrounded by pine trees. We were filled with anticipation, wondering what it would be like there now that two years had gone by.

As we stepped onto the grass, the green blades flattened by our sneakers, something felt different. The air was a little cooler this year. I could breathe easier. The sun was still vibrant filtering through the tree branches and illuminating the silhouettes of hundreds of pinecones. I scanned the horizon, looking for dragonflies but couldn't spot any. Two years earlier when we'd distributed her ashes, they were everywhere! I realized that I'd expected there to be dragonflies on every holiday or anniversary.

"It's ok," I thought to myself, "Just like last year, it doesn't have to be the same every year. Don't expect the same!"

So I slowed down as I passed brush and bushes, simply taking in the moment. My dad and sister had dispersed and were walking around, too, taking it all in. Marita was standing next to a pine tree looking up to the sky. Papi had reached the water's edge and was walking along the shoreline of the lake. I walked towards the general area where we'd spread most of Mami's ashes. And then I stopped dead in my tracks. My eyes grew big. My heart skipped a beat. I placed my hands on my heart as a joyful tear began to form in the corner of my eye. Could it really be?

I called Marita and Papi to my side and, together, we stood looking at it. Right there in a clearing surrounded by clusters of sixty-foot tall Florida pines, was a baby pine tree emerging from the earth. I recall very clearly two years earlier that clearing was blanketed in Mami's ashes. And now, before our very eyes, we witnessed that from her ashes had sprung new life.

Afterwards

A Prayer For You

I pray that you feel loved and that you find comfort during your times of need. I pray you feel God's presence and that you recognize your gifts and your purpose. You are here for a reason. I pray for you to have the courage to walk through all of your feelings, to acknowledge them in ways that serve you best and to release them whenever you feel ready. It's up to you. The love you think you've lost is already inside of you. The joy of which you feel you've been robbed is also there inside of you. It's been there all along. May you find peace.

With Love and Joy,
Michelle

About The Author

Author Photo taken by Mike Gill ©2018

Michelle Meier may have jumped out of a perfectly good airplane three times in her life but nothing scared her more than losing her mom. When the devastating news of her mom's imminent death struck her family, she learned to turn tragedy into triumph.

Despite a decades long struggle with the harmful belief that she's not good enough, she put her heart and this book out there for all to see in hopes of helping those going through the valleys in their own lives. Michelle is a practicing yoga therapist with a passion for assisting others on their own path of healing whether from injury, illness or a broken heart.

Visit her website at www.LoveJOYogaTherapy.com.

Made in the USA
Columbia, SC
26 March 2019